Why It's Hard to Be Good

An Introduction to Ethical Theory

Text and Illustrations
by

Donald Palmer

Professor Emeritus at College of Marin

...uque, IA Madison, WI New York
...kok Bogotá Caracas Kuala Lumpur
Lisbon London ....ico City Milan Montreal New Delhi
Santiago Seoul Singapore Sydney Taipei Toronto

Higher Education

To Mia and Jake, who are hardly ever naughty

This book is printed on acid-free paper.

1 2 3 4 5 6 7 8 9 0 DOC/DOC 0 9 8 7 6 5

ISBN 0-7674-2409-3

Editor in Chief: Emily Barrosse
Publisher: Lyn Uhl
Senior Sponsoring Editor: Jon-David Hague
Senior Marketing Manager: Zina Craft
Editorial Coordinator: Allison Rona
Senior Production Editor: Brett Coker
Manuscript Editor: Judith Brown
Senior Design Manager and Cover Designer:
    Violeta Díaz
Art Manager and Text Designer: Robin Mouat

Cover and Interior Illustration:
    Donald Palmer
Senior Production Supervisor:
    Richard DeVitto
Composition: 12/17 Tekton by
    TBH Typecast, Inc.
Printing: 45# New Era Matte by
    R. R. Donnelley, Crawfordsville

Library of Congress Cataloging-in-Publication Data

Palmer, Donald.
Why it's hard to be good: an introduction to ethical theory / Donald Palmer.
    p. cm.
Includes bibliographical references and index.
ISBN 0-7674-2409-3
    I. Ethics—History. I. Title.
BJ71.P35 2005
171—dc22   2004065630

www.mhhe.com

Prologue

This book is a presentation of the primary moral theories that have developed in the Western world between the times of classical Greek philosophy and our own. It is directed at students of ethics who are hoping to come away with a good grasp of ethical reasoning. I do not know if it will affect anyone's personal moral life, but, as the title indicates, it will show how much is demanded of us by the various ethical theories put forth. Even though these theories differ greatly one from the other as they contend among themselves for our allegiance, you will probably recognize the kernel of each of them, even if you've done no previous reading in moral philosophy, because all ethical theories have as their basis particular moral intuitions that we have all experienced—well, almost all of us; for the rest of us amoralism, immoralism, and sociopathology are also touched upon in this book.

I hope I have written this text in a clear, concise style that engages the reader in a manner that is serious but not free of humor. In fact, I hope that I have written the book that I wish had been available to me when I was an undergraduate student of ethics at the University of California all those years ago. (Yes, yes, it is among other things an attempt to recover my youth.) Most of the ideas presented here are in my opinion fairly easy to learn, and those that are hardest I've tried to break down into manageable units. At the end of each chapter there is an outline of the ideas presented that is meant as a study guide. As with my other books published by McGraw-Hill, the many pen-and-ink drawings throughout the book have several purposes. Some are intended as graphic explanations of philosophical concepts, some are meant as visual signifiers that can help students to remember key ideas, and some may simply help to lighten the load a bit. Having used the blackboard extensively as a teaching device for thirty-five years, I believe that even these small jokes serve students as mnemonic tools for hanging on to the more serious ideas on which the cartoon is riffing.

Much of the content of the book derives from material accumulated on the shelves of my mind after all these years of teaching philosophy at the College of Marin in California and, later, at North Carolina State University. It has involved research both with primary and secondary resources (the best and most accessible of which I've listed in bibliographies at the end of each chapter). I have occasionally borrowed paragraphs and illustrations from my previous books, *Looking at Philosophy*, *Does the Center Hold?* and *Visions of Human Nature*.

I would like to acknowledge several debts I've accumulated along the way. First, I am obliged to all those students in my classes (well, perhaps not *all* of them). My editor at McGraw-Hill, Jon-David Hague, has given me very welcome encouragement, and Allison Rona has also been a strong support. Thanks to the McGraw-Hill production team, TBH Typecast, and a special thanks to Judith Brown for her careful editing of the manuscript. Randy Carter, my colleague and friend at NC State, has given me some very good tips. I also owe thanks to the philosophy professors from a variety of colleges and universities across the country who have read my manuscript with a critical eye. Their suggestions and corrections, and even a few well-aimed insults, have been invaluable. Following are these intrepid workers:

SFC06330

- William J. Fitzpatrick
  Virginia Tech
- John M. Collins
  East Carolina University
- Douglas Fingal
  Iowa Lakes Community College
- Barbara Solheim
  William Rainey Harper College
- J. Jeremy Wisnewski
  East Carolina University
- John T. Kennedy
  Metropolitan State College

As always, my deepest gratitude is to my wife, Leila May, for her sharp eye, quick mind, and inexhaustible sense of humor.

Contents

VII. Contractualism   336

1

Moral Philosophy and Its Discontents

What Philosophy Is

Before I say what "ethics," or "moral philosophy," is, let me say something about philosophy itself, of which ethics, or moral philosophy, is supposed to be a part. First, let me admit that I do not think that the concept "philosophy" can be defined with precision. That is, when we try to define "philosophy," we can't state its **necessary conditions** (we can't say what is necessarily the case for something to be called philosophy in ways that would distinguish philosophy from other fields of activity), though perhaps we can state its **sufficient conditions** (we can say what features would suffice for something to be called philosophy). Typically, an exhaustive definition would provide both of these conditions. For some X to be called a mammal it is necessary but not sufficient that X be an animal, and it is both necessary and sufficient that X have mammary glands. For some Y to be called a square it is necessary but not sufficient that Y be a closed figure, and it is both necessary and sufficient that Y be an equilateral closed figure with at least three right angles. So, what I am saying is that we cannot give an exhaustive definition of philosophy—we can't say in advance what features philosophy must have if it is to count as philosophy. I don't think that this news is necessarily all that awful—we can't give exhaustive definitions of "art" nor of "love," yet

1

these concepts are important in the lives of most of us, and we seem to get through life without exhaustive definitions of them. Philosophy, art, and love are what some philosophers call **open concepts,** which, rather than being defined in terms of necessary and sufficient conditions, are defined in terms of what the Austrian philosopher Ludwig Wittgenstein called "family resemblances." Speaking of another open concept, "game," Wittgenstein denied that competition or winning and losing were necessary or sufficient conditions of the concept "game" by showing that there are games that do not involve these features (e.g., ring-around-the-rosy). And he denied that amusement, pleasure, or fun were necessary or sufficient conditions of games by pointing out that a game is still a game whether or not anyone is enjoying it, and that one can have fun without playing games. In Wittgenstein's own words,

> And we can go through the many, many other groups of games in the same way; we can see how similarities crop up and disappear. . . . [We] see a complicated network of similarities overlapping and criss-crossing: sometimes overall similarities, sometimes similarities of detail. I can think of no better expression to characterize these similarities than "family resemblances"; for the various resemblances

Family Resemblance

between members of a family, build, features, colour of eyes, gait, temperament, etc. etc. overlap and criss-cross in the same way.—And I shall say "games form a family."[1]

Having explained why I can't provide an exhaustive definition of philosophy, I will now offer you a perhaps slightly facetious definition provided by the American philosopher Wilfrid Sellars, who says that philosophy is "an attempt to see how things, in the broadest possible sense of the term, hang together, in the broadest possible sense of the term."[2] If we consider the ancient history of (Western) philosophy, we can perhaps see part of Sellars's point. The Greek philosophers now known as the **pre-Socratic philosophers** (between the seventh and fourth centuries B.C.E.) wanted to establish that the way the world presents itself to our senses is illusory, and that there is a systematic difference between reality and appearance. This difference could be revealed through a certain kind of rational discourse they called philosophy (literally, love of wisdom), which consisted of a kind of speculative logical analysis that was meant to pierce the veil of illusion to reveal the truth. These philosophers argued strenuously among themselves whether the basis of all reality was water (Thales), air (Anaximenes), fire (Heraclitus), or numbers (Pythagoras) and whether motion and change were illusions (Parmenides) or stability and permanence were illusions (Heraclitus). By the year 350 B.C.E. this debate had produced a primitive version of the atomic theory (Democritus), a more sophisticated version of which is now accepted by modern science. These early philosophers were certainly trying to figure out "how things hang together," in the broadest senses of the terms.

Sellars's definition of philosophy also emphasizes another usual but not necessary feature of philosophy that I would like to mention: its *general* and *abstract* nature (Sellars's "in the broadest sense of the term"). There are key categories of philosophy that are general and abstract, categories such as space, time, existence, sociality, beauty, justice, love, and death. If I ask you what time it is, I am certainly not asking a philosophical question. Or, if you tell me that it takes less time to fly from San Francisco to Reno than from Reno to St. Louis, in doing so, you are not making a philosophical assertion. But if I ask you not, "What time is it?" but, "What is time?" then I am asking a general, abstract question that is probably philosophical. (Again, without examining the context, I can't say for sure that it is philosophical and not scientific.)

Similarly, if I ask you what it means for something to be located in space, I am asking a philosophical question, but not if I ask, "How many chairs will fit around the dining room table?" It is true that in everyday discourse I am more likely to ask the practical questions than the philosophical ones, yet behind every practical question or statement lie the general concepts with which philosophy officially concerns itself. It's as if every practical statement entails some general, abstract presupposition, and philosophy sees part of its job as revealing those assumptions and critically scrutinizing them.

If, as I said, the earliest forms of philosophical discourse eventually led to the views of modern science, what is the difference between philosophy and science? It is a slight oversimplification, but still roughly correct, to say that when the general questions that philosophers ask can be posed in a way that promotes observable experimentation to test the truth or falsity of the general hypotheses, these questions break free from philosophy and become science. That is, there is a speculative or reflective or meditative (or armchair) feature of philosophical thought that cannot be reduced to empirical experimentation. (Philosophers sit at their desks a lot and think, or read, or write, but they don't go on many philosophical field trips.) But, we cannot say that speculation is a necessary or sufficient condition of philosophy, because some philosophical activities are not speculative after all (e.g., doing **logic,** or working out relations between certain concepts). Furthermore, as I just said, it is an oversimplification to distinguish between philosophy and science by rigorously contrasting speculation with **empirical** experimentation. Concepts like antimatter, dark holes, and the **big bang** are very much part of contemporary physics and astronomy, yet they have a distinctly speculative air about them. This is why we can't even say that speculation on abstract ideas is a sufficient condition of philosophy. Sometimes scientists engage in exactly this activity. Someone might say that they are doing it in their philosophical moments, but most people don't think that physicists who meditate on dark holes have stopped doing science at the moment they begin these speculations. All this does not show that there is no difference after all between science and philosophy; rather it shows how these two different families can indeed overlap and criss-cross.

I have been emphasizing the speculative nature of most philosophy, but this emphasis does not necessarily endorse wild speculation. Philosophical speculation usually wants to be restricted by the laws of logic. (In fact, logic is thought of as a branch of philosophy.) For example, the pre-Socratic philosopher Thales reasoned in this way:

A. The world (reality) must be either one thing or many things.
B. If the world were many things, there would be no unity in the world (i.e., no "world").
C. But B is impossible.
D. Therefore, the world must be one thing.

Using similarly logically constrained arguments, the pre-Socratics debated what that "one thing" must be, and, as you have seen, that debate produced the first atomic theory. (For this theory, the conclusion of the logical argument just presented was modified: There is one kind of thing in the world—atoms. But there are many,

many, many atoms—in fact, an infinite number, according to Democritus.)

One last way of beginning to think about philosophy is to look at the kinds of classes typically taught in philosophy departments in colleges and universities around the world. For example, typically, besides logic, there would be courses in **epistemology** (theory of knowledge); **metaphysics** (overall theory of reality); **aesthetics** (philosophy of art and beauty); **political philosophy** (theory of politics); and a number of courses beginning with the phrase "philosophy of . . ." such as philosophy of law, philosophy of science, philosophy of psychology, which would be the study of the meaning of the key concepts in these different fields and the structural relationships among them. And of course there would be a class called moral philosophy, or ethics, which brings us to our task at hand.

What Moral Philosophy Is

The word "ethics" derives from a Greek word meaning custom, more, or disposition. The words "morality" and "moral" derive from a Latin word also meaning custom, more, or disposition. Some philosophers use these words interchangeably, and others, such as the British philosopher Bernard Williams (1929–2003), argue that "ethics" is the broader term, and "morality" is a subset of ethics.[3] Williams does this, in part, because he notes that the concept of morality has taken on a sense of obligation, which he claims did not exist in ancient Greek discussions of our topic. It is also true that in everyday language there seem to be some differences between the two, though not exactly the difference that Williams points out. If you tell me that your dentist is unethical, I probably suspect that he or she is guilty of some billing impropriety, but if you tell me that your dentist is immoral, I think of other kinds of improprieties.

Similarly, we talk about "business ethics" and not so much about "business morality." Here, contrary to what Williams says, "ethics" seems to be more restricted than "morality." Ultimately, then, it all seems to be a bit arbitrary. Therefore, in this book I have decided to use the pairings "ethics/ethical" and "morality/moral" interchangeably.

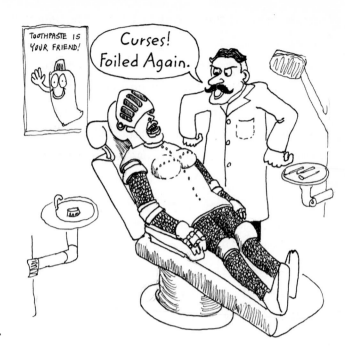

Precautionary Measures

So, ethics, or moral philosophy, is that branch of philosophy that deals with ethical theory. Part of the job of moral philosophy is what is sometimes called **meta-ethics** ("meta," from the Greek word for above, beyond, or after). This project of moral philosophy does not attempt to build moral theories or give moral advice; rather it involves the analysis of ethical concepts and language, determining the meaning of ethical terms and their status with regard to other forms of discourse. Typical of the kinds of questions asked are Can ethical claims ever be objective? Can they be deemed true or false? Are ethical terms like "good," "evil," "right," "wrong," "ought," "ought not" descriptions, or are they evaluations, or perhaps merely disguised expressions of emotion? These are good questions, and at one point in the twentieth century, **analytic philosophers**—that is, most philosophers in Britain, Canada, and the United States—believed that moral philosophy should restrict itself to meta-ethics, a purely analytical program. But today, most philosophers believe that in addition to answering these kinds of questions, another part of moral philosophy's job is indeed to formulate acceptable principles of behavior, to attempt to justify them, and to defend them against criticism.

The problems of ethics are not independent of other philosophical problems concerning reality and knowledge. Rather than thrust you into the many problems of philosophy related to ethics —which might involve loading more on you than you thought you were signing onto—I have placed an addendum at the end of this chapter, briefly discussing philosophical problems of meaning and truth that are presupposed by moral philosophy. If you (or your philosophy teacher) think you could benefit from this digression, it awaits your consultation, but the information is not required in order to engage in the study of ethics. However, before we can advance into the specific problems of moral philosophy, we must inspect certain challenges that have been made against various features of moral philosophy and can act as stumbling blocks to our progress.

David Hume Casting Stumbling Blocks

Stumbling Blocks

Like epistemologists (theorists of knowledge), moral philosophers have traditionally dreamed of building moral systems upon a foundation of certainty, in the manner in which the French philosopher René Descartes (1595–1650) built a whole metaphysical system. Descartes took as his foundation the simple proposition "I am"—a proposition that he claimed to be absolutely certain and irrefutable. (Every time it is uttered, it is shown to be true, and any attempt to negate it produces a self-contradiction.) From that basic foundation, Descartes deduced the rest of his whole system, including (believe it or not) the proof of the existence of God, the proof of the existence of the external world, the validity of mathematics, and the justification of scientific method for exploring material reality.

Ever since, the moral philosopher's dream has been to create such a moral edifice, based on a firm foundation that would support every column and beam in the structure. What would that foundation look like? One historical attempt to solve the problem is called **intuitionism**. It holds that there are certain moral principles, values, or qualities that are completely self-evident and need no analysis, explanation, or justification; and upon these self-evident moral features of the world an ethical system could be built. One early twentieth-century version of this view was put forth by George Moore (1873–1958)—usually referred to as G. E. Moore—in his book of 1903, *Principia Ethica*.[4]

SCIENCE
EXTERNAL WORLD
MATHEMATICS
GOD
SELF

See what you can do if you think clearly and distinctly?

René Descartes, the Arnold Schwarzenegger of the World of Philosophy

G. E. Moore believed himself to have solved the foundation problem by claiming that "the good" is some non-natural property that can be indicated (pointed at, revealed, called attention to) but that cannot be analyzed because it is "simple"—that is, has no parts or constituents. As an analogy, he uses the color yellow, which cannot be explained to a blind person because it can only be pointed at. (Presumably, telling a blind person that yellow is a primary color lying between green and orange on the color wheel, with a wavelength between 570 and 590 nanometers, would still not allow that person to know what yellow is.) Moore is the same philosopher who discovered the **naturalistic fallacy,** which we have yet to investigate. Most moral philosophers take seriously Moore's warning about this so-called fallacy, but, as far as I can tell, very few of them have accepted Moore's solution to the problem—nor any other version of intuitionism.

If there are no non-natural moral facts in the world to be intuited, perhaps there is some fact about the natural world, or about human nature or human desires, that is unshakable and that when studied correctly, tells us what we should strive to be and to achieve, and upon which a persuasive moral theory could be constructed.

The Relation Between Fact and Value

The Is/Ought Problem

Less than a hundred years after Descartes's death, this particular ethical dream of certainty was burst like a bubble by what is now called the **is/ought problem,** or sometimes, Hume's Guillotine.

It has to this day proved to be one of the greatest stumbling blocks for moral philosophers of all types. This guillotine consists of a philosophical blade first put into action by the astute Scottish philosopher David Hume (1711–1776), which seems to separate irrevocably all moral discourse from any factual discourse, thereby robbing the house of ethics of any possible foundation. (Hume also claims to have dismantled Descartes's "irrefutable, absolutely certain" metaphysical foundation, "I am," through **deconstruction** of the idea of self-identity—but that's another story.) Hume's idea is usually expressed in the form of the assertion, "No 'is' implies an 'ought'." (Hume's actual wording is more complex.) This means that no moral claims whatsoever can be logically derived from any merely factual claims. Let me clarify this point by choosing a moral principle with which almost everyone would agree: It is morally wrong to torture children just for the pleasure of doing so. Now,

I made it myself.

David's Hobby

Hume's point would be that there are no factual claims (no value-free descriptions of any facets of the world) from which this principle can be logically derived. For example, the following four sentences probably express facts about the world:

(a) Torture causes children great pain.
(b) Most people would be horrified to see children being tortured.
(c) Prolonged torture causes permanent harm to children.
(d) No child wants to be tortured.

But none of these assertions, nor any combination of them, logically entails the sentence

(e) [Therefore] It is morally wrong to torture innocent children.

In other words, you could assert (a), (b), (c), and (d), and deny (e) without contradicting yourself. Contrast this with the following set of sentences, all of which probably express facts about the world:

[Premise]	(f) All humans are mortal.
[Premise]	(g) Socrates is a human.
[Conclusion]	(h) Socrates is mortal.

This second group constitutes a genuine logical entailment. That is, if you assert (f) and (g), you are logically committed to (h). If you hold (f) and (g) to be true, and if you then deny (h), you are contradicting yourself, and nobody has any reason to take you seriously from that point on. Hume's point is that you can never logically derive a conclusion that has the word "ought" in it (that is, contains a moral judgment) from premises that contain only value-free descriptions of facts in the world. (By "value-free descriptions" I mean descriptions that have not sneaked in a disguised moral value. For instance, if I say, "X killed Y," I have described an event in value-free terms, but if I say, "X murdered Y," I have imported a value-loaded term into my description, because "murder" means wrongful killing.)

The Naturalistic Fallacy

G. E. Moore, whose intuitionism we looked at earlier, updated the debate that Hume initiated by producing an argument distinct from Hume's is/ought problem but closely related to it. It is distinct because it is logically possible to hold Moore's view and reject Hume's without logical contradiction, or vice versa; but it is related because both views attack attempts to derive moral value from morally neutral natural facts. As mentioned earlier, Moore called this supposed error the naturalistic fallacy. Moore's argument is not difficult, but it is a little complicated. You may need to slow down and perhaps read this a couple of times. His argument is meant to show that any attempt to define the concept "good," using only natural facts or processes as the defining terms, is doomed to failure. (One example of such an attempt would be "good" as defined by **hedonism** in terms of pleasure: "Good" means "pleasurable.") Moore asserted that all naturalistic definitions of "good," such as the hedonistic example, can be formulated in the following manner:

> "X is good" means "X has property P."
> (In our case: "X is good" means "X has the propensity to cause pleasure.")

Then Moore formulated two questions that he used to analyze the kind of naturalistic definition we are inspecting:

1. X has P, but does X have P?
2. X has P, but is X good?

Let us continue to use the same example, and let property P be "the propensity to cause pleasure." Then, question 1 means "X has the propensity to cause pleasure, but *does* X have the propensity to cause pleasure?" Now, the reason that this question sounds nonsensical is that it *is* nonsensical. If the first part of the formula asserts P's existence, the second part cannot ask whether P exists. (Consider two examples: "Water has two parts hydrogen, but *does* water have two parts hydrogen?" "Mexico is in the Western hemisphere, but *is* Mexico in the Western hemisphere?")

But now notice that the second question is not nonsensical in that same way. We can ask, "X has the propensity to cause pleasure, but *is* X good?" Someone might really want to ask this question, saying, "What if X is something that has the propensity to give

Hitler pleasure? Is X still *necessarily good?*" (There is a famous photo of Hitler kicking his heels together at the news that Paris had fallen to the German troops.) This is a reasonable question, and the point of using it as an example is to show you that if "good" were really defined in terms of pleasure, then question 2 (X has P, but is X good?) would be identical to question 1 (X has P, but does X have P?). That is, if the good is pleasure (by definition), then the question "X causes pleasure, but is X good?" is identical to "X causes pleasure, but does X cause pleasure?" According to Moore, the fact that it is not nonsense to ask whether something that causes pleasure is good, proves that there is a fallacy in arguing that "good" means "pleasurable."

For Moore, the same is true of any attempt to define "good" in terms of an empirical property. For instance, try out the argument on claims like these:

Is Sadistic Pleasure Good?

1. Good is the happiness of the greatest number of people. (Utilitarianism)
2. Good is whatever the majority says is good. (Rousseau)
3. Good is whatever best imitates **the Forms.** (Plato)

4. *Good is survival.* (Crude Darwinism[5])
5. *Good is being obedient.* (Crude authoritarianism)
6. *Good is obeying God's will.* (Crude moral theism)

Notice that Moore does not claim to have refuted assertions like "pleasure is good," or "happiness is good," or "survival is good," or "obedience is good," or "obeying God's will is good." Rather, he claims to have refuted all *definitions* of "good" in terms of those properties, on the grounds that, in each of these cases, it is never nonsense to ask questions like "But *is* happiness (majority opinion, imitation of the Forms, survival, obedience, obeying God's will, etc.) always good?" (The last example—6—shows that Moore's naturalistic fallacy is a misnomer, because his argument covers even properties that are not natural in the sense of being features of the natural world. Most people who agree with example 6 would think of God's will as being supernatural.)

For the entire twentieth century in the English-speaking world the is/ought problem and the closely related naturalistic fallacy have hounded discussions of moral philosophy. There have been basically two responses to this twin challenge: either to write moral philosophy in ways that do not become ensnared by these problems, or to write moral philosophy in ways that challenge either the correctness or the significance of the so-called problem and the so-called fallacy. But hardly any ethicist has simply ignored this thicket. As you will see, I have felt obligated to include a section about it in each of the six theories you will read about in the rest of this book.

The Problem of Determinism

Determinism

It is generally held, both by moralists and jurists, that "ought implies can"—that is, for morality or law to have any claim on us, it must be possible for us to perform the acts and maintain the attitudes required by moral or legal obligation. We cannot be demanded to do the impossible. By the same token, we cannot be held responsible for behavior over which we have no control. If this is so, then the claim of **determinism** seems to roll another giant stumbling block across the torturous path of moral philosophy.

The problem of determinism has been haunting us for a long time. In the ancient world the problem was perhaps better named **fatalism.** In Homeric times (ninth century B.C.E.) it was associated with the goddess Moira (Fate), who had dominion over all the other gods, including Zeus, the king of the gods. A form of fatalism was also derived from ancient astrology, according to which the heavenly constellations were mythical figures under whose power humans were born, their destinies forever fixed by the strength of the figure who reigned the night sky at the moment of their birth.

In the medieval period, some Christian and Muslim theologians derived a fatalistic determinism from the idea of God's omniscience. If God knows all, he knows every moment of the future, which must happen of necessity just as

Astrology at Work

God knows that it will. Therefore, the future (including our fate in heaven or hell) is predestined.

The French **Enlightenment** figure Pierre-Simon Laplace (1749–1827) presented a clear, modern version of the thesis of determinism based on his understanding of the laws of nature. Laplace said that if he knew all the natural laws and had one complete description of the whole universe at any given moment, then he could predict all future events and retrodict all past events. The fact that we do not have all this information, and probably never will, does not change the case that all events are rigorously determined by the strict laws of nature, according to Laplace.

There is a drunken ladybug on this leaf now. Therefore on June 19, 2020, there will be a mudslide in Rangoon.

Most contemporary physicists and philosophers of science use a less rigid model of natural laws than did Laplace in the eighteenth century. According to

Pierre-Simon Laplace (1749–1827)

the twenty-first-century view, natural laws should be understood as being probabilistic rather than absolute. Instead of saying with Laplace, "If event A happens, then event B necessarily follows," they say, "If event A happens, then necessarily either event B, C, or D follows," and these possibilities are rated statistically. (Even if B has a much higher statistical probability of following A than does D, the occurrence of A does not rule out the sequential occurrence of D rather than B.) But even this weaker version of **causality,** which is not a strict determinism, poses a threat to our ideas of responsibility and morality.

Now, there are basically four kinds of responses to either the stronger or the weaker deterministic claim: (a) agree with the deterministic model, and conclude that responsibility and morality are impossible; (b) agree with the deterministic model, and try to demonstrate that responsibility and morality are compatible with determinism; (c) disagree with the deterministic model, and conclude that freedom and responsibility exist; (d) admit that one is stumped by the problem, and draw no conclusion about its solution. Response (a) is sometimes called **hard determinism;** response (b) is sometimes called **soft determinism** or **compatibilism;** response (c) is sometimes called **libertarianism** (not to be confused with the political party of the same name). Response (d) has no name, but could be called "ignoramusism," from the Latin, *ignoramus*, meaning we do not know. People who hold position (d) probably would prefer to call themselves "agnostics," from the Greek, also meaning we do not know.

I know of no philosophers who have bragged about taking position (d), though some must have a sneaking suspicion that it corresponds best with the facts as they understand them. Few prominent philosophers and scientists have defended hard determinism, though the psychologist B. F. Skinner comes very close to doing so. Therefore, I will turn to compatibilism and libertarianism as the two most serious contenders.

Compatibilism

The thesis that one version or another of determinism is true (or may prove to be true) is currently popular with a large number of moral philosophers who believe that philosophy must be consistent with science, and therefore feel driven to treat determinism as true, even though it has not been proved true. But in fact the compatibility thesis has been defended by variously affiliated philosophers from Greek times to our own. At the end of the classical period, Augustine of Hippo (354–430) was one of those Christian philosophers who believed that God's omniscience did indeed entail God's knowledge of all events in the universe, including those that we humans call "future" events. According to St. Augustine, for God, there is no future or past, only an eternal present. Therefore, God knows all future events, and these events must necessarily happen just as God knows they will. Augustine saw it as his job to justify the rewards and punishments that God metes out to his creatures in such a deterministic world. Augustine agreed that only free acts could justly be punished or rewarded, but he concluded that freedom in the sense of "being in our power" was sufficient freedom to justify the concept of moral responsibility, which is the concept upon which rewarding and punishing are predicated. If I desire to do X, and if I can do X with no external impediments, then I am free to do X; and when I do in fact perform X, I am responsible for X. Thus, freedom and responsibility are compatible with these acts being in some sense necessary. Therefore, it is logically and morally legitimate for God to reward acts that are good and to punish acts that are evil.

In our own days, the philosophers who want to defend the compatibility of freedom and determinism are not motivated by a desire to exculpate God. Rather, they believe that the successes of scientific predictability point inevitably to the truth of some form or other of determinism, even if only a statistical one, and they believe that the apparent

St. Augustine as Judge—God as Accused

conflict between freedom and determinism must be shown to be illusory. (Unless God has created human beings as substantially different from anything else in the universe, it is difficult to see why humans should be exempt from the determinism that seems to hold in all other cases.) Despite the motivational differences between modern philosophers and Augustine, in many cases, the structure of their arguments remains similar to Augustine's. I will present a composite picture of such an argument.

In our daily lives, we all know how to tell the difference, in most cases, between events that simply happen to us—for example, being hit by lightning—and acts that we engage in—for example, tipping a waiter. There are, of course, occasional moments when we think everything is out of our control, and other moments when we feel that we are driven by compulsion; but in general we are familiar with the ideas of responsibility and of right and wrong, and recognize clear cases of their applicability. We learn these ideas in our childhood and we try to teach them to our children. We would be incredulous if we were told that, in terms of responsibility, an event like slipping on a banana peel and falling down the stairs is the same kind of event as robbing a bank or that, in terms of moral worth, there is no difference between helping the old woman who lives next door and burning down the house she inhabits because we want a better view from our house.

Now, says the compatibilist, it would be absurd to abandon the traditional commonsense concepts of responsibility, freedom, and right and wrong on the grounds that the new (no doubt correct) scientific picture of the world is one of a causal system expressed in scientific, statistical law–like propositions. If one wants to accept the scientific picture of the world—as one ought to do, according to the compatibilists—and maintain the traditional views of responsibility, the best way of doing this is to recognize that the model of the individual as author of her acts and the idea of freedom as the ability to act without impediments (roughly St. Augustine's freedom) is freedom enough. As the contemporary American philosopher T. M. Scanlon says when discussing both the hard-core and the statistical versions of determinism:

The mere truth of those theses would not imply that our thoughts and actions lack the continuity and regularity required of rational creatures. It would not mean that we lack the capacity to respond to and assess reasons, nor would it entail the existence of conditions that always disrupt the connection between this process of assessments and our subsequent actions. So, even if one of these theses is true, it can still be correct to say that a particular action shows a person to have governed herself in a way that is morally deficient.[6]

Libertarianism

Do the successes of science in fact force us to accept determinism as true? The libertarians answer in the negative. I will present what I take to be the mainstream libertarian argument, using ideas from two well-known articles, one by C. A. Campbell and another by Richard Taylor.[7] The first point to make (one that is perhaps a bit surprising) is that the libertarian sides with the hard determinist against the soft determinist on one important topic: The libertarian and the hard determinist agree that if determinism is true, then there is no freedom. As you saw, the soft determinist—or compatibilist—salvages freedom in a determined world by defining freedom as the coincidence of will and capacity ("I can"). Then the soft determinist claims that, given such a definition of freedom, freedom certainly does exist, even in a deterministic universe, and with it, responsibility. (The act that I can perform, and do perform, is my act, and I am responsible for it.) Now, libertarians such as Campbell argue that the soft determinist's definition of freedom is only half the truth. Freedom requires not only the ability to do what one desires to do ("I can") but also access to genuine alternatives, real choices ("I could have done otherwise"). That is, if I perform act X under conditions A, B, and C, X is a free act for which I could be held responsible only if under those identical conditions I could have performed act Y instead of act X. But it is precisely this ability that determinism denies. So the compatibilist theory does not generate a genuine concept of freedom; hence it does not generate a genuine concept of responsibility.

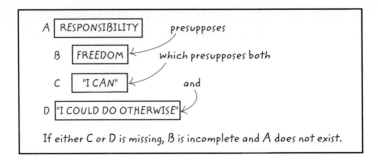

The Libertarian View of Freedom

Well then, is there such a thing as freedom as the libertarians define it ("I can" and "I could do otherwise")? Libertarians point out that if we appeal to our actual experience, we have to admit that we can never *prove* that we can do otherwise than we do, but in most cases we strongly *feel* that we can, and we certainly *believe* that we can. Our experience of ourselves in the world definitely tells us that we sometimes have freedom in the full sense of the word. Now, the theory of determinism—in both versions presented here—claims that our experience is illusory. The libertarian wants to stress that determinism is a theory (that is, an intellectual construct) and one that, like libertarianism, probably can never be proven true. Normally, a theory's function is to explain something that otherwise would be mysterious. Newton's theory of gravity is meant to explain certain features of the universe as we experience them. Freud's theory of the unconscious is meant to explain certain impulsive acts as we experience them. But the puzzling aspect of the theory of determinism is that far from explaining certain data of our experience (the strong feeling and the belief that we have genuine alternatives), this theory *denies* them. Furthermore, determinism is no part of any particular science; it is a part of philosophy.

Given this curious fact about the theory of determinism, the libertarian thinks we should be very skeptical of it. I'll make this point concrete. Let's say that I hold my index finger out and then consider the possible ways I can move it. For the sake of simplicity, I will arbitrarily limit my possibilities to four. I can move it up (call this act A), down (B), to my left (C), or to my right (D). And let us say that at times t^1, t^2, and t^3, I have held out my finger but not yet decided how to move it. Then at time t^4, I decide to move my finger to the left (act C) and do so. Now, I experience this act (as trivial as it might be) as a free act. I chose to do C, and I could have chosen to do A, B, or D instead. But determinism says that act C was a determined act—that it followed necessarily from the events that preceded at t^1, t^2, and t^3—at least, that's what the hard-core determinist claims. What does the soft-core (based on statistical probability) determinist say about this case? I'm not sure. But apparently she too must deny that the choice is totally up to me—that is, she must deny that I have freedom in the sense of "could do otherwise under identical conditions." Libertarians point out that no one has ever established that such an act was a necessary one, though we should remind ourselves that neither has anyone ever established that such an act is not necessary. The fact remains that I *feel* and *believe* that I am the cause of the act.

If determinists want to fly in the face of experience and claim that all acts, including act C, are necessary, or caused by events and processes over which we have no control, then the onus is on them to prove that counterintuitional claim. And until

Freedom in Action

they do, says the libertarian, the rest of us have good reason to believe determinism to be false.

Well, with the exception of ignoramusism, we have seen that two of the other three possibilities defend the ideas of freedom and responsibility. So we are batting almost 667 (i.e., getting on base 66⅔ percent of the time). That's enough to warrant proceeding carefully down the road of ethical theory.

The Problem of Cultural Relativism

The problem of **relativism** does not come from the field of philosophy but from the social sciences. Nevertheless, some believe that it represents a serious stumbling block to the possibility of moral philosophy.

Associated with some important names in anthropology and psychology, cultural relativism denies that there can be any universal or objective moral values on the grounds that moral values are the products of individual cultures, which differ from one another in such a fashion that the values central to

**Anthropologists Attacking
Moral Philosopher**

each society differ from one another. The anthropologist Ruth Benedict expressed the idea in a famous article in 1934:

> We recognize that morality differs in every society and is a convenient term for socially approved habits. Mankind has always preferred to say "It is morally good," rather than "It is habitual," and the fact of this preference is matter enough for a critical science of ethics. But historically the two phrases are synonymous.
>
> The concept of the normal is properly a variant of the concept of the good. It is that which a society has approved. A normal action is one which falls well within the limits of expected behavior for a particular society. . . . [I]ndividuals whose characteristics are not congenial to the selected type of human behavior in that community are the deviants, no matter how valued their personality traits may be in a contrasted civilization.[8]

Benedict's views were echoed a generation later by the psychologist B. F. Skinner:

What a given group of people calls good is a fact: it is what members of the group find reinforcing as the result of their genetic endowment and the natural and social contingencies to which they have been exposed. Each culture has its own set of goods, and what is good in one culture may not be good in another. To recognize this is to take the position of "cultural relativism." What is good for the Trobriand Islander is good for the Trobriand Islander, and that is that. Anthropologists have often emphasized relativism as a tolerant alternative to missionary zeal in converting all cultures to a single set of ethical, governmental, religious, or economic values.[9]

Well, cultural relativism may be a "tolerant alternative to missionary zeal," but it appears to be disastrous for moral philosophy. On this account, there can never be any universal moral reasoning, only acknowledgment of others' "good." ("I hear what you're saying," coupled with the advice, "When in Rome, do as the Romans do.")

And the data from the social sciences sometimes do seem to support such relativism. (It's not good for me to worship cows, but it is good for Hindus to worship cows because cow manure provides both fertilizer and fuel for Hindu culture.)

It cannot be denied that this kind of relativism is healthy as an antidote to puritanical uptightness and dangerous ethnocentric arrogance. ("Our values are right, and we'll impose them on you if we have to kill you to do it.") But our

relativism runs up against problems when we turn to questions like this: Must we withhold moral judgment about Nazi brutalities on the grounds that we are not members of a Nazi culture? Exterminating six million people is "good" for Hitler but not for me? This "different strokes for different folks" philosophy here seems to border on complicity in mass murder. So let's go back and take a closer look at what ethical relativism is saying. Under scrutiny, its thesis becomes less clear. Is the cultural relativist saying, (1) "There are no universally held values," or (2) "No value or set of values can be justifiably recommended for all people"? These are very different claims. Let's look at each of them.

A Texas Cow Worshipper

No Universally Held Moral Values

Notice that this first claim is an empirical one. In theory at least, it is capable of confirmation or refutation through scientific investigation. Now, there are several things to say about it. If it is meant to be interpreted *individually*, saying that there never has been a moral value accepted by *absolutely everybody*, then, no doubt, the claim is true but not very impressive. (Just because one person—Cronus perhaps—broke the law against eating one's children doesn't mean there is something wrong with the law.)

Then what about interpreting the relativist's thesis culturally rather than individually? Certainly not all social scientists are in agreement concerning the truth of this version of the claim. For example, the eminent anthropologists Alfred Kroeber and Clyde Kluckhohn argued that certain universal values have been accepted by all cultures: No culture tolerates indiscriminate lying, stealing, or violence within the in-group. The incest taboo is virtually universal. No culture places value on suffering as an end in itself. Every culture ceremonializes death. "All cultures define as abnormal [those] individuals who are permanently inaccessible to communication or who fail to maintain some degree of control over their impulsive life."[10] Kroeber and Kluckhohn do not deny that what counts as lying, stealing, violence, or even incest might be culturally defined, but they think that these values are universal behind the particulars.

Cronus Eating His Children (after Francisco Goya)

The social psychologist Solomon Asch holds a similar view. He claims that every society despises cowardice and honors bravery. In every society, modesty, courage, and hospitality are rewarded (even if these virtues are sometimes defined differently from culture to culture). Asch does not deny that there are indeed sometimes real differences in values, but even in cultures where acts that are horrible to us are routinely performed, it is often possible to find that the disagreement between their culture and ours is really more of a debate about apparently empirical facts than it is a debate over values. Ancient Chinese cultures commonly engaged in infanticide (leaving unwanted infants exposed to die in nature). But Asch claims that in ancient China infants were not considered human until their first year had passed. These Chinese and we may actually be seen to agree on the value of human life he facts concerning what constitutes a human

b..e thesis of cultural relativism is that there are no
.. or by most cultures, that thesis is probably false.
..s true? Would that put an end to moral philosophy?
..s' implies an 'ought'" certainly applies here. A Kantian or
..n would claim that some values are mistaken, and that
..ny can distinguish between sound and unsound values. Moral
..ns that make human sacrifice obligatory are mistaken, they
..uld say. Probably, you agree with them. This brings us to the second formulation of cultural relativism.

No Value or Set of Values Recommendable for All People

If the relativistic claim that "no value or set of values can be recommended to all people" is derived from an anthropology or sociology
that describes what people actually do in various cultures, then the
is/ought distinction invalidates the thesis. Even if it did turn out
that no values are universally held, it wouldn't follow from that discovery that no value is worthy of adoption by all. Even if we found out
that all people enjoy inflicting suffering on others, it wouldn't follow
that they *ought* to inflict suffering on others.

In *this* sense, anthropology
has nothing to offer to moral
philosophy. In this sense, it
doesn't matter what people
from other cultures do. This is
not to deny that the study
of anthropology can have a
salutary humbling effect, cutting
into our tendency to assume that
the values of our culture are
somehow "natural," hence superior, and provoking us to scruti-

**All People Enjoy Inflicting
Suffering on Others**

nize our values philosophically to justify them.

It's natural to keep your lawn mowed at one inch. I keep _my_ lawn mowed at one inch. You keep _yours_ mowed at one inch, too.

The Challenge of Logical Positivism

Between the two world wars in the twentieth century there developed a school of philosophy that came to be known as logical positivism, originally centered in Vienna, Austria. It was composed of a group of hard-nosed philosophers who thought that true philosophy was the **philosophy of science.** In their version, this meant that the correct analysis of all categories of propositions—ordinary language, philosophical language, moral language, aesthetic language—shows that only those propositions that could be restated in the language of science were truly meaningful. These philosophers were tremendously influential during their heyday. Most of them were forced to leave Europe when the Nazis came to power in Germany and Austria, but ironically this exile made them even more influential, as many of them were given positions in top British and American universities during and after World War II. Their views are no longer fashionable, but the ghosts of their ideas still abound. We will study logical positivism briefly because it offers one of the most dramatic challenges possible to the very idea of moral philosophy.

To see this, we will need to look at the positivists' theory of meaning, which actually derives from the eighteenth-century Scottish philosopher David Hume, whom we have already seen to be something of a troublemaker. According to this theory, there are only two kinds of meaning—what came to be called **analytic propositions** and **synthetic propositions.** Analytic propositions are true by definition. They tell us nothing about reality, only about how concepts are related (e.g., "all circles are round," "triangles have three angles," "sisters are female.") The negation of an analytic proposition produces a self-contradiction. For example, saying, "Triangles do not have three angles" is equivalent to saying, "Triangles are not triangles," because a triangle is defined in terms of its three angles. Analytic propositions, then, are **tautologies**—repetitions, redundancies. They are necessarily true, but they are empirically empty because they do not make assertions about the world, but only about relationships between concepts. Synthetic propositions, on the other hand, are empirical. They can be verified or refuted only by some actual or possible observation of facts in the world. Only these kinds of proposition are truly about reality. The negation of a synthetic proposition does not produce a self-contradiction; rather it produces another synthetic proposition, and one of the two is true, the other false. ("There are three books on the table"/"There are not three books on the table.") Any putative proposition that is neither analytic nor synthetic is cognitively empty, or, what amounts to the same thing, *nonsense.*

We've already seen another of Hume's distinctions—that between "is" and "ought"—dubbed Hume's Guillotine. Similarly, the division of all meaningful propositions into two types, analytic and synthetic, has been called Hume's Fork. This fork, in the hands of the logical positivists, devastated theology (e.g., "God exists" is neither analytic nor synthetic; same goes for "The soul is immortal"); it devastated metaphysics (e.g., Plato's "Justice exists as an eternal Form" is neither analytic nor synthetic; same goes for Parmenides' "Nothing changes; everything remains the same"); and it devastated aesthetics (e.g., "Painting stops time in its track and immortalizes the moment"; same goes for "This statue is more beautiful than that one"). So no surprise that it also eviscerates moral propositions.

The Three Possibilities		
ANALYTIC True by definition "Unicorns have one horn."	SYNTHETIC Established by observation "Pickles are sour."	NONSENSE . . . . . . "Twas brillig." "God loves you."

Take a sentence like "Torturing innocent children is immoral." I've already said that most people would probably agree with this claim, regardless of the moral system that grounds their beliefs. However, notice that it is not analytic; that is, it is not true simply by virtue of the meaning of its words (as is proved by denying the sentence and seeing that its negation, "Torturing innocent children is *not* immoral," is not a self-contradiction in the way that the sentence, "A sister is *not* a female" is self-contradictory). On the other hand, neither is the sentence synthetic. That is, there is no observation, actual or possible, that could confirm or refute the claim. If we watched a brute torturing a small child, we would feel horror, revulsion, and fury, but there would be nothing we could point at and say, "There it is! That's the immoral part" (in the way that we can say, look-

ing at a plant, "That's the yellow part," or, looking at a pancake with syrup, "That's the liquid part").

So what is the status of our moral claim, according to the logical positivists? Because it is cognitively empty, it is merely expressive, like your expression of the word "ouch!" when someone pinches you.

Find the Immoral Part

A British member of the school of logical positivism, philosopher A. J. Ayer, who as a young man went to Vienna to study philosophy, claimed that moral language was simply a disguised display of emotion, often coupled with commands in a misleading grammatical form. So the sentence "Torturing is immoral" really means something like this:

Only the third part of this division ("I don't like it!") could have truth value; therefore, the whole sentence "Torturing is immoral" can be neither true nor false. Ayer explains it this way:

TORTURING!
DON'T DO IT!
I DON'T LIKE IT!!

> Sentences which simply express moral judgements do not say anything. They are pure expressions of feeling and as such do not come under the category of truth and falsehood. They are unverifiable for the same reason as a cry of pain or a word of command is unverifiable—because they do not express genuine propositions. . . . [E]thical concepts are pseudo-concepts and consequently indefinable.[11]

Logical positivism inspired many in its day, and its influence is still seen here and there (e.g., in the **behaviorism** of B. F. Skinner's followers), but positivism's rather shocking views about morality need not stress the ethical philosopher too much. The consensus today is that, though its study is instructive, we do not have to take logical positivism all that seriously. It offers some good provisional tools for analysis, but it is fairly obvious that its theory of meaning is too restrictive. Even Hume's Fork (the analytic/synthetic distinction) has its critics.[12] Furthermore, logical positivism suffers from a deadly internal defect. If every proposition is analytic, synthetic, or nonsense, what is the status of the proposition that asserts that every proposition is analytic, synthetic, or nonsense? It is not analytic, because its negation does not lead to a self-contradiction. It is not synthetic, because no observation would tend to confirm or refute it. What status is left for it except that of nonsense according to its own criterion? Perhaps Professor Jon Wheatley was writing an obituary when he said, "Logical positivism is one of the very few philosophical positions which can be easily shown to be dead wrong, and that is its principal claim to fame."[13]

The Challenge of Existentialism

We need to look at one more radical challenge to the very idea of moral philosophy before proceeding, one that—like logical positivism—derives from mid-twentieth-century European philosophy. That is Jean-Paul Sartre's existentialism. Sartre (1905–1980), who coined the term "existentialism," was an **atheist.** (At least Sartre could call himself an atheist; the logical positivists could not call themselves atheists because an atheist denies that God exists— but for the positivists, the word "God" is a nonsense term, so either asserting or denying God's existence is to speak nonsense.) Yet Sartre derived many of his ideas from the nineteenth-century Danish Christian philosopher Søren Kierkegaard, who stressed our aloneness and our dread before the possibility of an alien, invisible God, and our need to decide (freedom) in the face of this anxiety-producing alienation. Kierkegaard and Sartre radicalized Immanuel Kant's claim (which you will study shortly) that human beings must recognize themselves as autonomous, free, and rational. From these three human characteristics, Kant built up a whole ethical code, which, according to him, makes absolute moral demands upon us. Kant could do this by emphasizing rationality over freedom. Kierkegaard and Sartre, to the contrary, stress our freedom over our rationality, and indeed, for them, our freedom overrides not only our rationality but everything else about us. The motto of Sartre's existentialism is "Existence precedes essence,"[14] To Sartre, this means that there is no human nature (essence) that determines our decisions, choices, and actions (existence); rather our decisions, choices, and actions determine our "human nature." Furthermore, even if we choose a certain moral code, that code not only cannot make us do anything, it can't even tell us what to do in concrete cases.

We see this feature of Sartre's thinking in a now-famous example he gave. Sartre cited the case of one of his students who, during the German occupation of France, approached him for advice. The young man came to Sartre under the following circumstances:

> His father was on bad terms with his mother, and, moreover, was inclined to be a collaborationist; his older brother had been killed in the German offensive of 1940, and the young man, with somewhat immature but generous feelings, wanted to avenge him. His mother lived alone with him, very much upset by the half-treason of her husband and the death of her older son; the boy was her only consolation.
>
> The boy was faced with the choice of leaving for England and joining the Free French Forces—that is, leaving his mother behind—or remaining with his mother and helping her to carry on. . . . Who could help him choose? Christian doctrine? No. Christian doctrine says, "Be charitable, love your neighbor, take the more rugged path, etc., etc." But which is the more rugged path? Whom should he love as a brother? The fighting man or his mother? Which does the greater good, the vague act of fighting in a group, or the concrete one of helping a particular human being to go on living? Who can decide *a priori*? Nobody. No book of ethics can tell him. The Kantian ethics says, "Never treat a person as a means, but as an end." Very well, if I stay with my mother I'll treat her as an end and not as a means; but by virtue of this very fact, I'm running the risk of treating the people around me who are fighting, as means; and, conversely, if I go join those who are fighting, I'll be treating them as an end, and, by doing that, I run the risk of treating my mother as a means. . . . You will say, "At least he did go to a teacher for advice." But if you seek advice from a priest, for example, you have chosen this priest; you already knew, more or less, just about what advice he was going to give you. In other words, choosing your advisor is involving yourself. The proof of this is that if you are a Christian, you will say. "Consult a priest." But some priests are collaborating, some are just marking time, some are resisting. Which to choose? If the young man chooses a priest who is resisting or collaborating, he has already decided on the kind of advice he's going to get.

Seeking Advice

Therefore, in coming to see me he knew the answer I was going to give him, and I had one answer to give: "You're free, choose, that is, invent." No general ethics can show you what is to be done; there are no omens in the world.[15]

If Sartre is right, then reason cannot compel anyone to behave in one way as opposed to another because reason can be an authority only if one chooses to authorize reason.

Once I decide that reason has value, then reason can force me to behave only in ways for which I can give cogent reasons. But what if rather than valuing reasons, I—like the "hero" of Fyodor Dostoyevsky's *Notes from the Underground*—choose unreason to guide me? Then I do not need to, nor can I give reasons for my choice. So we see that for Sartre, because we are free and autonomous, we cannot be naturally rational. We are only rational by choice. If we are free, then no moral code can be binding on us. For Sartre, this freedom produces a state of anguish, which is our true human condition. All we can do is face our anguish either in "good faith" (i.e., choose it) or in "bad faith" (i.e., deny its existence).

Sartre's position seems to me to be an overdramatization of certain truths—the

Reason Tries to Compel Sartre to Do the Right Thing

truth that reason by itself cannot force us to behave one way rather than another, and roughly the same truth that leads a number of the moral philosophers we will study to say that the power of moral claims can only be felt from "within" the world of morality. Usually, we are not surprised that sociopaths and some lunatics excuse themselves from that world; in fact, we are often prepared to excuse them ourselves. But we feel that the reason moral philosophy might mean

something to the rest of us is that normally people *do* want to "do the right thing," or perhaps I should say that normal people want to do the right thing. Sartre's argument is that "normality" is not a natural state, but one that we choose.

The Challenge of Feminism

Is there after all a fundamental flaw in traditional Western ethics—the flaw of being inappropriate for more than half of the human race? That is, is moral philosophy as it is traditionally expounded biased toward **androcentrism** (male-centeredness)? Does it fail to take into account the experience of women and to profit from the moral insights derived from female experience? Furthermore, is it possible that with what some call its "patriarchal discourse," moral philosophy has not only ignored women but has also participated in their oppression and perpetuated a bias against them? A good number of **feminist** critics of moral philosophy think that these questions are on target.

What differences exist in the experience of women that might be morally significant? An important step toward answering that ques-

I give unto you the tablets of the law (which may prove to be more burdensome to some than to others).

Patriarchal Discourse

tion was provided by the psychologist Carol Gilligan in 1982 with the publication of her book *In a Different Voice: Psychological Theory and Women's Development.* One of Gilligan's techniques was to interview children using a set of questions developed by the psychologist Lawrence Kohlberg. When Kohlberg performed the tests in the 1960s, it seemed to him that girls did not prove to have as clear a sense of justice as did boys, nor the same deductive capacity for deriving moral conclusions. Throughout the history of literature the claim keeps popping up that women have a lower developed moral sense than men. A typically brazen example is offered by the nineteenth-century German philosopher Arthur Schopenhauer:

But... she's a *girl!*

JUSTICE

> Women remain children for their whole life long. . . . [T]he fundamental fault of the female character is that it has *no sense of justice.* This is mainly due to the fact . . . that women are defective in the powers of reasoning and deliberation.[16]

The Challenge of Feminism   ◆

Gilligan replicated Kohlberg's interviews and reinterpreted the data. In one interview she posed the following question to a girl and a boy, both eleven years old: Should "Heinz" steal medicine from a pharmacist in order to save the life of his sick wife if the pharmacist refuses to lower the price so Heinz can afford it? The boy, Jake, is sure that Heinz should do so and is able to produce a principle ("life is worth more than money") and a logical argument applying that principle.

Jake's Solution

Amy, on the other hand, is less sure. She thinks it's wrong for Heinz to steal the drugs but insists also that it is wrong for the pharmacist to withhold them. She refuses to apply the rules of logic to the case—in fact, in a way she refuses the hypothesis. She thinks if we could talk with the pharmacist and make him understand the situation, he would freely donate the drugs.

Amy's Solution

Is Amy's answer an example of retarded moral development? Is Amy incapable of understanding the abstract concept of justice, of applying a principle to the case, and of drawing deductive conclusions from it? Gilligan does not believe that these are the lessons being taught here. She sees the girl's account as concentrating, not on "a contest of rights," but on a "network of relationships on whose continuation they all depend."[17] In short, Amy *does* refuse to apply abstract principles in a mathematical fashion to unrealistic scenarios as a solution to a human problem. She contextualizes and concentrates on the pragmatics of relationships between human beings.

A number of feminists think Amy got it right. (I say "a number" because there is no such thing as *the* feminist position. In fact, a few have disagreed with some of Gilligan's views.[18]) They think that Amy is correct to reject the typical extreme-case scenarios in terms of which moral philosophy is often argued (e.g., "the case of Sam," which you will read about in Chapter 4). She is right to stress relationships over rules, and she is right to demand more information regarding the context. That is, she is right to see moral judgment as emergent—flowing out from an understanding of the real situation.

Why would women have moral experiences that are distinct from those of men? Philosopher Agnes Heller believes that it is precisely women's historical confinement to the home and exclusion from the broader world of commerce, industry, travel, and war in Western society that has made their lives more alike over the generations and has given them a clearer insight into real human relations. They have had to learn to create and manage small communities involving real people with all their virtues and foibles. Because ethics must ultimately be about human relations, women may indeed have special insights into this sphere.

The feminist criticism of patriarchal ethics has two prongs. First, as philosopher Alison Jaggar says, feminist ethics "seeks to identify and challenge all those ways, overt but more often and more perniciously covert, in which Western ethics has excluded women or rationalized their subordination."[19] Second, it seeks to develop an ethics inspired by, or at least consistent with, the actual moral experience and intuition of women.

Concerning the first point, some feminists have worried that a masculine tendency toward artificially abstract thought may allow theories to be too distanced from actual human life. Conceptions of morality derived from such alienated thought may have "permeated human social life and institutions in a way that leads to a distorted and dangerous sense of human priorities; to a morality, in fact, that may be seen as underlying such things as militarism," feminist philosopher Jean Grimshaw says. Women's lives, Grimshaw asserts, may "provide the space for questioning the sorts of priorities that see human lives as easily dispensable in the service of some abstract idea or great cause; that see care for others or a life devoted to serving others as relatively unimportant."[20]

Furthermore, precisely because women have

to a great extent been historically excluded from the commercial and industrial world and from what Hegel calls "world-historical events," they ironically may be in the best position to criticize the morality of militarism and of the excesses of the capitalist market economy. Such social commentators need not be professional philosophers. Long-dead female novelists such as George Eliot (aka Marian Evans) in her *The Mill on the Floss* (1860) can be very instructive on such subjects.

A Quick Recap

What is the overall effect of these combined assaults on moral philosophy? Certainly no single attack has devastated the project of ethics, but has it been nibbled away, bite by bite, like a sugar cube set upon by ants? I do not believe so. There were some serious challenges, but things have been learned.

Hard determinism, if true, would make moral philosophy impossible as anything other than the study of customs. If every event and process in the universe, including human thought and behavior, is determined by immutable natural laws—if we could never have done otherwise than exactly what we did—then it is difficult to see how there could be such a thing as responsibility (except in the sense in which "P is responsible for X" means P did X). If the idea of responsibility is empty, it is hard to see how any moral judgments, whether of praise or blame, would make any sense. The modification of hard determinism into soft determinism (compatibilism) claims to defuse this problem by showing that a correct account of the laws of nature (and the sense in which the world is governed by them), along with a correct account of the ideas of freedom and responsibility, shows that the idea of moral responsibility is not incompatible with the idea of the universe being law governed. There is still a legitimate debate between the soft determinists and the libertarians, but that debate expands moral philosophy rather than shutting it down.

Cultural relativism believes itself to pose a threat to any ethical theory that attempts to impose general moral rules on us simply by virtue of our being human. But neither version of the relativist's thesis that we examined here seems sustainable, hence I believe there is no serious danger to the project of moral theorizing from the social sciences. Still, I think this anthropological attack must give the moral philosopher pause. What if Solomon Asch is correct that the ancient Chinese held that a birthed child becomes human only after its first year? Both the ancient Chinese philosopher and the modern Western ethicist can agree that it is immoral to kill human children, but how differently those two philosophers understand this principle! The moral of the story is not that the search for universal principles is futile, but rather that the contextualizing of such principles (situating them in a particular historical cultural milieu) is as important as the principles themselves. This, in my view, is the truth of relativism.

The only potentially career-ending challenge against ethics other than the one from hard determinism was from logical positivism, which wanted to reveal not just moral theory but morality itself as issuing only nonsense pseudo-statements. But ethics and morality have survived, and positivism itself has retreated, a victim of its own zealousness. (This is not to say that nothing has been learned from positivism. Almost all moral philosophers since the 1930s, including those who defend systems that were created earlier, have realized they must pay attention to the logical and **semantic** status of the positivists' key concepts.)

Hume's Guillotine and Moore's naturalistic fallacy have played a large role in the development of moral philosophy. Of course, neither Hume nor Moore meant to end moral philosophy—they each had one of their own, after all—but they did issue good advice on how *not* to do moral philosophy, advice that must be responded to by virtually all ethical theories represented in this text.

Like logical positivism, existentialism's star has now set, but each has left an afterglow. It is impossible, for me at least, to read Kierkegaard or Sartre (or even simply the short piece from Sartre

quoted in this chapter) without bringing to mind the idea that philosophical theories do not make moral decisions; individual human
beings must do that. Often these decisions are indeed made in
anguish, dread, and fear and trembling. In my view, the existentialists
were right to say that even if one dedicates oneself to a specific
moral theory, one must interpret the meaning of that theory in the
context of one's own life—or leave the decision to others, in what
Sartre calls "bad faith."

Feminism's critique of moral theory is not one that wants to
demolish such theorizing but to restructure it. Its complaint is that
the history of ethics is grounded in androcentric **ideology** that ignores women and even participates in their oppression. The program
of feminism is revisionist: Its goal is not to close down moral philosophy but to open it up more. To me, that does not seem like an attack
on moral philosophy itself. In fact, you will find in Chapter 6 that feminists have made a particularly large contribution to what is known as
"virtue ethics."

Finally, let me make a related point about the foundations of
ethical theories.

Foundationalism

So what is the ultimate influence of these various philosophical
assaults on the foundations of morality? Notice that, each in its own
way, the Humean, the positivistic, the relativistic, the existential, and
in some ways, the feminist critiques are just that—assaults on the
foundations of morality. Hume, with his is/ought problem, and the
positivists try to show that morality cannot have its foundation in
any true facts in the world; the relativist tries to show that morality
cannot have its foundations in human nature itself; Sartre tries to
show that morality cannot have its foundations in reason, and that
grounding morality on freedom produces a foundation that is subjective and unstable. Some feminists see the foundations of Western
morality in a now-outdated destructive form of patriarchy. But what

if talk about the *foundations of morality* turns out to be misconceived? It seems widely agreed upon in philosophical circles that the two-thousand-year attempt to find the foundations of knowledge was wrongheaded. Knowledge, it is supposed, is more like a net or a spiderweb than a house (it was Descartes who talked about "the house of knowledge").

The Assault on the Foundations of Morality

The same may be true in ethics. In the words of the influential British philosopher Bernard Williams,

> The foundational enterprise, [that] of resting the structure of knowledge on some favored class of statements, has now generally been displaced in favor of a holistic type of model, in which some beliefs can be questioned, justified, or adjusted while others are kept constant, but there is no process in which they can all be questioned at once, or all justified in terms of (almost) nothing. In Neurath's famous image we repair the ship while we are on the sea. (113)[21]

According to Williams, the same is true of ethics: "The aim of ethical thought," he says, "is to help us construct a world that will be our world, one in which we have a social, cultural, and personal life" (111). Now, for that activity, no foundation is needed. By virtue of being human, we find ourselves in it willy-nilly. I take it that Williams is suggesting that in this effort to build a world that will be our world, we are all "insiders," unless something goes terribly wrong with us.

Religious Ethics

I have not included a chapter on religious ethics in this book, but I will say a few things here about the attempt to base ethics on a religious foundation. I will begin by quoting a passage from Bernard Williams's *Ethics and the Limits of Philosophy*. Williams talks about what he calls "the crudest religious accounts, which represent ethical considerations as a set of laws or commandments sanctioned by the promised punishments or rewards of God." He says of an account such as this,

> It is a natural thing to say that this religious account is crude, meaning not that it is crude because it is religious, but that it is a crude piece of religion. A less crude religious ethics will not add the religious element merely as an external sanction, but will give an account of human nature that provides equally for ethical objectives and for a relation to God. (32–3)

If a person obeys, say, the Ten Commandments, based on the fear of hellfire and the enticement of eternal happiness, then, either religious ethics is a form of authoritarianism ("might makes right"), or, according

From the Cathedral of St.-Etienne, Bourges, France

to Williams's way of thinking, the philosophical grounding of that person's ethics is not religious but egoistic, because his or her motivation is the avoidance of punishment and search for rewards for him- or herself. (We will study egoism in Chapter 2.) This sounds correct to me. In his dialogue called *Euthyphro*—which I will paraphrase liberally—Plato has his spokesman, Socrates, ask Euthyphro, what is the good?[22] Euthyphro tells Socrates that the good is what the gods say is good. Socrates then asks, is it good because the gods say it's good, or do they say it's good because it is good? This is an instructive distinction. If a person believes that the good is good because God says it's good, then that person is accepting an authoritarian ethics: Power determines what is good. (I am aware, of course, that the religious person about whom we are talking believes that God *is* good, and is the source of all other goodness, but that does not refute Socrates' point.) If, on the other hand, the gods say that something is good because it *is* good, then the good has been conceptually separated from religion, and religion becomes the (correct) conduit of ethical instruction about a "good" that might be studied in ways independent of religion.

Now, when Bernard Williams says that a more sophisticated religious treatment "gives an account of human nature that provides equally for ethical objectives and for a relation to God," I think he means that the sophisticated religious thinker believes that God does tell us what is good—either through commandment or revelation—because it is good. That is, the sophisticated religious thinker acknowledges Socrates' point and feels free to do traditional ethical theorizing, but at the same time demands that his or her ethical framework not exclude his or her relation with God. An ethical theory like that of St. Thomas Aquinas (see Chapter 6, where Aquinas's moral theory is briefly discussed) meets both criteria. It gives us access both to the good and to God, and finds a way of conceptually relating the idea of the good with the idea both of God and the idea of the human being.

The Game Plan

Let me say briefly what we will be doing in the rest of the book. Chapter 2 is called "Egoism and Hedonism." Some people believe that morality's main job is to help individuals get out of their own skin, to see the world from the point of view of others, and to instruct them to think and behave in ways that overcome a natural childish propensity toward selfishness. These people may be surprised to discover that there are philosophies that advocate selfishness (or self-interest) as the correct moral stance. This philosophy is called "egoism." Some egoists argue that self-interest always cashes out as pleasure and that, therefore, true morality always involves the pursuit of pleasure. These philosophers are called "hedonists." We will inspect these related views in Chapter 2.

Chapter 3, "Kantian Ethics," presents one of the most important moral theories ever set forth, that of the eighteenth-century German philosopher Immanuel Kant. Kant tries to demonstrate that from our very nature as rational beings we can deduce a universal moral code that binds us all, and he argues that failure to abide by this code of reason is tantamount to self-exile from the human race. Kant's theory challenges every other theory treated in this text. It is so powerful that defenders of any other moral code feel obliged to attack Kant's views in order to defend their own.

Chapter 4, "Utilitarian Ethics," deals with a moral tradition at least as influential as Kant's—the utilitarianism of Jeremy Bentham and John Stuart Mill, British philosophers of the eighteenth and nineteenth centuries, respectively. The motto of this theory is "The greatest amount of happiness for the greatest number," and it tries to demonstrate that morality is exclusively concerned with human well-being and that this criterion allows us to judge the moral worth of any act whatsoever. Like Kantianism, with which it disagrees on most other issues, utilitarianism claims that you and I are at every minute under a moral obligation, whether or not we consciously choose to subscribe to the tenets of this philosophy. In the case of utilitarianism, that obligation is to promote human well-being.

Chapter 5, "Evolutionary Ethics," treats of a school of moral philosophy that has come to the fore in the past several decades. This cluster of theories holds in common the belief that moral theory must be revamped and made consistent with science because of Darwin's elimination of **teleology** (systems of goals, purposes, plans, and intentions) from the natural world and because of his placement of the human being right smack in the middle of nature. Ever mindful of the trap of the is/ought problem, evolutionary theorists do not try to deduce ethics from science, but to develop an ethics that is informed by science. In Chapter 5, two key features of this philosophy are foregrounded: the elimination of the **homocentric** (human-centered) bias in ethics and the demonstration that **altruism,** the foundation of most moral codes, is compatible with evolutionary theory.

Chapter 6, "Virtue Ethics," concerns itself with a contribution to ethics that is both very old and brand new: old in that it was first set forth in classical Greece, notably by Aristotle, and new in that contemporary efforts to revive and reformulate this ancient Greek conception of ethics have generated sizable enthusiasm. Much of Western ethics is act oriented—that is, it deals with the morality of specific actions, and it does so by judging them according to principles, or according to rules that follow from principles. Virtue ethics is more person oriented. It recommends as a moral ideal a certain kind of life over other types of life, and it studies the nature of the virtues associated with such a life. In doing so it produces an ethical theory that is less abstract than many and is more sensitive to context than to universal rules, thereby becoming more hospitable to related schools such as feminism and relativism.

Chapter 7, "Contractualism," discusses the theory that ethical values, rights, and obligations derive from agreements made between human agents. This idea goes back at least as far as the Stoics, a school of philosophy in ancient Greece and Rome. But, like virtue ethics, it has recently received much attention from philosophers who, in agreement with the evolutionary ethicists, believe that the underpinnings of much of traditional Western ethics have been undermined both by the advances of modern science and by the discovery of the is/ought problem. "Ethics by agreement," as contractualism is sometimes called, claims to demonstrate how moral values can be explained and justified without pinning them to now-discredited metaphysical claims.

I assume that it will be obvious that every one of these ethical schools of thought has both adherents and opponents. Both the defense and criticism of each position will be discussed in the various chapters.

Addendum: Moral Claims, Truth and Falsity

Beliefs, judgments, sentences, and **propositions** are the kinds of things that can be true or false. (A "proposition" is what a sentence expresses. It seems that now most philosophers hold that beliefs and judgments are propositional: Jane believes that lead is heavier than water; Jack judges that chocolate is better than vanilla.) But beliefs, judgments, sentences, and propositions cannot be true or false unless they are meaningful. Lewis Carroll's "Jabberwocky," which begins, "T'was brillig and the slithy toves did gyre and gimble in the wabe," is neither true nor false because it is nonsense (though in Looking-Glass Land, Humpty Dumpty tries to explain its meaning to the bewildered Alice. He begins his explanation with "There are plenty of tough words there.")

So, any viable ethical theory will have to establish that its key terms are meaningful. Different philosophers concentrate on different key vocabulary items,

'Brillig' means four o'clock in the afternoon—the time when you start broiling things for dinner. . . .'Slithy' means 'lithe' and 'slimy.' . . .

Whatever . . .

but typical among them are nouns such as pleasure, happiness, virtue, duty, obligation, contract, freedom, responsibility, reason, and passion. Also, there are adjectives such as good and bad, right and wrong and verbs such as ought and must.

After moral philosophers have secured the meaning of their key moral terms, they use those terms in presenting arguments defending certain principles that are meant to guide our conduct. Obviously, the moral philosopher believes that these principles are true and wants to convince us of this truth. But what is it for a claim—moral or otherwise—to be true?

Here, I will restrict my discussion of truth and falsity to sentences and propositions, even though I mentioned earlier that beliefs and judgments are also among the kinds of things that can be true or false. Now, even if *meaningfulness* is a necessary condition of a proposition's truth or falsity, it is not a *sufficient* condition. Commands and questions can be meaningful ("Don't throw the burning match in the gasoline barrel!" "Did you kill the dog?"), but they are never true or false. Also, whole philosophical theories are needed to establish the semantic value (the kind of meaning and subsequent relation to truth and falsity) in fiction and drama ("To be or not to be—that is the question"). The next complication is that there are a number of competing theories of truth. (This should come as no surprise to you.) The two most prominent theories of truth have been the correspondence theory and the coherence theory.

The correspondence theory is simply the assertion that a proposition is true if it corresponds with the facts. This theory is particularly attractive in empirical cases (cases where truth is established through observation) because "facts" are thought of as states of affairs in the world, and the kind of typical example given to illustrate the correspondence theory (such as the cat's being on the mat) are *observable* facts. The sentence "The cat is on the mat" is true if and only if the cat is in fact on the mat. The main attractions of this theory are its simplicity and its appeal to common sense. It has three main weaknesses:

1. It is difficult to explain how linguistic entities (words, sentences) or mental states (beliefs, judgments) can *correspond* to things (objects, facts, states of affairs) that are nothing like language.
2. It is difficult to state exactly *what it is* that sentences are supposed to correspond to (things in the world? facts? What is a "fact" if not that which a true sentence asserts?).
3. It is particularly awkward to apply to mathematics. (What is it to which the proposition "5 + 2 = 7" corresponds? If we say it corresponds to the "fact" that 5 + 2 = 7, aren't we simply repeating the claim that "5 + 2 = 7"?)

The coherence theory of truth asserts that a proposition is true if it coheres with all the other propositions taken to be true. This theory has been preferred by **rationalists** (philosophers who base their theories of knowledge on ideas, abstract concepts, and relationships rather than observation). Its greatest strength is that it makes sense out of mathematical propositions ("5 + 2 = 7" is true because it is entailed by "7 = 7," and by "1 + 6 = 7," and by "21 ÷ 3 = 2 × 3 + 1," etc.). Its greatest weakness is its vicious circularity. Proposition A is true by virtue of its coherence with propositions B, C, and D. Proposition B is true by virtue of its coherence with propositions A, C, and D. Proposition C is true by virtue of its coherence with A, B, and D, and so forth. Think of the belief system of the paranoid. All his beliefs cohere perfectly with one another. Everything that happens to the paranoid is evidence that everybody is out to get him.

Around the turn of the nineteenth century a theory called the "pragmatic theory of truth" was fashioned to respond to what its framers—the

The Paranoid Theory of Truth

pragmatists—took to be weaknesses in the other two theories. According to **pragmatism,** a proposition is true if believing it "works." On the face of it, this looks simplistic and subjective, and, indeed, William James (1842–1910), one of the founders of pragmatism, claimed that the sentence "God exists" is true for most people because it "works" for them; that is, it helps them get in a better relationship with the rest of their experience. But, of course, if "God exists" works for most people, the implication is that it is false for some people. This means that the same sentence is either true or false depending on who utters it. However, James also said this:

> True ideas are those that we can assimilate, validate, corroborate and verify. False ideas are those that we cannot. . . . The truth of an idea is not a stagnant property inherent in it. Truth *happens* to an idea. It becomes true, is *made* true by events.[23]

Here, we see that James seems to suggest using both the correspondence theory and the coherence theory as *tests* for truth, but not individually as *criterion* of truth. That is, one way of finding out if a proposition works is to see how many of these tests it can pass.

In the second half of the twentieth century, and on into the twenty-first, there have been a plurality of responses to the problems of the previous theories of truth that can all be subsumed under the title of **deflationism.** The deflationists are not so deflational that—like Pontius Pilate—they simply shrug their shoulders and walk away when someone raises the question "What is truth?" But they *do* seem to believe that the concept of truth is not a robust concept about which robust philosophical theories can be successfully articulated. (Many philosophers have arrived at a similar attitude toward the concept of existence. When someone says, "Dinosaurs no longer exist," that person is saying something about dinosaurs, not something about "existence." We may need to know more about objects called dinosaurs, but not about yet another object called existence.) Deflationist theorists agree with Aristotle (384–322 B.C.E.), who wrote, "To say of a thing that is that it is, or of a thing that is not, that it is not, is to speak the truth. To say of a thing that is that it is not, or to say of a thing that is not that it is, is to speak falsely."[24] In fact, deflationists seem to think that *everyone* agrees with Aristotle on this subject, but they don't think that his platitude should provoke a philosophical investigation of propositions, correspondences, and facts. As Simon Blackburn and Keith Simmons have put it, deflationists reject the view "that there is in fact any real prospect of discovering what truth is. . . . This deflationary view denies that there is an issue of 'the nature of truth' in general."[25] The deflationists realize that this claim may be considered not only deflating but disconcerting, and most of them do not want to appear to hold the view—attributed to some **postmodernists**—that no distinction between truth and falsity can be drawn. As Blackburn and Simmons say, "It is good or right to believe that cows fly if and only if cows fly; good to believe that cows swim if and only if cows swim" (6).

Therefore, Blackburn and Simmons feel that they have an obligation to explain their deflationist claim. However, at this stage of the development of the deflationary program, the various attempts to formulate a special theory explaining why no theory of truth is needed have divided these minimalists into warring camps with, in some cases, complicated formulations whose exposition would

go beyond the bounds of this text. Suffice it to say that some prominent philosophers have contributed to this effort.[26]

After an extended effort to articulate coherent accounts of
deflationism, some philosophers have come to believe that the whole
minimalist project may be a mistake, and that philosophers need to
go back to more robust theories of truth. At least for the purpose of
studying ethical theory, our job would be easier if deflationism were
true ("true"?) because, as Blackburn and Simmons note, deflationists not only evade the problem of truth, but they also "pride themselves on avoiding any engagement with the disputed notion of a
fact" (28), and among philosophers there is a "sense that ethical
'facts' are especially elusive, or difficult to place in the order of
nature" (5).

In any case, most of us can probably accept the commonsense
basis for claiming that the sentence "The cat is on the mat" is true if
and only if the cat is on the mat—a claim on which both correspondence theorists and deflationary theorists agree. But is it really so
easy to determine "truth" and "fact" (if that's what we are after) in
the following sentences?

> "The life of contemplation accompanied by virtuous action is the
>   best life for a human being." (Aristotle)
> "Lying is always immoral." (Immanuel Kant)
> "We should always act in such a way as to promote the great-
>   est amount of happiness for the greatest number of people."
>   (Jeremy Bentham)
> "We should treat individuals identically—whether these individu-
>   als are human or non-human animals—if their morally rele-
>   vant characteristics are identical." (James Rachels, speaking
>   for Charles Darwin)

With what *facts* are these sentences meant to correspond?
(Or, if there are no facts, with what objects or states of affairs in the
world?) This is not an easy question to answer, and I will not try to
suggest a general answer here; rather, in the chapters that follow,
we will attend to the various arguments that the philosophers provide to convince us that such facts, states of affairs, or objects
exist. Often, such attempts will bring the vessels of these philoso-

phers perilously close to the dangerous rocks and currents of the naturalistic fallacy, which you have already encountered.

The only general remarks I will make here concern the distinction made by some philosophers between **natural facts** and **conventional facts.** These remarks may help clarify how there could be such things as moral facts.

The following three sentences express natural facts:

Hot air rises.
The planets of the solar system orbit the sun in elliptical
  trajectories.

Light initiates the process of photosynthesis in most plants, and photosynthesis generates chlorophyll.

These three sentences express facts that would be the case even if there were no humans in the world to articulate those sentences. Contrast these sentences with the next group, which express conventional facts.

Susan is married to John.
Babe Ruth struck out.
Tom owns a cabin in the mountains.

The facts expressed in these three sentences are conventional because they could only be the case within the context of social conventions. The first sentence could be true only in a society with the convention of marriage. The second could be true only in a society with the convention of baseball (though in a society in which baseball is played, the sentence could also be metaphor- ically true, if, for exam- ple, Babe Ruth had been rebuffed by a woman to whom he had made overtures).

"The Babe" Strikes Out

The third sentence could be true only in a society with the conven- tions of private prop- erty. Some **Marxist** philosophers say that conventional facts are merely "legal fictions," but that implies that only natural facts are real facts, and that, to my way of thinking, is a mistake. Conventional facts are very real. ("The jury found the accused to be guilty of first-degree murder, and the judge condemned him to death.")

If moral philosophers or moral traditions try to base their ethical claims only on natural facts, they will be in danger of falling afoul of the dreaded naturalistic fallacy. If moral philosophers or moral traditions try to base their ethical claims on conventional facts, they will be in danger of falling into relativism. Still, moral facts, if they exist, may be more like conventional facts than like natural facts, because in real life, morality is a system of conventions. Therefore, we can learn something pertinent to our topic of moral philosophy if we consider the idea of conventional facts a bit more. First, it does not appear to me to be likely that conventional facts are reducible to natural facts. That is, a sentence like "Babe Ruth struck out" can be explained by appealing to the rules and history of baseball and, if needed, certain facts in addition about human persons and the conventions of naming such persons. But, as far as I can determine, no one has ever figured out how to explain the rules of baseball, the facts of personhood, and the conventions of naming in terms of descriptions of natural facts like bodies in motion and certainly not in terms of atomic configurations, or subatomic configurations, and the laws of physics. Even if you take the position of a hard-core **materialist** who believes that everything currently in the universe was present in it shortly after the big bang, several millions of years ago, and therefore believes that the facts of personhood, the conventions of naming, and the rules of baseball must have evolved out of the history of subatomic particles and the natural laws that govern them—even then, you can't show how to reduce conventional facts to natural facts. That is, you can't give a description of subatomic facts and an account of the laws that govern them in such a way that the sentence "Babe Ruth struck out" could be deduced from that description.

As an aside, I would like to say that my analysis of the irreducibility of conventional facts is provisional. Just because nobody now knows how to perform the reduction of conventional facts to **brute facts**, it doesn't follow that nobody will ever figure out a way of doing so. Certainly various theorists have tried. B. F. Skinner's behaviorism is one famous attempt, but I'll go out on a limb and say that behaviorism was a noble attempt but a spectacular failure.

The Author Out on a Limb

If I am right about the current irreducibility of the one kind of fact to the other, then it follows that sentences like "Babe Ruth struck out" are understandable only from *within* a particular world of conventions. I am not claiming that you have to become a member of that world to understand its conventions. With proper guidance, for-eigners can be made to understand baseball, and some of them may end up liking it, others not. In the same fashion, non-Christians can come to understand the Catholic mass of the Eucharist without becoming Catholics, and anthropologists can sometimes explain to us the conventions of societies alien to our own. Similarly, it is con-ceivable that moral claims can only be understood from within. In the case of morality, in my opinion, the question of how sympathetic one must be to the moral claims of competing ethical theories in order to see their point is still unresolved. Bernard Williams touches on this question:

> An insightful observer can indeed come to understand and anticipate the use of [an alien] concept without actually sharing the values of the people who use it: this is an important point. . . . But in imagina-tively anticipating the use of the concept, the observer also has to grasp imaginatively its evaluative point. He cannot stand quite out-side the evaluative interests of the community he is observing, and pick up the concept simply as a device for dividing up in a rather strange way certain neutral features of the world. (141–2)

So, it seems that to be able to see the force of a moral argument with which one has little sympathy initially, one has to get inside the system by being imaginative. Just *how* imaginative, I can't say.

At least three of the moral theories you will study here agree with this view that one can understand the ethical force of the argu-ments only from the inside. They are virtue ethics (Chapter 6), Rachels's version of evolutionary ethics (Chapter 5), and contractu-alism (Chapter 7). The other three theories you will study—namely, egoism (Chapter 2), Kantianism (Chapter 3), and utilitarianism (Chapter 4)—make universalistic claims and seem committed to the proposition that you can be persuaded to understand the demands that their respective ethical theories make on you even if you don't already have the desire to "do the right thing." But their claims can be challenged. If you are a **sociopath,** or an **immoralist**— that is, if you are truly outside the world of moral conventions—you may be immune to the claims of the determinists and to any of the arguments of the philosophers.

Questions for Consideration

1. Explain the concept of "necessary condition" and "sufficient condition," and then contrast the idea of definition based on these two concepts with the idea of definition (or characterization) based on Wittgenstein's "family relations."

2. What do you understand to be the relationship between ethics and meta-ethics?

3. Summarize the is/ought problem as posed by David Hume, and explain it.

4. Why does G. E. Moore think that any attempt to define the concept "good" in terms of natural facts is doomed to failure?

5. Explain why some philosophers believe that the problem of determinism provides a challenge to moral philosophy.

6. Defend either hard determinism, compatibilism, or libertarianism.

7. In what way might the doctrine of cultural relativism as propounded by some social scientists challenge the possibility of moral philosophy?

8. Why do the definitions of analytic and synthetic propositions as set forth by the logical positivists challenge the possibility of moral philosophy?

9. According to Sartre, what are the implications for moral philosophy of his story about his student during World War II?

10. In what ways would the feminist philosophers mentioned here wish to transform ethical theory?

11. What are the implications for moral philosophy of abandoning foundationalism?

12. Euthyphro says that the good is what the gods say is good. Socrates agrees, but finds this answer to be incomplete. Why?

Questions for the Addendum

13. Why do most philosophers claim that meaningfulness is a necessary but not a sufficient condition of truth or falsity?

14. Contrast the correspondence theory of truth with the coherence theory of truth.

15. What do you take to be the impetus behind the deflationary theories of truth?

16. Explain the distinction in the text between natural facts and conventional facts, using examples of your own.

17. Do you think that moral facts, if they exist, are more like natural facts or conventional facts? Why?

Study Guide: Outline of Chapter One

I. What philosophy is.

    A. It is probable that the necessary conditions of the concept "philosophy" cannot be stated.

    B. "Philosophy" is an open concept.

        1. The concept of philosophy explained on the analogy of "family resemblances."

        2. Wittgenstein's analysis of the concept "game."

    C. Sellars's facetious definition: Philosophy is "an attempt to see how things . . . hang together."

        1. The pre-Socratic philosophers and their search for a formula explaining how things hang together.

        2. This quest leads to a primitive atomic theory.

    D. The difference between philosophy and science? Roughly, philosophy's speculative (or armchair) activities, and science's experimental activities (with exceptions in both cases).

    E. Philosophy's general and abstract nature.

1. A concern with concepts such as space, time, existence, social-ity, beauty, justice, love, and death.

2. A concern with abstract concepts presupposed by concrete applications of everyday speech.

F. The divisions of philosophy: logic, epistemology, metaphysics, aesthetics, political philosophy, moral philosophy, etc.

II. What moral philosophy (or ethics) is.

A. The rather arbitrary distinction between "ethics" and "moral philosophy," and the author's decision to use the terms interchangeably.

B. Meta-ethics: an aspect of moral philosophy attending exclusively to the meaning, structure, and logic of ethical speech, without generating principles of behavior.

C. Theoretical component: the development of principles to guide conduct and of criteria of moral judgment.

III. Stumbling blocks on the road to moral philosophy.

A. The challenge of the is/ought problem (Hume's Guillotine).

1. No "is" implies an "ought."

2. There are no factual claims from which moral claims can be deduced.

B. The challenge of the naturalistic fallacy (G. E. Moore).

1. Any attempt to define the concept "good" in terms of natural facts is doomed to failure.

a. In the case of any legitimate definition having the form "X is Y" ("a triangle is a three-sided closed figure"), the question, "Yes, but is X (always) Y?" makes no sense.

b. But when we define "good" as, say, pleasure ("X is Y"), it does make sense to ask, "But is pleasure (always) good?"

c. Therefore, such attempts to define "good" in terms of natural qualities (such as pleasure) fail.

2. After Hume's is/ought problem, and Moore's naturalistic fallacy it seems there are only two ways to write moral philosophy:

a. Write so as consciously to avoid these related problems.

b. Write so as to challenge the validity of these two problems.

C. The problem of determinism: If natural laws govern all features of the universe, how are human freedom and responsibility possible?

    1. Hard determinism denies the existence of freedom and responsibility.

    2. Soft determinism, or compatibilism, defines freedom in such a way as to allow freedom in a deterministic world.

D. The challenge of cultural relativism.

    1. R. Benedict: "It is morally good" equals "It is habitual"; moral values are the products of individual cultures, which differ geographically and historically.

    2. B. F. Skinner:

        a. "What is good for the Trobriand Islander is good for the Trobriand Islander, and that is that."

        b. Cultural relativism is a "tolerant alternative to missionary zeal."

    3. Moral reasoning between members of different cultures is impossible; there can only be acknowledgment of the others' "good" or the advice to imitate others.

    4. Demand for a clarification of cultural relativism: Does it claim that there are no universally held values, or that no value can be justifiably recommended for all people?

        a. No universally held values.

            i. An empirical, not philosophical, claim.

            ii. Not all social scientists agree with this claim: Kroeber, Kluckhohn, and Asch claim there are universal values.

        b. No value recommendable to all people.

            i. Hume's Guillotine seems to rule out this thesis because it illegitimately derives an "ought" from an "is."

            ii. From the claim that all values are culturally bound it does not follow that no value is worthy of universal recommendation.

E. The challenge of logical positivism.

    1. According to the school of logical positivism:

        a. Meaningful propositions must be either analytic or synthetic.

b. Analytic propositions

   i. Are true by definition, hence tautological.

   ii. When negated become self-contradictions.

   iii. Are necessarily true, but are always empirically empty.

c. Synthetic propositions

   i. Are empirical, i.e., are about facts in the world.

   ii. When negated are not self-contradictory.

   iii. Can be verified or refuted by observation.

d. The propositions of theology and metaphysics are neither analytic nor synthetic, hence they are nonsense.

e. The propositions of ethics are similarly neither analytic nor synthetic; they are merely

   i. Expressions of emotion combined with . . .

   ii. Disguised commands ("I don't like it! Don't do it!")

f. "Ethical concepts are pseudo-concepts and consequently indefinable."

g. If logical positivism is correct, "ethics" is a form of pseudo-philosophy.

2. Weaknesses of logical positivism.

a. The absolute distinction between analyticity and syntheticity has been challenged as unsustainable.

b. The positivist theory of meaning has been attacked as too restrictive.

c. The principles of logical positivism have been shown to be self-defeating.

F. The challenge of existentialism.

1. According to Sartre, our individual freedom overrides everything else about us, including our rationality and our moral sentiments.

a. If this is so, then rationality and morality cannot make demands on us unless we choose to authorize them to do so.

b. Even if we do choose a moral code, it cannot tell us what to do in concrete cases; we still must decide how to interpret the moral code we have chosen, and that interpretation will be a choice.

2. Weaknesses of existentialism.

    a. Sartre's radical conclusion derives from an exaggeration and overdramatization of certain features of the human condition.

    b. Nevertheless, some aspects of Sartre's view may be pertinent.

        i. E.g., the claim that, by itself, rationality (reason) cannot force us to do anything.

        ii. E.g., the claim that every moral code must be interpreted and decided upon contextually.

G. The challenge of feminism.

  1. The androcentric bias of traditional ethics ignores women and participates in their oppression.

  2. An adequate moral theory must be informed by the moral experience of women.

H. Foundationalism.

  1. Many of the stumbling blocks on which moral philosophers have tripped may be the result of their using a "foundationalist" model of moral philosophy.

    a. The view that morality is structured like a building, with foundations and a superstructure.

    b. The superstructure is solid only if the foundations are solid.

    c. Therefore, each moral system must be built on a solid foundation.

  2. But perhaps the "building" model was a bad metaphor and should be replaced with the metaphor of a net, or a spiderweb, or a ship at sea.

I. Religious ethics.

  1. Crude accounts (according to Williams).

    a. Ethical values are considered as laws or commandments sanctioned by the rewards and punishments of God.

    b. A form of authoritarianism: Might makes right.

    c. A form of egoism: motivated by the desire for reward and desire to escape punishment.

  2. The separation of ethics and divinity in Plato's *Euthyphro*.

    a. Euthyphro's thesis: The good is what the gods say is good.

  b. Socrates' question:

   i. Is the good good because the gods say it's good (authoritarianism), . . .

   ii. Or do the gods say it's good because it is good (separation of ethics from divinity)?

 3. Sophisticated accounts of religious ethics (according to Williams) "give an account of human nature that provides equally for ethical objectives and for a relation to God" without reducing ethical considerations to being simply orders from God.

Outline of the Addendum

IV. Truth, falsity, and moral claims.

 A. Meaningfulness is a necessary but not a sufficient condition of truth and falsity.

 B. Theories of truth:

  1. The correspondence theory: A sentence is true if and only if the proposition it expresses corresponds with the facts.

  2. The coherence theory: A sentence is true if and only if the proposition it expresses coheres with all the other propositions we take to be true.

  3. The pragmatic theory: A sentence is true if believing the proposition it expresses "works," i.e., puts us in a more satisfactory relationship with the rest of our experiences than do its alternatives.

  4. Recently a number of philosophers, dissatisfied with traditional theories of truth, have developed deflationary theories, demoting truth to a nonphilosophical status.

 C. Moral truths:

  1. With what facts do moral claims correspond? The distinction between natural facts and conventional facts suggested as an aid in answering this question.

   a. The claim that there are moral truths, and they correspond with natural facts, runs the risk of committing the naturalistic fallacy.

   b. The claim that there are moral truths, and they correspond with conventional facts, runs the risk of cultural relativism.

2. Nevertheless, moral facts, if they exist, may be more like conventional facts than natural facts.

    a. In this case, moral facts, like conventional facts, could only be understood from within—but how far in?

    b. Can only converts to moral system X understand the moral facts that system X claims to be true?

    c. Or can one put oneself "within" system X and come to understand what system X claims to be moral facts and, at the same time, remain neutral with regard to system X?

For Further Reading

General

Nagel, Thomas. *What Does It All Mean?: A Very Short Introduction to Philosophy.* New York and Oxford: Oxford University Press, 1987.

Rawls, John. *Lectures on the History of Moral Philosophy.* Barbara Herman, ed. Cambridge, Mass.: Harvard University Press, 2000.

Williams, Bernard. *Ethics and the Limits of Philosophy.* Cambridge, Mass.: Harvard University Press, 1985.

Cultural Relativism

Benedict, Ruth. *Patterns of Culture.* New York: Pelican, 1946.

Ladd, John, ed. *Ethical Relativism.* Belmont, Ca.: Wadsworth, 1973.

Determinism

Bergmann, Frithjof. *On Being Free.* Notre Dame, Ind., and London: University of Notre Dame Press, 1977.

Skinner, B. F. *Beyond Freedom and Dignity.* New York: Bantam Books, 1972.

Existentialism

Kierkegaard, Søren. *Fear and Trembling.* Alastair Hannay, trans. London and New York: Penguin Books, 1985.

Sartre, Jean-Paul. *Existentialism and Human Emotions.* Trans. Bernard Frechtman and Hazel Barnes. New York: Citadel Press, 1987.

Feminism

Grimshaw, Jean. *Philosophy and Feminist Thinking.* Minneapolis: University of Minnesota Press.

Is/Ought Problem and the Naturalistic Fallacy

Hudson, W. D., ed. *The Is—Ought Question.* London: Macmillan, 1969.

Moore, George Edward. *Principia Ethica.* Cambridge, Mass.: University of Harvard Press, 1960.

Logical Positivism

Ayer, Alfred Jules. *Language, Truth and Logic*. New York: Dover Publications, 1952.

Reichenbach, Hans. *The Rise of Scientific Philosophy*. Berkeley and Los Angeles: University of California Press, 1961.

Addendum: For Further Reading

Blackburn, Simon, and Keith Simmons, eds. *Truth*. Oxford: University of Oxford Press, 1999.

James, William. *Pragmatism and the Meaning of Truth*. Cambridge, Mass.: Harvard University Press, 1979.

Searle, John R. *The Construction of Social Reality*. New York and London: Free Press, 1995.

Notes

1. Ludwig Wittgenstein, *Philosophical Investigations* (New York: Macmillan, 1964), 32.

2. Wilfrid Sellars, quoted in Richard Rorty, "The Fate of Philosophy," *New Republic* (Oct. 18, 1982): 28.

3. Bernard Williams, *Ethics and the Limits of Philosophy* (Cambridge, Mass.: Harvard University Press, 1985), 6. Future references to this book will be cited parenthetically in the body of the text.

4. G. E. Moore, *Principia Ethica* (Cambridge, Mass.: Cambridge University Press, 1960).

5. I use the word "crude" here because, as we shall see, there are more sophisticated forms of Darwinism, just as there may be more sophisticated forms of authoritarianism (though I doubt it) or of moral theism.

6. T. M. Scanlon, *What We Owe to Others* (Cambridge, Mass. & London: Harvard University Press), 281.

7. C. A. Campbell, *In Defence of Free Will, An Inaugural Lecture* (Glasgow: Jackson, Son and Co., 1938); Richard Taylor, "I Can," *Philosophical Review* 69 (1960): 78–89.

8. Ruth Benedict, "Anthropology and the Abnormal," *Journal of General Psychology* 10 (1934): 73–4.

9. B. F. Skinner, *Beyond Freedom and Dignity* (New York: Bantam Books, 1972), 122.

10. Alfred Louis Kroeber and Clyde Kluckhohn, "Values and Relativity," in *Culture: A Critical Review of Concepts and Definitions*, Papers of the Peabody Museum, Harvard University 47, no. 1 (1952): 174–9.

11. Alfred Jules Ayer, *Language, Truth and Logic* (New York: Dover Publications, 1952), 108–9, 113.

12. Notably, in a famous essay by W. V. Quine, "Two Dogmas of Empiricism," (1951) reprinted in Quine's *From a Logical Point of View* (Cambridge, Mass.: Cambridge University Press, 1952). (But even in Quine's work the influence of logical positivism is obvious.)

13. Jon Wheatley, *Prolegomena to Philosophy* (Belmont, Calif.: Wadsworth, 1970), 103.

14. Jean-Paul Sartre, *Existentialism and Human Emotions* (New York: Citadel Press, 1987), 15.

15. Ibid., 24–8.

16. Arthur Schopenhauer, "On Women," in *Self and World: Readings in Philosophy*, ed. James A. Ogilvy (New York: Harcourt Brace Jovanovich, 1973), 395–6.

17. Carol Gilligan, *In a Different Voice: Psychological Theory and Women's Development* (Cambridge, Mass.: Harvard University Press, 1982), 130.

18. See Judy Auerbach, Linda Blum, Vicki Smith, and Christine Williams, "Commentary on Gilligan's *In a Different Voice*," *Feminist Studies* 11, no. 1 (Spring 1985).

19. Alison M. Jaggar, "Feminist Ethics: Some Issues for the Nineties," *Journal of Social Philosophy* XX: 1-2 (Spring/Fall 1989): 91–107.

20. Jean Grimshaw, *Philosophy and Feminist Thinking* (Minneapolis: University of Minnesota Press, 1986), 194, 196.

21. The reference is to the Austrian sociologist and philosopher Otto Neurath (1882–1945).

22. Volumes have been written attempting to determine how many of the words that Plato puts into Socrates' mouth in his dialogues truly represent Socrates' thoughts and how many represent exclusively Plato's views. Plato was the student of Socrates, so he was certainly familiar with Socrates' views, but Socrates wrote nothing—on principle, according to Plato—so we can only speculate on which features of Plato's many dialogues contain Socratic philosophy and which are truly Plato's innovation.

23. William James, *Pragmatism and the Meaning of Truth* (Cambridge, Mass.: Harvard University Press, 1979), 97.

24. Aristotle, *Metaphysics*, Book Gamma, 7.27. Kirwin's translation is "to say that that which is is and that which is not is not, is true." Aristotle, *Metaphysics: Books Gamma, Delta, and Epsilon*, trans. Christopher Kirwin (Oxford: Clarenden Press, 1993), 23.

25. Simon Blackburn and Keith Simmons, eds., *Truth* (Oxford: Oxford University Press, 1999), 2, 3. Future citations from this book will be included parenthetically in the body of the text.

26. Among others, Alfred Tarski promoted the "semantic theory of truth"; W. V. Quine developed the "disquotational theory of truth"; Paul Horowich supports the "minimalist theory of truth"; and Paul Churchland defends the "disappearance theory of truth." Blackburn and Simmons's book, *Truth*, gives a good overview of the debates.

2
Egoism and Hedonism

The seventeenth-century French mathematician and philosopher René Descartes (to whom you were briefly introduced in Chapter 1)

René Descartes

is sometimes called "the father of modern philosophy." Descartes sought an absolutely solid foundation on which to build a theory of knowledge, and after rejecting several possibilities—such as sense perception and mathematics—he claimed to have discovered such a foundation in the reality of his own existence. All other candidates were susceptible to philosophical doubt. For example, what we take to be the evidence for the existence of an external physical world could prove to be merely images from a dream; what we take to be the certainty of mathematics could be the product of a malevolent unrecognized force— what Descartes called an "evil genius." In other words, when I say,

"This is a table," I may be wrong, as I may waken later to realize that what I took to be a table was only a phantasm in my dream life; and when I say with a feeling of certainty, "two plus two equals four," that sense of certainty could be the consequence of tricks played on my mind by a malevolent force. But when I assert, "I am," or, "I think, therefore I am,"[1] I express a truth that cannot be subverted by the dream state, nor by a potential evil genius, because every attempt to doubt it fails. Having established the certainty of his own selfhood, Descartes's remaining project was to build a bridge from his **solipsistic** state of self-awareness to the external world and the world of other humans. Most critics think that Descartes has failed to secure that bridge and that he is eternally stuck in his solipsistic echo chamber eternally repeating, "I am, I am, I am."

It may seem surprising that ethics has a parallel problem, because we normally think of moral philosophy as being about relations among the vast number of humans that exist. Yet, a version of Descartes's ontological and epistemological dilemma exists in the field of ethics. Just as **Cartesian** philosophy begins necessarily with the subject "I," so must ethics begin with an "I" (as in "What must I do?"), says

Descartes Drifting Alone in the Universe

a school of philosophy known as egoism. Indeed, according to the egoist, ethics must not only begin with the individual subject—"I"—but must also end with the "I." The **psychological egoist** claims that the goal of every act is to achieve a benefit for the subject. The word "egoism," from the Latin *ego*, meaning "I," is the opposite of "altruism," from the Latin *alter*, meaning "other." We are all aware of the fact that people—usually *other* people—sometimes act out of their own selfish interests, and we sometimes think it is the job of moral instruction to teach people not to act selfishly. But egoists—at least, those called psychological egoists—claim that motivation based on anything but self-interest is impossible.

Psychological egoists denounce as impossible the altruistic demand that we should sometimes sacrifice our own interests for the interests of others. These egoists claim that apparent altruism is really a disguised form of self-interest. We may well be acting in the interest of others, but only if at some deeper level we believe we are acting for ourselves. Notice the importance of insisting not that we always *do* act in our own interest but

I would be glad to help you, but as far as I can determine, there's nothing in it for me. Make me an offer.

that we always act in *what we take to be* our own interest. This claim is necessary to keep psychological egoism consistent with observable facts, because it is clear that people do not always act in their own best interest.

Psychological egoism, then, is a theory about human nature—or about organic nature at large. But in a textbook on moral philosophy, we must concern ourselves with **moral egoism,** the theory that we ought always to act in what we take to be our own best interest. Historically, it turns out that almost all moral egoists are psychological egoists as well. Logically, there are two awkward features of holding both views. First, it seems odd to advocate egoism if it's the only show in town—something like advocating that Christmas should always fall on the day after Christmas Eve. Nevertheless, it seems that most philosophers who advocate acting in terms of self-interest do so because they hold that doing so is "natural." This raises the second awkwardness: that of trying to derive an "ought" from an "is."

Now, when egoists say that we always do, or always should, operate in terms of our own best interest, what do they mean by "best interest"? Is there any general category in terms of which "best interest" can be defined? Some philosophers have suggested that *power* or *survival* would be the real objectives of "self-interest," and each of these is plausible; but historically most egoists have held that self-interest should be understood in terms of *pleasure*, and therefore the two ideas of egoism and hedonism are often in association.

Here, we will take moral egoism seriously, not because there has been a continuous school of egoism, but because egoism doesn't seem to want to go away. In almost every philosophical epoch there have been vociferous defenders of it. We will first look at the theory of Epicurus, the most famous defender of egoistic hedonism from the Hellenistic period, then at the theory of Thomas Hobbes in the seventeenth century, and finally at the theory of Ayn Rand in the twentieth century.

Epicurus

The classical age of Athens is called the **Hellenic** period; the period that followed it is the **Hellenistic** period, which is often thought of as an era of decline in philosophy and the arts. Aristotle's death in 322 B.C.E. typically dates the end of Hellenism. Those historians who claim to detect degradation in later Greek philosophy can point to the devastations in Greek life during the fourth century B.C.E. The Greek city-states were ravaged by the plague and further debilitated by the political collapse caused by the Greek city-states' failure to solve the problem of disunity among them. The **Peloponnesian War,** fought among the various city-states, decimated much of the population, destroyed agriculture and commerce, and ended Greek dreams of glory.

Hellenic Vigor and Hellenistic Malaise

Epicurus (341–271 B.C.E.) was nineteen years old when Aristotle died; nevertheless, his philosophy is usually designated as Hellenistic rather than Hellenic. When we consider Aristotle's much more subtle and sophisticated account of the good life (as we will in Chapter 6), we detect in Epicurus a less rigorous mode of reasoning and a simpler account of human motivation, and a narrower scope of application. The same historians who call the Hellenistic period decadent often claim that Epicurus's philosophy is typical of the period insofar as it is **quietistic** and demotes ambition, politics, and efforts to engage vigorously with the world, choosing instead to turn inward, escaping from the anxieties and uncertainties caused by the collapse of the old communal traditions of the city-states.

Epicurus

Atoms

Before talking about Epicurus's ethics, I need to say something about his physics, because in his mind, the correct moral stance could only be taken if one understood the true nature of the world. Epicurus was a follower of Leucippus (ca. 460 B.C.E.–?) and Democritus (ca. 460–

ca. 370 B.C.E.), both of whom
espoused a philosophy called
atomism. Some people are
surprised to discover
that there was a
primitive version of
atomic physics so
early in our history,
but in fact it arrived
on the scene only
after several hundred
years of **cosmological**

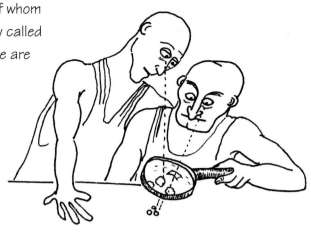

Leucippus and Democritus

speculation. According
to the atomists, atoms are the invisible foundational units of all that
exists. Atoms are minuscule basic physical bodies that are "indivisible and unalterable."[2] They have size, shape, weight, location, and are
in constant movement, though the composite bodies they produce
can be in states of rest. Based on his understanding of the theories
of Leucippus and Democritus, Epicurus became a materialist. In his
"Letter to Herodotus," he wrote that "the universe is bodies and
space" (B4). By "bodies," Epicurus, like Democritus, meant atoms or
compilations of atoms.

The Soul, Gods, and the Afterlife

Human bodies have souls, but souls are material, being composed of
"fine particles distributed throughout the whole structure." The soul
"most resembl[es] wind with a certain admixture of heat" (B10).
Atoms are eternal and indestructible, but entities composed of
atoms, such as bodies and their parts, including the soul, are not
eternal.

Despite Epicurus's materialism (or physicalism), he does include
gods in his universe. But, consistent with his initial premise, gods are
also material bodies; they too are atomic structures, but structures

that last a long time. The gods are sufficiently unlike human beings that they are indifferent to the concerns of humans and even to human existence.

These are radical views, but their acceptance is, according to Epicurus, a large step in the direction of happiness. This is because one of the greatest sources of human unhappiness is the fear of death. People fear death itself, and they fear the punishments of the gods in the afterlife. But the gods do not punish us humans; the gods are in fact unconcerned with us or our comportment. Furthermore, there is no afterlife. Death is nothing but the dissolution of the atomic components of the individual. Therefore, there is no such "thing" as death:

> Death, the most terrifying of ills, is nothing to us, since so long as we exist, death is not with us; but when death comes, then we do not exist. It does not then concern either the living or the dead. (B31)

Hamlet Considers the Punishments of Hell

Freedom

One of the major problems that Epicurus's moral philosophy faces is the problem of freedom. Epicurus was well aware of the strict determinism of the views of Leucippus and Democritus, the founders of atomism. According to them, everything is composed of atoms, and all atoms move through empty space traversing absolutely necessary paths that are determined by rigid laws of nature.

We do not know Leucippus's complete thoughts on this or any other topic, because only one fragment of his works remains. However, it is a telling one: "Naught happens for nothing but

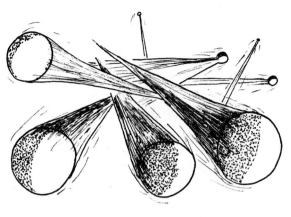

everything from a ground of necessity." Epicurus saw, as Democritus apparently did not, that the absolute determinism of atomism was incompatible with moral responsibility and, perhaps, even with agency. Epicurus's solution was to adjust atomistic physics in a puzzling way. He agreed with Leucippus and Democritus that atoms move through infinite space, and despite saying that in space there is no "'up' or 'down'" (B9), he nevertheless went on to say that in space atoms "fall," and sometimes collide, and in this veritable rainstorm of atoms, some atoms "swerve" from their paths (B5). These "atomic swerves" break the backbone of determinism and allow for the possibility of agency and freedom.

The so-called atomic swerve was never explained by Epicurus and over the years has seemed to many to be a desperate measure to save his theory of freedom, a **deus ex machina.** But in the twentieth century the Nobel Prize–winning German physicist Werner Heisenberg developed a theoretical construction that might be called the "subatomic swerve." According to his **principle of uncertainty,** at the subatomic level of reality (i.e., at the most basic level), the causal model does not work and must be replaced with a statistical model. Subatomic particles such as electrons occasionally behave in such unpredictable ways that their movements must be called *uncaused* events, or events that did not happen of *necessity.* Heisenberg himself, like Epicurus before him, tried to derive a theory of freedom from this discovery,[3] but most commentators claim that theories of indeterminacy do not generate the idea of freedom but the idea of randomness. Random behavior (**indeterminism**) does not appear to be any more free than necessary behavior (determinism).

Pleasure as the Motive and Goal of Life

Like almost all classical moral philosophers, Epicurus wanted to establish a program whose fulfillment would lead to the good life, which he called eudaimonia, or happiness.[4] Other Greek thinkers, such as Socrates, Plato, and Aristotle, asked what role pleasure (hêdonê) plays in happiness, but Epicurus claimed that happiness *is* pleasure. He wrote, "Pleasure is the starting point and goal of living blessedly. For we recognize this as our first innate good, and this is our starting point for every choice and avoidance."[5] Indeed, he claimed, "No pleasure is a bad thing in itself," but he went on to say that "the means which produce some pleasures bring with them disturbances many times greater than the pleasures" (B35). So we see in this qualification that the immediate sensation of pleasure is not the criterion of goodness. Epicurus was looking for an overall state of pleasure, and it was that which he equated with happiness. He created a philosophy not of crass sensualism (as did some of his followers in the Roman world) but of enlightened self-interest, where self-interest is defined in terms of pleasure spread over a lifetime.

Almost all of Epicurus's readers have noticed that his idea of pleasure is unusual in a number of ways. First, unlike some hedonists, he did not feel that the individual is necessarily an expert on his or her own pleasures—the philosopher may be able to convince someone that she is not leading a pleasant life, even if she is convinced that she is. Also, Epicurus made what seems to many to be the odd claim that pleasure does not have degrees. He wrote, "The pleasure in the flesh is not increased, when once the pain due to want is removed, but is only varied" (B36). When pain is removed, we are, according to him, in a state of the highest pleasure.

| Before Pain | Pain | After Pain |

To the uninitiated, it seems that Epicurus made an inexcusable error, confusing a neutral state with an intense sensation. But we discover that Epicurus defined pleasure negatively, as an absence of disturbance. Therefore the highest pleasure is a state of repose (*ataraxia*).

Desire

Epicurus's views on pleasure are derived from his analysis of desires. According to him, "of desires some are natural, others vain, and of the natural some are necessary and others merely natural; and of the necessary some are necessary for happiness, others for the repose of the body, and others for very life" (B31). There are, then, two fundamental kinds of desires, hence two kinds of pleasure as a result of gratifying these desires:

I. Natural desire

    A. Necessary (e.g., desire for food and sleep)

    B. Unnecessary (e.g., desire to scratch an itch or for sex)

II. Vain desire (e.g., desire for decorative clothing or exotic food)

In the words of Epicurus,

So when we say that pleasure is the goal we do not mean the pleasure of the profligate or the pleasures of consumption . . . but rather the lack of pain in the body and disturbance in the soul. For it is not in drinking bouts and continuous partying and enjoying boys and women[6] or consuming fish and the other dainties of an extravagant table, which produce the pleasant life, but sober calculation which searches out the reasons for every choice and avoidance and drives out the opinions which are the source of the greatest turmoil for men's souls (IG, 30–1).

Let us return to the category of "natural unnecessary desires." Is there any reason not to fulfill the desire to scratch one's nose? Epicurus said, "We must not violate nature, but obey her; and we shall obey her if we fulfill the necessary desires and also the physical, if they bring no harm to us, but sternly reject the harmful" (B41). So scratching your nose could be resisted, but it's all right to scratch if doing so will bring no harm to you. What about the desire for sex? It is natural, but usually can be overcome; and when it can be, it should be, because satisfaction of sexual desire gives intense pleasure, and all intense emotional states are dangerous. Also, the desire for sex puts people in relationships that are usually ultimately more painful than pleasant, and these relationships are often extremely painful.

Epicurus wrote, "Sexual intercourse has never done a man good, and he is lucky if it has not harmed him" (B45).

In *Epicurus' Ethical Theory*, Phillip Mitsis points out that Epicurus has a strong theoretical reason for advocating the fulfillment of only the simplest desires in the simplest ways possible. Mitsis demonstrates that, according to Epicurus, true

Love Is a Many-Splendored Thing (for a day or two)

happiness has three formal conditions, which Mitsis lists as (1) self-sufficiency, (2) invulnerability to chance, and (3) completeness. Self-sufficiency means that our pleasures must be under our control. If we choose to slake thirst by drinking water and overcome hunger by eating bread, then we very much have our pleasures in our power, but the moment that we opt for more delicate pleasures, we begin to lose control of our own fate. Epicurus said, "Self-sufficiency is the greatest of all riches" (B51) and, "[t]he greatest fruit of self-sufficiency is freedom" (B44). Invulnerability to chance is closely related to self-sufficiency. Bread and water are usually available even in harsh conditions; if we demand more than that, we will become vulnerable to the vicissitudes of the external world and hence to frustration, disappointment, and failure.

Epicurus said, "[B]read and water produce the highest pleasure, when one who needs them puts them to his lips" (B32) and, "[n]othing satisfies the man who is not satisfied with little" (B51). Epicurus can advocate "completeness of pleasure" only to those who accept his minimalistic account of the nature of pleasure. This qualification demonstrates to Mitsis that Epicurus "must subordinate his requirements for completeness to the demand that our happiness be under our control."[7] Epicurus tells us to eat bread,

and he is forced to deny that white bread may taste better (produce more pleasure) than brown bread. What about those who think of bread and water as prisoners' fare, desiring for themselves something a bit more exciting? As Mitsis points out, Epicurus can only look with disdain upon the person who rejects the bread because she is in the mood for steak and lobster, and certainly upon the individual who, though no longer hungry, "might take pleasure in eating a rich dessert" (47).

Because Epicurus was a rationalist, he could claim that nothing can produce more pleasure than simple freedom from pain and disturbance. He believed that the correct understanding of his philosophical arguments could transform the experience of sensation itself. Once we understand why frivolous pleasure is not true pleasure, the very experience of frivolous pleasure is demeaned and diminished.

Epicurus's rationalistic account of pleasure allows him to utter two of his most notorious remarks: his assertion that knowledge of one's impending death cannot decrease one's pleasure (because as a philosopher one knows that death holds no fear), and his assertion that even on the torture rack one can be perfectly happy. Mitsis astutely observes, "To see the real force of Epicurus' claim here, we should remember that he argues not only that one can be happy on the rack but he also is committed to the claim that one can be just as happy on as off the rack" (122). Even Epicurus's most dedicated readers usually part company with him here. In fact, it looks as though Epicurus should agree with his Roman critic Cicero (106–43 B.C.E.), that a dead person has as much pleasure as a live one. Two thousand years later, Sigmund Freud would reach a similar conclusion, when, after arguing in all his earlier books that the pleasure prin-

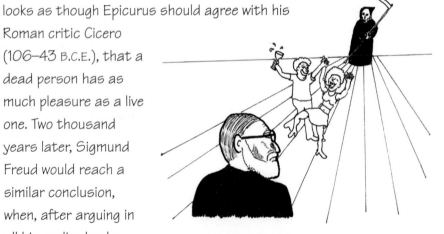

Beyond the Pleasure Principle

ciple was the ultimate guide of all behavior, he concluded in his book *Beyond the Pleasure Principle* that behind the pleasure principle is **Thanatos,** the death instinct.

The Virtues

Epicurus knew that the Greek moral tradition preceding him equated the good life with the virtuous life. It might be thought that a hedonist like Epicurus would see the pursuit of pleasure as hindered by the pursuit of virtue. Especially the demands of virtues like justice, generosity, and bravery seem to require that one sacrifice one's pleasure in the name of honor. But, to the contrary, according to Epicurus,

> It is not possible to live pleasantly without living prudently and honourably and justly, nor again to live a life of prudence, honour, and justice without living pleasantly. And the man who does not possess the pleasant life, is not living prudently and honourably and justly, and the man who does not possess the virtuous life, cannot possibly live pleasantly. (B 35)

The reason that only virtuous individuals can be happy is that the chief virtue for Epicurus is prudence, which in turn "is the source of all other virtues" (IG 31). Prudence—judicious reasoning about one's own good—is the one virtue that is dedicated to self-interest. According to Epicurus, if I am honest, loyal, trustworthy, and kind, it is only because I know that these virtues will bring to me inner calm (*ataraxia*), which is the highest form of pleasure for Epicurus.

Even though Epicurus chose a retiring life, he understood that human beings must live among other humans, and that these others are capable of disturbing our repose. What others think of us matters; offended parties are capable of causing us pain. Therefore the most peaceful form of life is the virtuous one. Epicurus infamously asserted, "Injustice is not an evil in itself, but only in consequence of the fear which attaches to the apprehension of being unable to escape those appointed to punish such actions" (B38). But this concern that one will have to pay for one's injustice means that "[t]he just man is most free from trouble, the unjust, most full of trouble" (B36).

In Plato's *Republic*, Glaucon, a companion of Socrates, tells the story of the magic ring of Gyges. In the story, the man who possesses the ring is able to become invisible and avoid the normal consequences of his actions. He seduces the queen, kills the king, and takes over the kingdom.

The implication of the story is that anybody would do the same and would be a fool not to. If we condemn Gyges, we do so because we are envious or don't want people to think badly of us. In the *Republic*, Glaucon's story provokes Socrates to defend the view that the wise man, even if invisible, would not behave

Gyges and His Magic Ring

immorally as Gyges does. Epicurus, it seems, has no such response. On his account, it certainly appears that an individual who knew he could not be held responsible for his actions would have no reason to be just, except in the rare cases when being just suited his wishes. Epicurus, who emphasized repose as the greatest pleasure, would certainly never advocate seduction, murder, or usurpation, even if we could perform these acts with impunity, but he gave no reason for being just to others except to avoid the consequences of being unjust.

Friendship

When we consider Epicurus's egoism and hedonism, we might be surprised to discover how important friendship is for him. Indeed, we see that the friendship that Epicurus advocated is altruistic friendship, evidenced by his claim that true friendship is worth the sacrifice of one's very life. How is it possible for an egoist to advocate altruism? In the fragments of his books remaining to us, Epicurus never gives an account of the workings of friendship, so we don't really know exactly how he defended his claim. There are possible arguments to which Epicurus could appeal, but most of them are too modern to be attributed to him. For example, as Phillip Mitsis points out, there is a Freudian argument according to which all pleasure is narcissistic in its origin, but under certain conditions the desire whose fulfillment produces the pleasure can be displaced onto another object—such as a friend—producing a relationship in which pleasure is taken from friendship. This relationship then becomes so routine that certain features of the friendship are pursued even if no pleasure is available for the agent. At this stage, even the egoist might be willing to risk her life for the friend. But Epicurus did not have the pleasure of reading Freud.

What did Epicurus actually say about friendship in the fragments that are still available? Epicurus wrote, "All friendship is desirable in itself, though it starts from the need of help" (B41). This tells us that we are more dependent on others than Epicurus

HOW TO TRAIN THE ID TO MAKE FRIENDS AND INFLUENCE PEOPLE

All you need is love, love,... Love is all you need

by Prof. SIGMUND FREUD, M.D.

A Recently Discovered Lost Manuscript

must have wanted to admit, as this dependency sins against one of the three formal requirements for happiness: invulnerability. We see that other humans—in the form of friends—are required in order to meet the need for completeness, which is another of the three formal conditions of happiness. Epicurus said, "Of all the things which wisdom acquires to produce the blessedness of the complete life, far the greatest is the possession of friendship" (B37). A passage that seems to demonstrate Epicurus's altruism informs us, "The wise man feels no more pain when he is tortured than when his friend is tortured, and will die on his behalf." But when we look at Epicurus's reason for being prepared to die for a friend, we see him saying, "[F]or if he betrays his friend, his entire life will be confounded and utterly upset because of a lack of confidence" (IG 39). Apparently there is some problem with the language in the original Greek manuscript containing this passage, so we cannot be certain of the meaning. For example, Bailey's translation is remarkably different from that of Inwood and Gerson. Bailey translates the passage "[B]ut if his friend does him wrong, his whole life will be confounded by distrust and completely upset" (B43). The 1994 translation of Inwood and Gerson is more recent, hence perhaps more researched. According to it, the reason one should be loyal to one's friend and even risk death protecting a friend is roughly the same as the reason for practicing justice: failing to do so may disturb one's peace of mind (ataraxia). On this reading, despite Epicurus's calling friendship "desirable in itself," the real value of friendship for me—like everything else in Epicurus's system—is in the pleasure it provides me.

I've discovered that throwing money at people is a good way to make friends.

If today the term "Epicurean" seems to hint at gluttony, debauchery, and bacchanalian orgies, that is not Epicurus's fault but the fault of some of his Roman interpreters who understood the idea of pleasure in a way that would have horrified Epicurus—thinking of it in terms of sensual titillation. Epicurus himself led a life of sobriety and simplicity: eating bread, cheese, and olives; drinking a bit of wine; napping in his hammock; and enjoying conversation with his friends while strolling through his garden. He died with dignity and courage after a painful disease.

What shall we in the twenty-first century say about Epicurus's moral philosophy? It is certainly replete with distracting flaws, such as the absence of an explanation of how a hedonistic egoist can sacrifice her life for a friend and how such a person can be equally content whether being tortured on the rack, or enjoying bread, cheese, and cool water with friends in the shade of her garden. However, some of Epicurus's ideas that might be unattractive to us may make more sense if we historicize them. His quietism might have looked compelling after the political upheaval, the chaos of war, and the horrors of the plague that afflicted the Greek peninsula during his time. Indeed, they may look attractive to us in our day for roughly the same reasons. As odd as most Westerners have found many of the Asian religions, the West has always seemed to have a secret admiration and even an envy of the calm and tranquility that Asian philosophies promise, a stance in the world similar in many ways to Epicurus's ataraxia—repose, tranquility, calm. Sigmund Freud, near the end of his life, when he was riddled with painful cancer, wrote that two sources of great misery for humans are the overwhelming power of nature and the frailty of the body, but that the greatest misery by far derives from the need of human beings to have dealings with other human beings. Freud suggested various possible attempts to escape such compounded misery, including hermitism, intoxication, "the mass delusion" of religion, neurosis, and madness ("the desperate attempt at rebellion seen in psychosis"[8]), each of which is described by Freud as an existential choice. Given this panoply of options, perhaps Epicurus's recommendation of *ataraxia* doesn't look so bad after all.

Thomas Hobbes

Epicurus had a number of disciples in the late classical period, the most noteworthy of whom was the Roman philosopher and poet Lucretius (ca. 98–55 B.C.E.), who wrote "On the Nature of Things," a philosophical poem expostulating on the virtues of hedonism. During the thousand years of the medieval period—roughly between 400 and 1400—neither egoism nor hedonism had many published defenders, mostly because of the intellectual domination of the Catholic Church during this period. However, at the end of the Renaissance and the beginning of the Baroque period, these two related theories found their ablest defender in the person of Thomas Hobbes.

Hobbes's Life

Thomas Hobbes was born on April 5, 1588, near the town of Malmesbury in Wiltshire, England. His father was a parson in the local church, but rather than being a scholarly and peaceful man of God, he was apparently uninterested in learning and somewhat disposed to angry outbursts. He fled from the village after assaulting one of the parishioners, leaving his wife and son to fend for themselves.

Thomas's wealthy uncle assumed responsibility for his education, sending him off to school at age four. Having excelled in Greek and Latin, Thomas entered Oxford University

Little Thomas Says Good-bye to His Daddy

at age fifteen, where he found his instruction to be so deficient that he developed a lifelong suspicion of traditional academics. (He may have been right; four years after his death, Oxford University ordered his *Leviathan* to be burned because of its "heretical," "blasphemous," and "destructive" doctrines.) After graduating from Oxford, Hobbes became the tutor to the children of the wealthy

Thomas Hobbes

and politically powerful Cavendish family, a family with which he remained in contact throughout most of his long life. Hobbes was one of those few philosophers who published nothing of significant originality until after his fiftieth birthday (Immanuel Kant, whom you will study in Chapter 3, was another such late bloomer), but luckily he was intellectually active for his last forty years.

Hobbes lived during a difficult time in English history. A weakened King Charles I was contemptuous of the Parliament, whose support he needed to raise the funds for his projects, and the more he became dependent upon the Parliament, the stronger and more resistant toward him it became. Finally, in 1642 the first of two civil wars broke out between the king's supporters and those factions that supported the Parliament. Charles lost the war and was publicly beheaded in 1649. The unhappy supporters of the king, along with those who disliked the amount of power that fell to the Puritan minority in England after the first war, rallied in revolt, provoking a second war. The Puritan army, led by Oliver Cromwell, triumphed, and Cromwell was named Lord Protector of England in 1650. Upon Cromwell's death, ten years later, the monarchy was restored and Charles II was proclaimed king of England.

During parts of these conflicts, Hobbes felt the need to absent himself from England and to visit the Continent, because he had somehow managed to alienate all sides in the disputes. The Royalists were sure that he defended a parliamentary form of government (and, indeed, by criticizing the theory of the divine right of kings, he had attacked the mainstay of the Royalist argument), while the Parliamentarians were certain that Hobbes supported a monarchy (and, indeed, he was suspicious of democratic governments and believed in the nearly absolute power of the sovereign, whatever form such sovereignty took). In his travels throughout France and Italy, he had interviews with the leading intellectual leaders of the day, conversing with Descartes in Paris and with Galileo in Padua. Hobbes wrote what is considered his most important philosophical work, *Leviathan*, in Paris, starting in 1648. It was published in London in 1651. But his book produced anger not only in England but in Paris, where its challenge to the legitimacy of the Catholic Church's claims to political power outraged many traditionalists. He returned to England, where, with the help of his friends in the Cavendish family, he almost managed to stay out of trouble. He died on December 4, 1679, at age ninety-one.

Hobbes's Egoism

Hobbes's egoism is presented in a simple and straightforward manner in *Leviathan*, where he set forth the following views:

> Of the voluntary acts of every man, the object is some *good to himself*.[9]
>
> For no man giveth, but with intention of good to himself; because gift is voluntary; and of all voluntary acts, the object is to every man his own good. (100)
>
> Every man by nature seeketh his own benefit, and promotion. (126)
>
> By necessity of nature [men] choose that which appeareth best for themselves. (195)

All voluntary acts, then, have as their motive and goal a benefit to the agent. Hobbes contrasted "voluntary acts" with "vital motions," such as heartbeats, breathing, and intestinal activity (all of which also seem to be programmed for the advantage of the individual), and with accidents. If I trip and fall down the stairs, I do not, according to Hobbes, do so with the hope of achieving a benefit for myself.

(Hobbes did not go so far as to erase the distinction between voluntary and accidental behaviors, as Sigmund Freud would do three hundred years later, assigning conscious intentions to "voluntary" acts, and unconscious motives to [many? most? all?] "accidents.")

Hobbes, then, is what was designated earlier in the chapter as a psychological egoist.

This could really work out to my advantage.

(I should mention at this point that I believe I am presenting the standard interpretation of Hobbes's theory of motivation when I call him a psychological egoist, but that there is at least one philosopher—Bernard Gert— who takes issue with that interpretation. I believe his argument is erroneous and will say why in an endnote.[10] Here I will proceed with what I take to be the traditional view of Hobbes's views.) If Hobbes's view is true, it rules out the biological possibility of altruism. As you have seen, altruism as a psychological theory is the claim that people sometimes do sacrifice what they take to be their own interests for the interests of others, and as a moral theory it is the claim that people sometimes ought to sacrifice what they take to be their own interests for the interests of others. Egoism, which may seem offensive to many people today, seemed perfectly natural to the ancient Greeks, such as Aristotle, whom you will study in Chapter 6. Its opposite, altruism, is a view we often associate with Christianity, expressed for example in Jesus's instruction to the rich man that he sell all his possessions and give the money to the poor (Mark 10:21). Certainly egoism is overturned when Jesus asserts in the King James version of the New Testament, "If any man cometh unto me and hateth not . . . his own life, . . . he cannot be my disciple" (Luke 14:26). On the other hand, Jesus tells us, "Love thy neighbor as *thyself*" (Luke 6:31, emphasis added) and, "[d]o unto others as you would have them do unto you" (Luke 6:31).

Love Thy Neighbor as Thyself

If altruism is impossible, as Hobbes seems to have held, then surely it cannot be a moral duty. (As David Hume said, "ought" implies "can." If some moral philosopher tells you that you have a duty to do something that is impossible, that philosopher is wrong.) Well then, *is* altruism impossible? Is it ever possible to sacrifice what one takes to be one's own interests in order to act in the interests of another? Hobbes said sacrifice is possible only if one perceives it to be in one's interests. Certainly most of us are surprised by Hobbes's claim because we tend to draw certain distinctions that he rejected. For example, in the case of a person who at great risk to his own life saves a drowning child from the surf, consider the kinds of explanations he might give after the fact: I saved her because . . .

A. I saw that she would drown if I didn't go in after her. (Somebody had to do it!)   (responsibility)

B. I recognized that it was my duty to try to save her.   (duty)

C. Only an animal would have stood by and let her drown.   (natural sentiment)

D. I know that family, and I love that little girl.   (love)

E. Her father helped me once when I was down and out.   (debt)

F. Well, I don't know why I did it. I'm as surprised as you are.   (?)

G. My conscience would have plagued me for the rest of my life if I hadn't tried.   (guilt)

H. I didn't want people to say that I was a coward.   (reputation)

I. I hoped I would get some recognition out of all this.   (reputation)

J. I wanted to satisfy a need I have to help others. (self-aggrandizement—perhaps out of guilt or feelings of inferiority)

K. I wanted to achieve a benefit for myself.   (Hobbesian honesty)

L. I wanted the pleasant sensation that heroism affords me.   (hedonism)

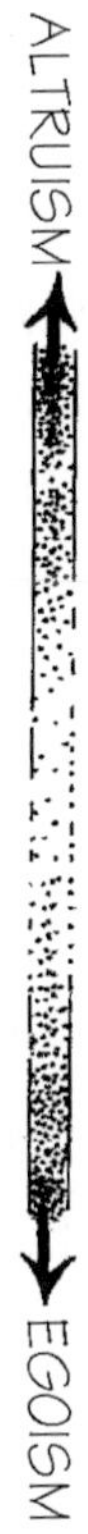

(Right margin, vertical axis: ALTRUISM ↑ ... ↓ EGOISM)

Hobbes would say that reasons A through J are really versions of K, and indeed that K is a version of L because he defined "benefit" in terms of pleasure. ("*Pleasure . . . or delight, is the appearance or sense of good, and molestation or displeasure, the appearance or sense of evil*" [36]). Therefore, Hobbes's egoism, like Epicurus's egoism, is a form of hedonism. It is also a form of **monism,** reducing all types of motivation to one kind. Our everyday conception of motivation is pluralistic: There are many different kinds of reasons for action.

There is another complication in Hobbes's theory. He wrote, "So that in the first place, I put for a general inclination of all mankind, a perpetual and restless striving of power after power, that ceaseth only in death" (66). It is not clear to me whether Hobbes thought that, without

power, we will be unable to prevent others from obstructing our quest for pleasure, or whether he meant that power itself gives pleasure, or whether he meant that this power-mongering is independent of the hedonistic principles that also motivate us. In any case, this power-mongering is at least compatible with hedonism and with psychological egoism and is probably meant to be an aspect of them.

Criticism of Psychological Egoism

Psychological egoism has had many more critics than defenders. The most accessible criticism—one that goes back at least as early as Bishop Joseph Butler (1692–1752) and has a number of twentieth-century exponents (e.g., C. D. Broad, Thomas Nagel, and Joel Feinberg)—accuses the psychological egoist of illegitimately deriving egoism from the fact that people (often, and in varying degrees) derive pleasure from the successful achievement of their intentions. According to these critics, I may or may not derive pleasure from helping someone climb out of a cesspool into which he has fallen, but my motive was not to achieve pleasure but to help out someone in trouble. Whether I do or do not derive pleasure from the act is indifferent to my motive—the primary reason I did it, what moved me to do it.

In my opinion this is a good argument, but not a conclusive one. To establish that egoism is false, the argument would have to demonstrate that we would have the same intentions and engage in the same behavior that we do now, even if we never achieved pleasure from our actions.

Another line of criticism derives from what has come to be known as the **principle of falsifiability** (associated with the British-Austrian philosopher of science Sir Karl Popper). From the perspective of this principle, the question to be asked is How does the psychological egoist—Hobbes, in this case—know that human action is always motivated by self-interest? Is the claim to this knowledge based on empirical fact? Is it the result of a scientific investigation?

In fact, Hobbes has not only failed to conduct a scientific investigation, he has subverted the very possibility of any such investigation. This subversion takes place because truly scientific theories must always be open to possible refutation if new disconfirming data are discovered. According to the principle of falsifiability, for a hypothesis to be truly scientific, its expositor must be able to state the conditions under which it would be admitted that the hypothesis had been refuted. For example, Isaac Newton would admit that his theory of gravity was false if, all other things being equal, repeated instances were reported and confirmed of heavier-than-air objects hovering, floating, or rising. Precisely what makes Newton's theory convincing is

Things Going Up

the fact that no such events have been confirmed, or, where they have been confirmed—in cases like airplane and rocket liftoffs—explanatory theories consistent with the theory of gravity have been presented. But what makes Newton's theory *scientific* is that we know what it would be like to be false.

Now, in the face of the principle of falsifiability, what is the status of Hobbes's thesis? What kind of data, if discovered, would refute Hobbes's view? The answer to this seems to be: *none*. No matter what possible counterevidence we could imagine, Hobbes would claim that his theory can account for it. For example, let's try to imagine an event that we believe to be paradigmatic of altruism. What about the case of the soldier who throws himself on the grenade, thereby saving the lives of his comrades at the cost of his own life? Such heroic acts are possible—in fact, they have taken place. Are these acts not evidence of altruism, hence evidence against Hobbes's egoism? Not at all, Hobbes would say. If the soldier sacrificed his life, it was because

(whether foolishly or not) he construed it as being in his interest to do so. (He knew he would be dead either way and preferred to be remembered as a hero; he was raised in such a way that his concept of self-esteem was intimately tied to the performance of heroic acts; or he thought people would like him; etc.)

Hobbes probably believed that it was to his theory's credit that it could account for any possible contingency, but those who respect the principle of falsifiability believe that the opposite is true. Any theory that accounts for every possible case in effect accounts for no case. Or, to put it slightly differently, any "theory" that is compatible with every possible state of affairs is no theory at all because real theories must exclude some possibilities. Confucius is supposed to have said, "If the mind is too open, everything falls out." The same goes for theories.

If Hobbes had stated his proposition differently, it might have escaped being targeted by the principle of falsifiability. What if Hobbes had said, "There is more self-interest in most motivation than is usually admitted. One should be generally suspicious when estimating an agent's intentions. When thinking of the agent's action, one should ask, 'What's in it for the agent?'" In that case Hobbes would be admitting the possibility, though not the likelihood, of altruistic acts, and the question concerning which acts are egoistic and which altruistic would be an *empirical* one (i.e., one to be determined by observable evidence). It is still not obvious that such an empirical investigation would be truly scientific, but it would at least be meaningful. But no doubt Hobbes would be loath to give up his psychological egoism and hedonism, because he believed that his views provided a scientific insight into human motivation that would be needed before any adequate theory of society was possible. But, as the British philosopher Richard Peters says, Hobbes does not give us "a new theory of motivation with concrete evidence to support it but a re-description of the familiar process of living," in which he simply redefines all motivation as egoistic.[11] What if, perhaps under the influence of having eaten too many Big Macs in one afternoon, I put forth the theory, "Everything is hamburger"? You point to a rock, and ask, "What about this?" to which I answer, "That's hard hamburger"; you point to water, and I say, "Wet hamburger";" you ask about the wind, and I say, "Cool, forceful, invisible hamburger." In that case, I have slipped into what might be called "tautological hamburgerism," which is hardly a real theory. Hobbes, it has been said, slipped into tautological egoism.[12]

Hamburgerism

Not all commentators are convinced that an appeal to the principle of falsifiability demonstrates that versions of psychological egoism like Hobbes's are merely tautological. In their book *Unto Others: The Evolution and Psychology of Unselfish Behavior*,[13] philosopher Elliott Sober and biologist David Sloan Wilson argue against egoism on evolutionary grounds (as you will see in Chapter 5). They believe that their empirically based argument produces a likely refutation of psychological egoism, and that their success contrasts with the stalemate produced by arguments based on the principle of falsifiability. Now, from these ideas, Sober and Wilson conclude that we cannot accept the claim that by its very nature psychological egoism is indifferent to empirical evidence. They write about the current state of the theory of psychological egoism, "[H]ow do we know that new theories will not be developed and confirmed?" (289, emphasis added). I believe this is an inadequate criticism of the application of the principle of falsifiability to the theory of psychological egoism. It is true that psychological egoists may find new and better formulations of their theory, but the principle of falsifiability reveals a serious internal weakness in all versions so far presented, in my opinion. We will wait and see if any better versions are forthcoming.

According to Sober and Wilson, the paradigmatic case of altruism is the one mentioned earlier of a soldier who throws himself on a live grenade, saving the lives of his buddies at the cost of his own life. The psychological egoist tries to undermine the theory of altruism by saying that rather than sacrificing his life for his comrades (altruism) in the face of inevitable death, the soldier prefers knowing that people will think of him as a hero after his death, or prefers the pleasure of knowing that he will die as a hero over the pain of simply dying (psychological hedonism). Now, according to Sober and Wilson, those who say that the egoist's thesis is untestable, fail to notice that, strictly speaking, neither the egoist's nor the altruist's thesis is testable. The soldier's real motive can never be established empirically.

In my view, this is a good point, and it does dull somewhat the edge of the "falsification" attack. It does not change the fact, however, that the altruist's claim is derived from our standard way of thinking about motivation, and the egoist's response seems artificial and contrived in trying to overturn our standard belief that altruism is possible. Still, philosophy often shows that our normal ways of thinking are wrong. Perhaps this is why Sober and Wilson reject all philosophical refutations of egoism and seek a scientific one. They will derive their view from Charles Darwin's biological theories, as you will see when you read about evolutionary ethics in Chapter 5, and they will conclude that most likely, we humans, along with many other living organisms, have the capacity for genuinely altruistic acts built into our genes. Furthermore, we act altruistically because groups composed of individuals motivated exclusively by egoistic goals would have less survival value than those composed of individuals who sometimes are willing to act on behalf of others at their own expense.

Hobbes's Dilemma: How Is a Society of Egoists Possible?

In some ways, Hobbes's egoism seems quite cynical (everybody looks out only for Number One) and very pessimistic. Hobbes himself recognized the potential for **anarchy** entailed by our egoistic, hedonistic, power-mongering propensities, and (as you will see in Chapter 7, where Hobbes's version of "ethics by contract" will be discussed) he worried about the difficulty of conceiving a society in which egoists could live together in peace. According to him, if there were no powerful authority to keep the individuals in such a society in a state of awe, life would be "solitary, poor, nasty, brutish, and short" (84). On the other hand, once Hobbes had drawn up the contractual articles of legitimate authority, the society he imagined looks fairly normal, as you will see. Furthermore, he insisted throughout *Leviathan* that people can and should cooperate with each other, and that they should consider other people's interests as they go about large and small daily activities. (Doing so is in *everybody's* interest.)

So, what are the implications of egoism for us, according to Hobbes and Epicurus? Despite the radical appearance of the doctrine at first glance, in their cases, it is mostly "business as usual."

Ayn Rand

Our final defender of egoism—Ayn Rand—does see radical implications for hedonistic egoism, perhaps to her credit. For her, these implications are **utopian.** She envisioned a society of pure egoists, with responsibility only to themselves individually and none, or virtually none, to the less fortunate (the poor, sick, downtrodden, handicapped). Any service to them must be a gesture of generosity made from within the bounds of selfishness, freely chosen by the egoist from his accumulation of power, wealth, or material surplus. Should one attempt to save a drowning swimmer? In *The Virtue of Selfishness*, Rand wrote that "it is morally proper to save him only when the danger to one's own life is minimal; when the danger is great, it would be immoral to attempt it."[14] Similarly, Rand recommended that we help to save strangers from a sinking ship. But she strongly qualified her advice: "It is only in emergency situations that one should volunteer to help strangers. . . . But this does not mean that after they all reach shore, he should devote his efforts to saving his fellow passengers from poverty, ignorance, neurosis or whatever other troubles they might have" (54–5). This, I believe, is the way we expected our egoists to talk. Let us now turn to Rand's defense of egoism.

Rand's Life

This dramatic and influential version of egoism was introduced into American philosophy in the twentieth century by the Russian émigré and naturalized American novelist and philosophical essayist, Ayn Rand.

Rand, who was contemptuous of academia itself, influenced thousands of high school and university students, primarily through her two best-selling novels, *The Fountainhead* (1943) and *Atlas Shrugged* (1957). These books, years after her death, still sell about 400,000 copies a year in English and in numerous translations. The artistic value of these novels is debated by defenders—

Ayn Rand

some of whom believe Rand to be the greatest novelist of all time—and detractors—some of whom see the novels as clunky vehicles for her controversial philosophy. (At one point in *Atlas Shrugged*, the novel's Olympian hero, John Galt, delivers a 35,000-word speech.)

Rand was born in 1905 as Alisa Rosenbaum in Petrograd, Russia (soon to be Leningrad; today, St. Petersburg). She was twelve years old when the Bolshevik revolution broke out, and her middle-class Jewish family fled Petrograd to escape the havoc wreaked by the subsequent civil war between the Bolsheviks (defending a radical version of Communism) and the White Russians (defending the old Russian monarchy). After the Bolshevik victory, her family returned to Petrograd—newly dubbed Leningrad—and at the age of sixteen, Rosenbaum entered the University of Leningrad, completing a three-year diploma. In 1926 she arrived in Chicago, ostensibly to visit relatives, but clearly with the intention of fleeing the Soviet Union, whose Communist regime she detested. Upon her arrival in the States she began calling herself Ayn (pronounced "Eye-n") rather than Alisa, and she soon changed her last name to Rand. While seeking work in Los Angeles in 1929, she met and married a part-time actor, Frank O'Connor. This marriage provided her with permanent resident status. A fortunate chance meeting with the Hollywood director Cecil B. DeMille led to a job as a scriptwriter. Rand worked on her English—always heavily accented but soon grammatically and stylistically mastered—and began writing plays and working on her novel *The Fountainhead*, whose publication in 1943 brought her fame and financial stability. In 1947 Rand testified as a friendly witness before the House Un-American Activities Committee (HUAC), which was investigating Communist influence in Hollywood.

The movie version of *The Fountainhead* was released in 1949, and, as her fame spread, Rand gathered around her a close-knit group of disciples, including Alan Greenspan, later chairman of the Federal Reserve Board, Nathan Blumenthal (soon to change his name to Nathaniel Branden), and his wife, Barbara. The Brandens, through the establishment of the Nathaniel Branden Institute, quickly became the chief purveyors of Objectivism, the title chosen by Rand for her philosophy. In 1957, Rand's masterpiece, *Atlas Shrugged,* was published to popular acclaim and, mostly, to critical disdain. In 1964, *The Virtue of Selfishness* was published, setting forth in a series of articles the main principles of her philosophy and selling to date more than a million copies.

Rand's inner circle was dubbed "the Collective," an insider's joke, because Rand's philosophy rants against all forms of collectivism. As Rand's power and influence grew, she demanded ever-stricter dedication from the members of the Collective and occasionally excommunicated those members whose loyalty she suspected. One such expulsion on August 23, 1968, rumbled like an earthquake through the Objectivist movement: Nathaniel Branden himself—Rand's closest associate, friend, and lover, and the person to whom she had dedicated *Atlas Shrugged*—along with all of Branden's sympathizers, was violently severed from any connection with the movement.

Branden and Friends Excommunicated

Apparently it was at this moment that Branden

told Rand that the twenty-five years of age difference that separated them had made a continued romantic liaison impossible for him. (She was soon to learn that in fact there was already another woman involved.) The split between Rand and Branden provoked the dissolution of the Nathaniel Branden Institute, and the schism among the various groups of Objectivists proved almost fatal to the Objectivist movement that Rand had created. The reason for the split was generally kept a secret until after Rand's death in 1982. In 1989 Branden spilled the beans in his book *Judgment Day: My Years with Ayn Rand*. Explaining why Rand had not publicly denounced him at the time of the rupture, Branden wrote, "She could hardly say to the world that she repudiated Nathaniel Branden as a spokesman for Objectivism because he failed her romantically, because he refused to sleep with her."[15]

Despite this near meltdown at the core of Objectivism, the high rate of sales of Rand's books since her death in 1982 has provided the Objectivist movement with new generations of members, who seem to be less disturbed by the in-house sexual scandal than were those of the late 1960s and early 1970s.

Egoism and Reason

As you saw, Ayn Rand called her overall philosophy Objectivism. In Objectivism, egoism—or, as she usually preferred to call it, selfishness—plays a large role. The clearest fairly systematic exposition of her ideas about egoism is presented in her book of 1964, *The Virtue of Selfishness: A New Concept of Egoism.*[16]

Why did Rand prefer the term selfishness to the term egoism? Apparently this is a stupid question that a true Objectivist would never ask. Her book opens with this passage:

> The title of this book may evoke the kind of question that I hear once in a while: "Why do you use the word 'selfishness' to denote virtuous qualities of character, when that word antagonizes so many people to whom it does not mean the things you mean?"

To those who ask it, my answer is: "For the reason that makes you afraid of it." (vii)

Rand said that the very asking of that question reveals "moral cowardice" (viii) on the part of the questioner.

Despite Rand's insult to her potential reader (an insult because virtually every reader who picks up her book puzzles at the **oxymoronic** character of Rand's title),[17] Rand deigns to explain why she chose as a virtue what is generally thought of as a vice. "The meaning ascribed in popular usage to the word 'selfishness' is not merely wrong: it represents a devastating intellectual 'package deal,' which is responsible, more than any other single factor, for the arrested development of mankind" (vii). Rand supports this amazing assertion by saying that "the exact meaning and dictionary definition of the word 'selfishness' is: *concern with one's own interests.*" She goes on to say, "This concept does *not* include a moral evaluation." (vii).

This explanation may not convince everyone. Webster's New Universal Unabridged Dictionary provides this definition:

Me, me, me . . .

How admirable!

1. devoted to or caring only for oneself; concerned primarily with one's own interests, benefits, welfare, etc., *regardless of others.* 2. characterized by or manifesting concerns or care *only* for oneself. (Emphases added.)

It seems all too convenient for Rand to delete from the definition the passages I have left in italics, for their inclusion does indeed seem to imply a moral criticism, as does the dictionary's entry for synonyms of selfishness as "self-interested, self-seeking, egoistic; illiberal, parsimonious, stingy."

Rand makes it clear throughout her book that she advocates a version of moral egoism (one ought to think and behave egoistically) and rejects psychological egoism (one has no alternative but to think and behave egoistically). As you saw, psychological egoism denies the very possibility of being motivated by altruism, while Rand believes that altruism—the sacrifice of (what one takes to be) one's own interests for (what one takes to be) the interests of others—is not only possible, but actual, and that it is *always* morally wrong. In *The Virtue of Selfishness*, Nathaniel Branden, Rand's key spokesman before he fell into disgrace, is the one who addresses the issue head-on. In an essay titled "Isn't Everyone Selfish?" he writes that it is sometimes claimed that because "every purposeful action is motivated by some value or goal the actor desires, one always acts *selfishly*, whether one knows it or not" (66). Branden (correctly, in my view) calls this thesis a form of "intellectual confusion." Branden says, "Obviously, in order to act, one has to be moved by some personal motive; one has to 'want,' in some sense, to perform the action. The issue of an action's selfishness or unselfishness depends, not on whether or not one wants to perform it, but on *why* one wants to perform it" (68). By taking this line of reasoning, Branden and Rand avoid the criticism aimed at egoists like Hobbes, according to which the egoistic theory of motivation is really only a tautology. (One defines egoism as doing only what one wants, therewith claiming that all acts are egoistic, because people only do what, in some sense, they want to do.)

Rand is for selfishness and against altruism. What is altruism, according to her? She defines it in the following manner: "Altruism declares that any action taken for the benefit of others is good, and any action taken for one's own benefit is evil" (viii). She then describes altruism as the requirement that one sacrifice oneself, and calls it "the ethical theory which regards man as a sacrificial animal" (37). She then defines "sacrifice": "A sacrifice, it is necessary to remember, means the surrender of a higher value in favor of a lower value or of a nonvalue" (45).

I would like to pause here and say that Rand's definition of altruism ("Altruism declares that any action taken for the benefit of others is good, and any action taken for one's own benefit is evil" [viii]) produces a **straw man**—that is, it produces an artificial opponent.

Arguing with a Straw Man

Nothing in the definition of altruism, nor in any well-known version of altruistic theory (e.g., Christianity or Kantianism) implies that any action taken for the benefit of others is good. Many dictators and lunatics believe that they are acting for the benefit of others (e.g., the madwoman who drowns her babies so they won't have to suffer in this terrible world), yet their acts are condemned by almost all moral systems. Similarly, neither the definition of altruism nor any well-known theory of altruism claims that all actions taken for one's own benefit are evil. The result of Rand's stilted definitions is that she produced a caricature of altruism that is all too easy to attack. In addition, Rand's definition of "sacrifice" as "surrender of a higher value for a lower value" is not correct. Many people who make sacrifices do so believing that the object they sacrifice is of lesser value than that for which they make the sacrifice (e.g., national security, or God's will). Again, it is easy to attack "sacrifice" if it is defined as giving up something of higher value for something of lower value.

Such a definition of altruism as she gave allows Rand to write, "The rational principle of conduct is the exact opposite: always act in accordance with the hierarchy of your values, and never sacrifice a greater value to a lesser one" (50). Now, according to Rand, if a man values his wife because he correctly believes that it is in his interest to do so, then he might give up other values for her or even risk his life for her. In such a case, "his action is *not* a sacrifice" (51). Similarly, if a man[18] risks his life working against a vicious dictator because that man would not value his life if he were a slave, undertaking such a risk is not an act of self-sacrifice. Like Aristotle, Rand held that a truly *human* life is the life of reason; therefore she believed she could square the idea that one might be willing to lose one's life in certain circumstances with her original assertion that the source of all value is survival. A merely animalistic form of existence, or the existence of a slave (a person who does not enjoy the freedoms that Rand claims are natural for man), is not a *human* existence. Finally, Rand makes the rather astounding statement, "Altruism is incompatible with freedom, with capitalism and with individual rights" (112).

According to Branden, not everybody is selfish (i.e., moral), but there is indeed such a thing as "a genuinely selfish man" (i.e., a genuinely moral man). Such a man operates under "the guidance of reason" (67) in seeking that which is in his best interest. Almost all egoists throughout history believe that humans should pursue *rational* self-interest. In this respect, Rand falls into line with a long tradition of egoists. In *The Virtue of Selfishness*, she writes that "man must act for his own *rational* self-interest" (x). In the case of Epicurus and

Hobbes, pursuing rational self-interest involves my recognizing that I must compromise what I take to be my most immediate interests because reason tells me that pursuing such immediate interests is not in my long-term interest. The difference here seems to be that for Rand, rational self-interest does not involve compromise (which is a form of self-sacrifice, hence a form of altruism). Furthermore, for Rand, only those who pursue *rational* self-interest are really egoists. Those who follow only their desires or impulses are not egoists. Being rationally self-interested means accepting as absolutes the principles of rationality as determined by Ayn Rand herself. That is to say, anyone who does not accept the whole of Objectivism (with its commitment to capitalism as the natural exemplification of human activity, and to minimalism in government as the only legitimate form of political organization, and its refusal to accept any obligation to the less fortunate) is not being rational, and therefore is not truly selfish. I do not mean this as a criticism of Rand's views, rather as a paraphrase of them. Let's see how this all plays out.

Rand claimed that her strongest commitment is to reason. In *The Objectivist* of September 1971, she wrote, "I am not *primarily* an advocate of capitalism, but of egoism; and I am not primarily an advocate of egoism, but of reason."[19] In other words, a commitment to reason entails a commitment to egoism, which in turn entails a commitment to capitalism. Well, then, what about the commitment to reason? A main thrust of Rand's is to distinguish reason from emotions and to advocate a form of life in which motives are never based on the emotions. However, the concept of reason itself is never carefully analyzed in *The Virtue of Selfishness*. We are told that it is a faculty that directs the process of conceptualization, which is "an actively sustained process of identifying one's impressions in conceptual terms," which in turn is identical to the process of *"thinking"* (22). Furthermore, we are told that an "acceptance of reason as one's only source of knowledge, one's only judge of values and one's only guide to action. . . . means one's total commitment to a state of full, conscious awareness, to the maintenance of a full mental focus in all issues, in all choices, in all of one's waking hours" (28). Evidently, one conclusion that such an intense form of thinking produces in a man is "that *concern with his own interests* is the essence of a moral existence, and that *man must be the beneficiary of his own moral actions*" (x). In other words, again, clear thinking leads to egoism. This clear thinking is achieved, apparently, by directing one's attention to the idea of "value," and establishing the true nature of values.

Egoism and Value

Rand rejects the fact/value distinction discussed in Chapter 1. Value is "based on a *metaphysical* fact, on an unalterable condition of man's existence" (14). (Rand says she uses the word "metaphysical" to mean "that which pertains to reality, to the nature of things, to existence" [14]).[20] The "unalterable condition of man's existence" is the struggle for survival. She says, "Life can be kept in existence only by a constant process of self-sustaining action. The goal of that action, the ultimate *value* which, to be kept, must be gained through its every moment, is the organism's *life*" (17). Rand continues, "An organism's life is its *standard of value*: that which furthers its life is the *good*, that which threatens it is the *evil*" (17).

Because Rand will base so much of her philosophy on this idea, I think it should be scrutinized carefully. She knows very well that she is trying to derive a value statement from a factual one. If she believes that such a derivation is possible, she owes us an explanation of the logic that she will use to do so. In the absence of such an explanation, I think we must suspect a logical fallacy. It is true that almost all of us do value life, but from that fact we cannot deduce as an objective fact that one's own life has an ultimate value that goes beyond the subjective value that we attribute to life. From the obvious fact that without life one can hold no values, it does not logically follow that life must be the ultimate value. She makes a similar error, in my view, when she says that the goal of all action is life. The correct formulation is that life is the necessary condition of the pursuit of any goal whatsoever. From this **truism,** Rand seems to deduce that life is the ultimate goal of all action.

Rand approaches the goal of proving that the individual's life has an ultimate value by another avenue as well. Like Aristotle (Rand's favorite philosopher) and Thomas Aquinas, Rand asserts, "It is only an ultimate goal, an *end in itself,* that makes the existence of values possible" (17–18). This means that if there is no absolute value, then there can be no lesser values either. (It is not at all clear to me, by the way, why anyone should buy into this claim.) Rand concludes, "The standard of value of the Objectivist ethics— the standard by which one judges what is good or evil—is *man's life,* or: that which is required for man's survival *qua* man" (25). This idea of "man's survival *qua* man" is important in Rand's philosophy, as it was in Aristotle's. If there were a philosophical toad who asserted, "The standard of value is a *toad's* life, that which is required for a

toad's survival *qua* toad," we would get a very different prescription from the one Rand offers us. Rand says to us humans (what she would not say to toads, even though she often speaks of "organisms"), "'Man's survival *qua* man' means the terms, methods, conditions and goal required for the survival of a rational being through the whole

"Bufo Americanus Shrugged."
New Hit Novel about Rugged Individualism among Tailless Amphibians

of his life span—in all those aspects of existence which are open to choice" (26). This is very Aristotelian—as you will see in Chapter 6—and, in my opinion, is commendable. The basic requirements for a truly human life are not simply biological in nature. As almost all of the ancient Greek philosophers knew, the mind as well as the body must be nourished. I am not sure what my imaginary philosophical toad would say in this case. It would probably have something to do with worms and insects.

Egoism and Hedonism

Unlike Epicurus and Hobbes, Rand has so far been characterized here as an egoist, but not necessarily as a hedonist. However, she too makes her gesture toward hedonism:

> Now in what manner does a human being discover the concept of "*value*"? By what means does he first become aware of the issue of "good and evil" in its simplest form? By means of the physical sensations of *pleasure* or *pain*. . . . He has no choice about it, and he has no choice about the standard that will make him experience the physical sensation of pleasure or pain. What is that standard? His *life*. . . . The physical sensation of pleasure is a signal indicating that the organism is pursuing the *right* course of action. The physical sensation of pain is a warning signal of danger, indicating that the organism is pursuing the *wrong* course of action. (18)

A consideration of pleasure and pain as natural indicators of value leads Rand to conclude that "man must live for his own sake, neither sacrificing himself to others nor sacrificing others to himself. To live for his own sake means that *the achievement of his own happiness is man's highest moral purpose*" (30).

At this point it may appear to you that Rand has defended a pure form of hedonism, but Rand next refers to the "alleged happiness" (31) of the mystic or the masochist. What is the relation between pleasure and happiness, according to Rand? The happiness of the mystic and the masochist is not true happiness; is their pleasure also false pleasure? Branden, writing in 1964—a few months before his excommunication for "immorality"—asks us to observe the alleged happiness of "the modern 'beatniks'—for instance, their manner of dancing. What one sees is not smiles of authentic enjoyment, but the vacant, staring eyes, the jerky, disorganized movements of what looks like decentralized bodies, all working very hard—with a kind of flat-footed hysteria—at projecting an air of the purposeless, the senseless, the mindless. *This is the 'pleasure' of the unconscious"* (75).

Happiness, then, as in Aristotle, is not to be determined by the individual based on his actual sensations. It is (again) *reason* and not sensation that will determine happiness, and particularly the reason of Objectivism. You

Happy Beatniks Dancing

may have thought you are happy, but Ayn Rand will be the judge of that. She writes, "If you achieve that which is the good by a rational standard of value, it will necessarily make you happy" (32). Reason, for example, tells us that happiness derived from the unhappiness of others is not true pleasure (34). We see, then, as in Epicurus, for Rand pleasure is not merely a sensation; rather it is a rationally informed sensation. An uninformed, unthinking individual is not in a position to know whether he is experiencing pleasure.

Egoism and Individual Rights

The idea of "individual rights" is as important to Objectivism as is the idea of "egoism." Let us try to get clear on Rand's idea of the nature of a right. Rand says that "altruism erodes man's capacity to grasp the concept of rights or the value of an individual life" (94). According to this assertion, a right is a kind of value, and values, as we have seen, are derived from needs. Indeed, Rand equates rights and needs, as we observe in the introduction to *The Virtue of Selfishness*, where she writes, "The first step is to assert *man's right to a moral existence*—that is: to recognize his need of a moral code to guide the course and the fulfillment of his own life" (x). This *right* to a moral existence turns out to be identical to a *need* for a moral code. It is difficult to see how Rand can sustain such a definition without committing once again a blatant version of the naturalistic fallacy (illegitimately deriving a value judgment from a factual assertion). If I need X (where X is anything at all: clean air to breath, or a dry martini, or a moral code), do I therefore have the right to X? As far as I can determine, Rand never explores the logic of rights.

> I *need* to rule the world; therefore I have the *right* to rule the world!

"Rights," we are told, "are a moral concept. . . . *Individual rights are the means of subordinating society to moral law*" (108). But this still does not tell us what a right is or what its source is. To say that rights are derived from needs is, to my way of thinking, not satisfactory. The same is true of claims such as "A 'right' is a moral principle defining and sanctioning a man's freedom of action in a social context" (110). Hobbes had the same problem; he claimed there was only one natural right, but never said what the source of that right was. Indeed, on this topic, Rand follows closely on Hobbes's heels. She says, "There is only *one* fundamental right (all others are its consequences or corollaries): a man's right to his own life" (110). She continues, "The source of rights is man's nature" (111). The implication is that man *needs* his own life (which in some sense is true); therefore, he has a *right* to his own life—"is" implies "ought." Rand also quotes from a character in one of her novels (something she is wont to do) —John Galt in *Atlas Shrugged*—to prove that individual rights are derived from logic. Galt says, "The source of man's rights is not divine law, but the law of identity. A is A—and Man is Man. *Rights* are conditions of existence required by man's nature for his proper survival" (111). It is almost unanimously agreed by philosophers that no factual claims whatever can be deduced from the principle of identity. Certainly no rights can be logically derived from the fact that Man is Man, or the claim that man requires (needs) rights to live fully. And when John Galt adds, "If a man is to live on earth, it is *right* for him to use his mind, it is *right* to act on his own free judgment, it is *right* to work for his values and to keep the product of his work" (111), it appears to me that "he" has confused something's *being* right (it's right to peel potatoes using a sharp blade) with a *right* (there is a right to peel potatoes).

It must be stated that Ayn Rand is not the

John Galt, Architect, Exercises His Right to Peel Potatoes

only philosopher who has failed to solve the problem of the source of rights. The Declaration of Independence asserts that there are certain God-given rights, rights that will be incorporated in the Constitution. However, many political analysts, perhaps embarrassed by such an apparent breach of the so-called doctrine of the separation of church and state, treat this assertion as elliptical for the fact that "We the people" in association with each other have created this state and bestowed political power upon it with our consent to bequeath these rights upon the citizens of this new state (and to hold in contempt states that do not bequeath the same rights upon its citizens). The Bill of Rights bequeaths its rights upon the citizenry, but these rights are not absolute because under certain conditions they can be amended, added to, or even deleted. One group of philosophers simply denies that absolute rights exist at all. For example, Alasdair MacIntyre, a prominent British-American philosopher whose work will be discussed in Chapter 6, says about natural rights, "Belief in them is one with beliefs in witches and unicorns."[21]

Another British philosopher, Alan Brown, says that claiming that I have a *right* to something is just an emblematic way of saying, "All things considered, there is a good moral reason to respect or promote my freedom in this case."[22]

Well-known legal philosopher Ronald Dworkin states his belief that there are such things as basic rights, but points out that sometimes claims of rights conflict, and there is no way to determine the priority of one kind of right—such as property rights—over others.[23]

As you saw, Rand holds that the individual's right to life is the primary right, and all other rights are corollaries or derivations from that right. Following Hobbes, she holds that this basic right gives each man not only "the right to self defense" (126) but "the right to take the actions he deems necessary to achieve his happiness" (114). Apparently, as in Hobbes, one must be prepared to transfer contractually this right to the government as the price for peace.

What other rights are there, according to Rand? The key subsidiary right is the right to property ("the right of use and disposal" [100]; "the right to gain, to keep, to use and to dispose of material values" [111]), but sometimes it seems that the right to property takes priority even over the right to life. "No human rights can exist without property rights. Since material goods are produced by the mind and effort of individual men, and are needed to sustain their lives, if the producer does not own the result of his effort, he does not own his life" (106). This right and "the right to free trade" (114) are inalienable. They cannot be taken away by a government; no collectivity can take them away, though some "group rights" can be "derived from the rights of its members through their voluntary, individual choice and contractual agreement" (119). I read this as claiming that taxation is morally and legally valid only as long as each taxpayer has agreed individually to the process and the amount of the tax. Anyone who disagrees can morally and legally refuse to be taxed. Rand says, "Since only an individual man can possess rights, the expression 'individual rights' is a redundancy. . . . But the expression 'collective rights' is a contradiction" (119).

Egoism and Capitalism

The concept of individual rights is the medium through which Rand deduces capitalism from selfishness. She says, "If one wishes to uphold individual rights, one must realize that capitalism is the only system that can uphold and protect them" (108) and, "[t]hose who advocate laissez-faire capitalism [capitalism free of governmental control] are the only advocates of man's rights" (117). As much as she admired America, the term "capitalism" is not the equivalent of "the American way of life," for Rand. She puts it this way:

> When I say "capitalism," I mean a full, pure, uncontrolled, unregulated laissez-fair capitalism—with a separation of state and economics, in the same way and for the same reasons as the separation of state and church. A pure system of capitalism has never yet existed, not even in America; various degrees of government control have been undercutting and distorting it from the start. Capitalism is not the system of the past; it is the system of the future—if mankind is to have a future. (37)

For Rand, capitalism is *natural*.

Neanderthal Capitalism

Because the primary human right is the right to survival (individual survival; egoism), and because only capitalism can guarantee survival ("The great merit of capitalism is its unique appropriateness to the requirements of human survival" [143]), it is the logical extension of egoism. Therefore, one has a moral duty to promote capitalism.

Egoism and Minimalist Government

If capitalism is the logical extension of egoism and if government can have no controlling power over the development of capitalism, the question arises, What, if anything, is the role of government in a Randian world? Rand answers this way:

> The only proper, moral purpose of a government is to protect man's rights, which means: to protect him from physical violence—to protect his right to his own life, and to his own liberty, to his own property and to the pursuit of his own happiness. Without property rights, no other rights are possible. (36)

For Rand, this is an either/or proposition. To allow the government to have even a few controls beyond this minimalism "is to surrender the principle of inalienable individual rights and to substitute for it the principle of the government's unlimited, arbitrary power" (79–80). It is only the acceptance of an "altruist-collectivist" (93)—i.e., socialist—premise that allows us to ask the question What should be done about the poor? Even asking this question implies an acceptance of the premises of the enemy. Medicare (new in 1963 when Rand wrote against it) receives the brunt of her vitriol. It involves the "enslavement and, therefore, the destruction of medical science" (95). As Rand puts it,

> The proper functions of a government fall into three broad categories, all of them involving the issues of physical force and the protection of men's rights: *the police*, to protect men from criminals—*the armed services*, to protect men from foreign invaders—*the law courts*, to settle disputes among men according to objective laws. (131)

Now, in our contemporary (un-Randian) world, these services and many others—including welfare for those who, through no fault of their own,[24] fall below the minimally acceptable standards of living; fire protection; building of roads; monitoring of transportation (civil air traffic control), monitoring of medical products (FDA); monitoring of environmental pollutants (EPA); postal service; foreign aid; and educational, scientific, and artistic subsidies—are paid for by taxes.

We can ask, in a Randian world, who pays for even the minimalist governmental services that Rand finds necessary?

**Mother Nature Protects
Laissez-Faire Economics**

Egoism and Taxation

According to Rand, the sole function of the government is to protect the rights of each individual egoist. No consideration is given to needy citizens, to the protection of individuals or the environment against industrial abuses, nor to government strategies overseas (with the exception of the invasion of states whose governments are totalitarian—Rand says that a free state has the right to invade a totalitarian state; somehow this right is apparently derived from individual rights, hence from egoism [122]). Road building and postal services will be paid for by those who use them, and those who need the courts to control business contracts will pay an insurance fee that will constitute only a small part of the profit they make from the existence of such courts. Apparently, this fee will be in excess of the actual cost of the maintenance of these courts and of the police activity that enforces the courts' rulings; and, Rand assures us, this excess will be more than enough to pay the few additional costs of this minimalistic government. The cost of this insurance fee could be raised in time of war (136–7). (It seems to me that, to be consistent, Rand must say that those who object to the war do not have to pay the increased fee, but I am not sure that this represents her view correctly.) From my point of view, one advantage of Rand's scheme is that those on the lower end of the economic scale—those who receive very few or no benefits from contract courts—would pay a very small part, if any, of the rest of the cost of government. (Rand herself says this [139].) Such a scheme eliminates taxation's "'redistribution of wealth'—for the unearned support of some men by the forced labor and extorted income of others" (140).

Paying One's Fair Share of Taxes

No Real Conflicts of Interest

A number of times I have pointed to similarities between Hobbes's and Rand's views. Both hold that there is a fundamental individual natural right to life and that such a right entails the further right of self-defense and the right to engage in any act that one believes is conducive to one's survival. Both hold a version of the view summarized in Rand's words, when she says that if one wants to live with other human beings, one must accept "the principle of renouncing the use of physical force and delegating to the government his right of physical self-defense, for the purpose of an orderly, objective, legally defined enforcement" (129). However, among the serious differences between them (besides the earlier-mentioned distinction between

Hobbes's psychological egoism and Rand's moral egoism) is Hobbes's picture of a war of every man against all others and Rand's more benign view captured in her assertion that "there are no conflicts of interest among rational men" (57). The emphasis here is obviously on the word "rational." Rand admits that in the case of people who are motivated by their desires rather than their reason, "men have no choice but to hate, fear, and fight one another, because their desires and their interests will necessarily clash" (33). Rand thinks that it is impossible that a man's interests can conflict with reality. For her, any agent's interest that conflicts with reality is not truly in the interest of the agent, because one's interests must be realistic. She gives an example of two men who compete for the same job, which can be given to only one of them. She asks, does this not involve a conflict of interests? She answers that nothing is in one's interest unless it is "right" (58). What is right? Competition in the free market. The rational man understands that this competition (which Rand calls "struggle" [60]) is in his own interest: "So he does not judge his interests by any particular defeat" (61). Apparently the market is rational, hence right, and it is in both parties' interest to realize this fact.

I suspect that many will remain unconvinced. For example, if the "man" who fails to get the job is a woman, who correctly believes her qualifications are stronger than those of her competitor and senses a whiff of good-old-boyism in the hiring process, she may have a hard time convincing herself that the result is in her interest. To her credit, Rand may have sensed the justification of such a loser's anger and

Reason at Work

disappointment when she wrote, "Whoever gets the job, has earned it (assuming that the employer's choice is rational)" (64; italics added).

The Is/Ought Problem

On a couple of occasions I have claimed that Rand seems to commit the naturalistic fallacy by trying to derive a definition of the good from the natural world or that she runs afoul of the related is/ought problem by trying to derive an "ought" (moral obligation) from an "is" (a fact about human nature). I have made these suggestions particularly related to her claims about the individual's life as an absolute value and about natural individual rights. Now, Rand had certainly heard these objections before. She writes in defense of herself,

> In answer to those philosophers who claim that no relation can be established between ultimate ends or values and the facts of reality, let me stress that the fact that living entities exist and function necessitates the existence of values and of an ultimate value which for any given entity is its own life. Thus the validation of value judgments is to be achieved by reference to the facts of reality. The fact that a living entity *is*, determines what it *ought* to do. So much for the issue of the relation between "*is*" and "*ought*." (18)

I said that Rand was aware of the charge against her, but nothing in this passage indicates that she understood the charge. I take it that the centerpiece of this passage is just plain false—"the fact that living entities exist and function necessitates the existence of values and of an ultimate value which for any given entity is its own life." Try replacing "living entities" with "amoebae." No statement about values can be logically deduced from the fact that amoebae exist, *unless* one presupposes a general teleological metaphysics in which there are either goals and purposes built into nature or supernatural goals driving nature. Aristotle held the first view (see Chapter 6), and certain religious thinkers hold the second view. Rand herself contemptuously rejected the religious view, and, it seems to me, no one can hold such an archaic view as that of goals and purposes in nature, without rejecting modern science (see Chapter 5).

If Amoebae Could Philosophize . . .

Now, what if instead of amoebae, we try "human beings" in the formula, so that it reads, "the fact that human beings exist and function necessitates the existence of values and of an ultimate value which for any given human being is its own life." This sounds more sensible, because human beings—unlike amoebae—can value things. But the best we get out of this is that (most) human beings *do* value their lives highly. (And why not? As Rand points out, without their lives they can't value *anything*.) However, from the fact that (most) human beings value their lives highly, we cannot logically deduce that they *ought* to value their lives, or that there is an ultimate value called "the value of the individual's life." What we can do, with Immanuel Kant (see Chapter 3)—whose philosophy Rand detested—is offer advice in the form of what's called a "hypothetical imperative": *If you value your life, then you ought to do X, Y, and Z; or, in reverse, if you value X, Y, and Z, then you ought to value your life (because without it, you can't have X, Y, and Z).*

There is one widely accepted philosophically unproblematic way of deducing values from facts, in certain kinds of contexts. For example, we can say, "This knife is light, handled easily, and cuts smoothly; therefore this is a *good* knife." In this case, the knife is an artifact intentionally created to cut, so we have placed the artifact in a teleological context that already has values built into it. (This X serves its intended purpose; therefore, this X is a good X.) And we can extend this model to natural organs that function in ways we humans require or approve of. Think, for example, of an animal organ like the heart. Charles Darwin would reject as unscientific the sentence *The heart is in the body in order to pump blood* (or, *the osprey has fine eyesight in order to detect prey*).

It's the "in order to" part that Darwin would object to, because that phrasing implies purposes in nature. Darwin would not object to phrasing these ideas like this: *The heart functions in such a way as to pump blood throughout the body, and such bodies are more likely to survive and reproduce than are bodies whose heart does not so function* (or, *the*

I'm considering contact lenses.

Myopic Osprey

osprey's keen eyesight functions in such a way that the bird is able to detect prey, and such ospreys are more likely to survive and reproduce than ospreys whose eyes do not so function). In other words, the correct phrasing deletes the teleological context. Nevertheless, Darwin, other scientists, philosophers, and "normal people," have no trouble with sentences such as *Her blood pressure is 120 over 80, therefore she has a good heart,* or *this osprey is unable to detect* the fish just below the surface, therefore it has *bad* eyesight. Here, we do indeed derive values from facts, but only because we impose a teleological model upon nature by virtue of the language we employ to describe it. Now, none of this is of help to Rand's project. The sense in which we are deducing values from facts here cannot produce any ultimate metaphysical values on which to base a whole philosophy. Rather than discovering independent values, this technique builds values into the way it characterizes parts of the world.

I conclude that the two moral facts that Rand uses as pillars on which to base her philosophy—the ultimate objective value of the individual's life, and the natural right to one's individual life—cannot bear the weight she places on them.

Perceived Strengths and Weaknesses
Epicurus's Strengths

— Epicurus's emphasis on calm, peace, and repose (*ataraxia*) and his appeal to simplicity can be attractive to citizens of the twenty-first century caught up in the hustle and bustle of a hectic world.

— Those who fear death or punishment in the afterlife can find solace in Epicurus's philosophy.

— Epicurus's deemphasis of immediate gratification and his insistence that happiness should be the project of a whole life constitute good, practical advice.

— Almost everybody likes a philosophy that says that it's OK to have fun.

Epicurus's Weaknesses

— There is a logical tension involved in holding both psychological and moral hedonism.

— Epicurus's Hellenistic style of thought sometimes seems overly simplistic (as when he reduces happiness to mere pleasure and claims that one can be happy on or off the torture rack).

— The "atomic swerve" as a solution to the problem of freedom in a deterministic world is unconvincing.

— Epicurus seems unable to avoid self-contradiction when he amalgamates his three conditions for happiness: self-sufficiency, invulnerability to chance, and completeness.

- Epicurus's justification of the virtuous life and the value of friendship seems stilted if not cynical.
- Epicurus's definition of pleasure as the good commits the naturalistic fallacy.

Hobbes's Strengths

- Hobbes offers us a clear, forthright, no-nonsense statement of egoism, a theory that every moral philosopher must eventually confront.
- Hobbes's theory pulls us as moral theorists away from overly optimistic, naïve assumptions about human nature and forces us to deal with the selfish, pleasure-seeking, power-mongering tendencies of human nature.
- Hobbes lays the foundations for a naturalistic philosophy of "morals by agreement" rather than one based on unrealistic or overly metaphysical premises. (See Chapter 7 for development of this idea.)

Hobbes's Weaknesses

- The single-minded reductiveness of Hobbes's theory of motivation seems unwarranted.
- Hobbes's defense of his psychological egoism becomes tautological.
- Hobbes's account of human nature may be overly pessimistic.

Rand's Strengths

- Rand has inspired many a young person to take moral philosophy seriously.
- Rand recognizes the folly of adopting both psychological and moral egoism.
- Against Epicurus and Hobbes, Rand recognizes the reality of altruism.
- Like Epicurus, Rand recognizes that a successful hedonism cannot base itself on immediate sensations of pleasure but must look at a whole life-time.
- Rand's assertion that human survival is not simply a question of biology is laudable.

Rand's Weaknesses

- Rand has a tendency to make bombastic claims and to defend them with aggressive certainty rather than with arguments.
- Rand's commitment to what she calls "reason" seems too intense and exhausting.
- Rand's separation of the emotions from reason is too extreme.

- There is a blatant commission of the naturalistic fallacy in Rand's definitions of "value" and "individual right."

- Rand's deduction of egoism, capitalism, and governmental minimalism from the concept of reason seems too facile and ideological.

- Rand provides a very artificial defense of her claim that among rational men, there is never a conflict of interest.

Questions for Consideration

1. Distinguish carefully between psychological egoism and moral egoism. Explore the relation between the two views by answering the following question: Is it possible to hold one of these views and reject the other? How do Epicurus, Hobbes, and Rand fit into this discussion?

2. Why, according to Epicurus, is the philosophy of materialism conducive to happiness?

3. Epicurus says, "No pleasure is a bad thing in itself," but he goes on to qualify this assertion significantly. What effect on his hedonism do his qualifications produce?

4. Explain Epicurus's distinctions among desire that is natural and necessary, desire that is natural but unnecessary, and desire that is vain (unnatural). Show how these categories fit into the moral advice that he gives.

5. According to Epicurus's philosophy, happiness is the goal of life, but there are three "formal conditions" to true happiness. What are they, and why does failure to meet them produce moral failure?

6. Explain Epicurus's theories of the value of a virtuous life and the value of friendship.

7. In what ways does the motivation of Thomas Hobbes's egoist contrast with our standard manner of thinking about motivation?

8. Using examples observed by you, explain what you take to be the criticism attributed to Bishop Butler of Hobbes's egoism.

9. Describe the criticism of psychological hedonism based on Karl Popper's principle of falsifiability.

10. According to Ayn Rand, the morality of altruism is responsible, more than any other single factor, for the arrested development of mankind. What do you take her to mean when she says this?

11. Rand is a moral egoist. Why does she reject psychological egoism?

12. Explain why Rand thinks that there are no conflicts of interest between rational men.

13. Rand claims that a commitment to reason entails a commitment to selfishness that in turn entails a commitment to laissez-faire capitalism and to governmental minimalism. Briefly show how she makes these moves.

14. What is the key "individual right" in Rand's philosophy? What is the source of this right, and what role does it play in her Objectivism?

15. I suggested that scrutiny of Rand's account of the sources of "values" and "rights" in her philosophy reveals that she commits logical fallacies involving the is/ought problem. Explain this accusation, and give Rand's response to it.

Study Guide: Outline of Chapter Two

I. Epicurus.

    A. Egoism.

        1. Psychological egoism defined:

            a. All acts are motivated by self-interest.

            b. Altruism (acting for the interests of others at the expense of one's own interests) is impossible.

        2. Moral egoism defined:

            a. All acts ought to be motivated by self-interest.

            b. Altruism is possible, but wrong.

    B. Hedonism.

        1. Psychological hedonism defined: All acts are motivated by the pursuit of pleasure.

        2. Moral hedonism defined: All acts ought to be motivated by the pursuit of pleasure.

    C. Epicurus's marriage of psychological and moral egoism with psychological and moral hedonism.

        1. All acts are motivated by self-interest, and self-interest is defined in terms of pleasure.

2. All acts ought to be motivated by self-interest (pleasure).

3. Philosophy's role: the demonstration of enlightened self-interest (enlightened pursuit of pleasure).

4. General criticism:

    a. Is there a logical tension in the marriage of psychological and moral egoism/hedonism?

    b. Are all forms of moral egoism/hedonism condemned to fall afoul of the is/ought problem?

D. Historical setting of Epicurus's philosophy.

  1. Hellenistic period: 4th and 3rd centuries B.C.E.

  2. Generally considered a period of cultural decline after the classical age of the preceding Hellenic period.

E. Epicurus's atomistic materialism.

  1. The world is nothing but atoms.

    a. Souls are composed of subtle atoms.

      i. Death is the dispersal of the soul's atoms.

      ii. Death is never experienced.

      iii. Therefore there should be no fear of death.

    b. Gods are composed of atoms:

      i. Gods last a long time, but eventually their atoms disperse.

      ii. Gods have no interest in human existence.

      iii. Therefore, there should be no fear of punishment in an afterlife.

  2. The atomic swerve preserves freedom in an otherwise deterministic universe.

F. Epicurus's hedonism: Happiness is the motive and goal of life.

  1. Happiness is defined as a life of pleasure.

  2. Though no pleasure is bad in itself, some pleasures have painful consequences.

  3. Pleasure does not admit of quality, only quantity.

  4. Pleasure is the lack of disturbance (pain).

  5. Pleasure is the result of sating desire (which is a kind of disturbance).

G. Kinds of desires:

    1. Natural desire:

        a. Necessary desire.

        b. Unnecessary desire.

    2. Vain desire (unnatural desire).

H. Life should be spent avoiding vain desires, reducing unnecessary natural desires to a minimum, and fulfilling necessary natural desires.

I. The fulfillment of necessary natural desires best meets the three conditions of happiness:

    1. Self-sufficiency.

    2. Invulnerability to chance.

    3. Completeness.

J. Pleasure as related to virtue and friendship.

    1. Only the virtuous individual surrounded by friends leads a life of pleasure.

    2. Friendship and the virtues are chosen only because they lead to pleasure.

K. Standard criticisms of Epicurus:

    1. Does Epicurus's negative definition of pleasure constitute a death wish (is death the most pleasant state)?

    2. Does Epicurus escape the snares of the is/ought problem?

II. Thomas Hobbes.

A. Hobbes's psychological egoism.

    1. "Of the voluntary acts of every man, the object is some good to himself."

    2. "No man giveth, but with intention of good to himself."

    3. This rules out the possibility of altruism.

B. Contrast between the standard (everyday) conception and Hobbes's conception.

    1. Standard conception: pluralism—there is a range of motivation running from the most altruistic to the most egoistic.

    2. Hobbes's conception: monism.

        a. All motives are egoistic.

b. Motives that seem to be nonegoistic are really cases of disguised egoism.

c. All egoism is really hedonism.

C. Criticism of psychological egoism/hedonism.

1. Bishop Butler's criticism:

a. Egoistic hedonists correctly see that we derive pleasure from the accomplishment of our intentions, . . .

b. but illegitimately deduce from this fact that pleasure must be the intention of every act.

c. In fact, acts usually have as their intention exactly what they seem to have as their intentions (I want to help you out in order to help you out).

2. The criticism based on the principle of falsifiability.

a. Karl Popper's principle of falsifiability:

i. Every (scientific) hypothesis must be incompatible with some possible states of affairs.

ii. Psychological hedonism's hypothesis about motivation is compatible with every possible state of human affairs.

iii. Therefore, psychological hedonism is not a genuine (scientific) hypothesis.

b. Sober and Wilson's rejection of the argument from falsification.

i. New versions of psychological egoism may prove testable.

ii. If the theory of psychological hedonism is not testable, then neither is the theory of altruism testable.

III. Ayn Rand.

A. Rand's egoism (or selfishness).

1. Rejection of psychological egoism.

a. Psychological egoism is based on an "intellectual confusion."

b. Altruism is possible.

2. Advocacy of moral egoism.

a. Altruism involves the sacrifice of the self.

b. Self-sacrifice is always wrong.

3. Advocacy of rational egoism (pursuit of rational self-interest).

a. Desire and impulse cannot determine true self-interest.

b. Reason determines true self-interest.

B. Rand's commitment to reason (rationalism).

1. Reason contrasted with emotion, desire, impulse, and whim.

2. Reason as a process of conceptualization, source of knowledge, judge of value, guide to action.

3. Reason involves constant conscious awareness and mental focus.

C. What Randian reason tells us about egoism and value.

1. The goal of all action is the preservation and maximizing of the organism's life.

2. The organism's life is the standard of all value.

a. That which furthers the organism's life is good.

b. That which threatens the organism's life is evil.

3. Human survival is not simply biological survival, but also survival of the life of the mind.

D. Hedonism and value.

1. Pleasure and pain are the first and most natural indicators of good and evil.

2. "The achievement of his own happiness is man's highest moral purpose."

3. But there can be false pleasure and "alleged happiness" too.

4. False pleasure and happiness are those uninformed by reason, for example:

a. Following impulse, desire, or whim.

b. Beatniks dancing.

E. Egoism and individual rights.

1. There are only individual rights, not collective rights.

a. The primary right: man's right to his own life.

b. The source of this right is "man's nature."

2. All other rights are corollaries or derivatives:

a. The right to property.

b. The right to free trade.

F. Capitalism: a natural corollary of egoism.

    1. Capitalism is natural because it is the embodiment of

        a. The struggle for survival.

        b. The natural right to property and trade.

    2. Therefore, there is a moral duty to promote capitalism.

G. Minimalist government: a natural corollary of egoism.

    1. The moral function of government: to protect life and property of citizens (i.e., to protect their natural rights).

    2. Any additional power held over individuals by government is immoral.

    3. Therefore, the only system of government consistent with egoism is minimalist government.

    4. Taxation:

        a. Any taxation beyond financing the protection of lives and property (police, military, courts) is illegitimate.

        b. Perhaps the court system could be funded by privatized user fees rather than by taxes.

H. There are no real conflicts of interest.

    1. According to Hobbes, the state of nature is a war of each against all.

    2. According to Rand, there are no conflicts among rational men (not even in a state of nature).

        a. There are such conflicts among irrational men, or between rational men and the irrational men (those motivated by desire, etc.).

        b. The main function of government is to protect the rational from the irrational.

    3. Rational interests can never conflict with reality (can never be unrealistic).

        a. Competition is the main fact about life and reality.

            i. Nothing is in one's interests unless it is morally right.

            ii. Competition on the open market is morally right.

        b. Competition in business or love will be resolved morally and realistically (the best man will win).

I. Rand and the is/ought problem.

1. Rand rejects the fact/value distinction: values are facts.

2. Values are derived from (human) nature: "is" implies "ought."

   a. Living organisms have needs, and these needs are values.

   b. The needs of humans give them basic values and rights.

3. Is Rand's deduction of "ought" from "is" logically valid?

For Further Reading

Primary Literature:
Works by Epicurus, Hobbes, and Rand on Ethics.

Epicurus

The Stoic and Epicurean Philosophers, ed. Whitney J. Oates, trans. C. Bailey. New York: Modern Library, 1940.

The Epicurus Reader: Selected Writings and Testimonia, Brad Inwood and L. P. Gerson, eds. and trans. Indianapolis and Cambridge: Hackett Publishing Co., 1994.

Thomas Hobbes

Leviathan: Or the Matter, Forme and Power of a Commonwealth Ecclesiasticall and Civill. 1651. Oxford and New York: Oxford University Press, 1998.

Ayn Rand

Atlas Shrugged. New York: Dutton, 1992. [Fiction]

The Fountainhead. New York: Bobbs-Merrill Company, 1993. [Fiction]

The Virtue of Selfishness: A New Concept of Egoism. New York: New American Library, 1964.

Secondary Literature:
Studies of the Ethical Theories of Epicurus, Hobbes, and Rand.

Epicurus

Mitsis, Phillip. *Epicurus' Ethical Theory: The Pleasures of Invulnerability.* Ithaca and London: Cornell University Press, 1988.

Strozier, Robert M. *Epicurus and Hellenistic Philosophy.* Lanham, N.Y., and London: University Press of America, 1985.

Hobbes

Boonin-Vail, David. *Thomas Hobbes and the Science of Moral Virtue.* Cambridge and New York: Cambridge University Press, 1994.

Broad, C. D. *Five Types of Ethical Theory.* Totowa, N.J.: Littlefield, Adams, 1965.

Feinberg, Joel. "Psychological Egoism," in S. Cahn. P. Kitcher, and G. Sher, eds., *Reason at Work*, pp. 25–35. San Diego: Harcourt Brace Jovanovich, 1984.

Gert, Bernard. "Hobbes and Psychological Egoism," *Journal of the History of Ideas*, 28, 1967, 503–20. Reprinted in *Hobbes*, ed. Robert Shaver. Aldershot, Brookfield, Vt.: Dartmouth Publishing, 1999.

Nagel, Thomas. *The Possibility of Altruism*. Oxford: Oxford University Press, 1970.

Peters, Richard. *Hobbes*. Middlesex and Baltimore: Penguin, 1967.

Rand

Branden, Nathaniel. *My Years with Ayn Rand: The Truth behind the Myth*. San Francisco: Jossey-Bass, 1999.

Gladstein, Mimi Reisel. *The New Ayn Rand Companion*. Westport, Conn. and London: Greenwood Press, 1999.

Peikoff, Leonard. *Objectivism: The Philosophy of Ayn Rand*. New York: Dutton, 1991.

Walker, Jeff. *The Ayn Rand Cult*. Chicago and La Salle: Open Court, 1999.

Notes

1. See, for example, *The Essential Descartes*, ed. Margaret D. Wilson, trans. Haldane and Ross (New York: New American Library, 1969), 171 and 127, respectively.

2. Epicurus, in *The Stoic and Epicurean Philosophers*, ed. Whitney J. Oates, trans. C. Bailey (New York: Modern Library, 1940), 4. Future references from Bailey's translation will be included parenthetically in the body of the text, designated with the letter B before the page number. The fact that we now talk about "splitting the atom," means that there is a wide gap between "atomism" and contemporary atomic theory.

3. Werner Heisenberg, *Physics and Philosophy: The Revolution in Modern Science* (New York: Harper & Row, 1962).

4. We will see in Chapter 6, when we study Aristotle's more nuanced theory of eudaimonia, that "happiness" is not a perfect translation of the Greek word. Sometimes Epicurus's translators call it "blessedness." Aristotle's translators often call it "well-being," or "flourishing."

5. Epicurus, *The Epicurus Reader: Selected Writings and Testimonia*, eds. and trans., Brad Inwood and L. P. Gerson (Indianapolis and Cambridge: Hackett Publishing Co., 1994). Future references to Inwood and Gerson's translation will be included parenthetically in the text, designated with the letters IG before the page number.

6. Bailey leaves the "boys" out of his translation, rendering the passage as "For it is not continuous drinkings and revellings, nor the satisfaction of lusts, . . ." (B32).

7. Phillip Mitsis, *Epicurus' Ethical Theory: The Pleasures of Invulnerability* (Ithaca, N.Y., and London: Cornell University Press, 1988), 50. Future references to this book will be included parenthetically in the body of the text.

8. Sigmund Freud, *Civilization and its Discontents,* trans. James Strachey (New York and London: W. W. Norton and Co., 1961), 35–6.

9. Thomas Hobbes, *Leviathan: Or the Matter, Forme and Power of a Commonwealth Ecclesiasticall and Civill* (Oxford and New York: Oxford University Press, 1998), 88. Emphases in the original. Future references to this work will be included parenthetically in the text.

10. Bernard Gert describes his article "Hobbes and Psychological Egoism" (originally in the *Journal of the History of Ideas,* 28 [1967], 503–20; reprinted in *Hobbes,* ed. Robert Shaver [Aldershot, Brookfield, Vt.: Dartmouth Publishing, 1999], 255–72) as being the "attempt to show that the almost unanimous view that Hobbes held psychological egoism is mistaken." (Shaver, 255). Gert says that psychological egoism claims that "men never act in order to benefit others, or because they believe a certain course of action to be morally right" (Shaver, 257). But Gert is mistaken. Psychological egoism does not deny that sometimes men so act; it claims that when men do so act, they are motivated by the belief that it is in their interest to so act, and this motive has priority over the secondary intention of benefiting others or behaving morally. Gert continues, "It is the claim that *all* actions of *all* men are motivated entirely by self-interest that is philosophically interesting" (*ibid.*). But Gert seems to confuse "in order to do X" with "motivated by X." A person can act in order to save another person's life at great risk to himself, and be motivated by self-interest. Psychological egoism claims that if one chooses to risk danger to save another's life, one is motivated by self-interest, and that if one chooses not to risk danger to save another's life, one is also motivated by self-interest. Gert admits that Hobbes holds exactly this view, but he claims such a view is not psychological egoism. Gert calls this view "tautological egoism" (Shaver, 259) and admits that Hobbes is a tautological egoist. In conceding that Hobbes is a "tautological egoist" and denying that he is a "psychological egoist," Gert is insisting that, by definition, psychological egoism be empirically decidable. In doing so, Gert robs the psychological egoist of his fallback strategy. Of course nobody would defend psychological egoism if that view could be refuted, for example, by finding one smoker who admits that smoking is not in her best interests. So-called tautological egoism is just the stronghold of psychological egoism—the place to which the psychological egoist retreats when under heavy fire.

11. Richard Peters, *Hobbes* (Middlesex and Baltimore: Penguin, 1967), 142.

12. Bernard Gert; see note 10. I repeat my disagreement with Gert, who claims that tautological egoism is a different theory from psychological egoism. I contend that tautological egoism is an essential feature of the defense strategy of psychological egoism. Similarly, in my view, "tautological astrology" is a key feature of the defense strategy of astrology and in some ways explains its longevity. (No matter what happens to you, it was predicted by your astrological chart.)

13. Elliott Sober and David Sloan Wilson, *Unto Others: The Evolution and Psychology of Unselfish Behavior* (Cambridge, Mass., and London: Harvard University Press, 1999). Future references to this book will be included parenthetically in the body of the text.

14. Ayn Rand (with additional articles by Nathaniel Branden), *The Virtue of Selfishness: A New Concept of Egoism* (New York: New American Library, 1964), 52. Future references to this work will be included parenthetically in the body of the text.

15. Nathaniel Branden, *My Years with Ayn Rand* (San Francisco: Jossey-Bass Publishers, 1999), 334–5. In the 1999 version of his book, Branden dropped the phrase "Judgment Day" from the title. Future references to Branden's book will be to this later edition, and citations will be included parenthetically in the body of the text.

16. The book comprises articles written for the newsletter "The Objectivist" between 1961 and 1964. Five of the book's nineteen chapters were written by Nathaniel Branden, whom, at the time, Rand thought of as a primary expositor of her ideas. In printings from 1970 forward, Rand ends her introduction to the book with this notice: "P.S. Nathaniel Branden is no longer associated with me, with my philosophy or with *The Objectivist* (formerly *The Objectivist Newsletter*)."

17. This is a rather ironic beginning for an author who accuses her opponents of "argument by intimidation." See Chapter 19 of *The Virtue of Selfishness*, "The Argument from Intimidation."

18. In my discussion of Ayn Rand's Objectivism I will follow her style and intention and employ the word "man" to mean "human being." Branden writes, "I should mention that in 1956, it would not have occurred to us to question the use of the word *man* to denote both sexes. . . . Ayn, of course, would have been vigorously opposed to the search for a better word" (Branden, 155). Rand said, "I am not a feminist" and "I am a male chauvinist." (Quoted in Jeff Walker, *The Ayn Rand Cult* [Chicago and La Salle, Ill.: Open Court, 1999], 117.) Nevertheless, there is an interesting anthology involving a debate over the extent to which Rand may be considered a feminist. See Mimi Reisel Gladstein and Chris Matthew Sciabarra, eds., *Feminist Interpretations of Ayn Rand* (University Park, Penn.: Pennsylvania State University Press, 1999).

19. Quoted in Nathaniel Branden, *My Years with Ayn Rand*, 117.

20. Notice that Rand's use of the term "metaphysics" is quite different from the one in this book's glossary.

21. Alasdair MacIntyre, *After Virtue* (Notre Dame, Ind.: University of Notre Dame Press, 1981), 67.

22. Alan Brown, *Modern Political Philosophy: Theories of the Just Society* (New York: Penguin, 1986), 106.

23. Interview with Ronald Dworkin, in Bryan Magee, *Men of Ideas: Some Creators of Contemporary Philosophy* (London: British Broadcasting Corporation, 1978), 254.

24. Ayn Rand would of course deny the existence of this category.

3
Kantian Ethics

The German philosopher Immanuel Kant (1724–1804) was born in the old Hanseatic city of Königsburg in the northeastern corner of Prussia (today the city of Kaliningrad, Russia). The Hanseatic League was a powerful and successful economic and political organization linking a number of German, Danish, and Swedish ports along the North Sea in the seventeenth and eighteenth cen-turies. This efficient and domineering cartel created prosperity for its members, and its cities were controlled by the new bourgeois class and its rather stuffy values. Kant spent his whole life in this prosperous town, passing his days complacently as a respected professor of philosophy at the University of Königsberg. This dedicated bachelor's personal life was Spartan, and his personal life was so methodical that his neighbors used to set their clocks by his afternoon walks along a path that is still called "The Philosopher's Way."

Immanuel Kant is one of the outstanding intellectual figures of the historical epoch known as the Enlightenment. This philosophical, political, economic, and artistic movement developed in the last half of the eighteenth century, culminating in the American Revolution (1775–1789)—of which Kant approved—and the French Revolution (1789–1799)— which Kant also supported, though he was horrified by the excesses of its aftermath, known in history as **the Terror.** The Enlightenment thinkers saw themselves as guiding the human race out of the medieval overgrowth of irrationality, superstition, fear, and oppression that, in their view, had dominated the past several hundred years of European history. One of their favorite targets was the absurdities of traditional religious belief (they became atheists, or **agnostics,** or they believed that reason itself could produce a rational religion). Another target was the claim of monarchists that they governed by divine right. (There was an antimonarchic, pro-democratic thrust to the Enlightenment, corresponding with demands for power by the working and bourgeois classes, leading in 1793 to the execution on the guillotine of the king and queen of France.)

Other objects of their hatred were the censorship, inquisitions, exploitation, and oppression of the masses by the authorities of the Church. (The Enlightenment had a distinctive **anticlerical** edge to it, leading eventually to the murders and executions of many priests and nuns during the French Revolution.) Some Enlightenment figures paradoxically simply replaced God and the

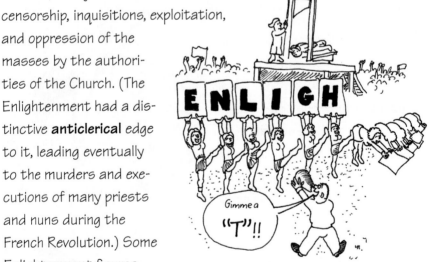

Gimme a "T"!!

The Enlightenment

Monarch with Reason and Man, and they bowed unthinkingly before them. But not Immanuel Kant. He had *arguments* to support the great respect he had for rationality.

But Kant's arguments in defense of reason did not come easily nor early. The philosophy that he wrote as a young man is not remarkable. He made no major contribution to philosophy until he was in his late middle age, when he discovered the works of the Scottish philosopher David Hume (1711–1776), whose radical theories "awakened him from his dogmatic slumber," as Kant put it, and caused him to rethink all of his own ideas.

Kant Awakens from his Dogmatic Slumber

Kant and Hume: What Can We Know?

After his "awakening," all of Kant's works are responses to Hume's radical **skepticism.** They show a genius and an originality that are missing in his earlier writings; and in the fields of metaphysics, epistemology, and ethics, they have earned him a permanent place of honor in the history of philosophy. In a few scandalously short paragraphs I will sketch some of the main ideas of Kant's epistemology. Despite the fact that Kant's ethical theory can be studied independently of his overall *Weltanschauung* (worldview), I think you will see that in his own mind, metaphysics, epistemology, and ethics are closely linked.

The shock that Kant experienced while reading Hume was based on a specific series of Hume's ideas. First, Hume divided all judgments into two categories, what Kant called "analytic" and "synthetic" judgments. (You should already be somewhat familiar with these categories, because they were also used in the twentieth century by the logical positivists, whom Hume deeply influenced, and whose philosophy you studied in Chapter 1.) Analytical propositions only exhibit relationships between ideas, as is seen in such examples as "no unmarried woman has a husband" and "Tuesday precedes Wednesday." Hence they are *a priori* (independent of observation), tautological, and give us no information about the world. Synthetic propositions, such as "Immanuel Kant takes a stroll every afternoon" and "his neighbors set their clocks by his passing," are the only category of propositions that provide factual information about the world. They, and only they, are **a posteriori** (derived from observation). For Kant, this was an impossible pill to swallow. Kant was a Lutheran Christian, a metaphysician, and an ethicist, but Hume's methodical analysis seemed to doom to the status of nonsense all the propositions of theology, metaphysics, and morality, as you saw in Chapter 1, where the logical positivists, using Hume's ideas, arrived at just such a conclusion.

But, to add insult to injury, Hume's attack also undermined even everyday common sense and science, because, as Hume looked into the nature of synthetic propositions, even he seemed shocked by the conclusions that he was forced to draw about their epistemological status. Though scholars still argue over the true meaning of Hume's most radical statements, what Kant (and, indeed, most readers of Hume) understood him to be saying is this: The information that the senses provide us is not sufficient on which to base a science, nor is it even strong enough to justify most of what we call our common-sense picture of reality. Both science and common sense require the idea of substantiality ("thingness") and continuity (causality) in the world. But the senses only give us sensations (which philosophers now call "**sense data**": colors, tastes, textures, sounds, and odors), and from these sensations we illegitimately draw the conclusion that there is a substantial physical world "out there" causing these sensations in our minds. In fact, the senses only provide sense data, and there is no sense datum of substance ("thing") nor of cause and effect. Hume must have done his empirical work in the pool hall because a number of his examples are about billiard balls. He points out that when we say that ball A strikes ball B and causes ball B to move, in fact, the only datum that the senses

provide is the motion of ball A (strictly speaking, not even "ball A," just "gray, circular sense datum moving left to right"), then the contact between ball A and ball B, then the motion of ball B. We never see a third thing called "the cause." No matter how many times we observe this series, we see exactly the same thing: ball A rolls, hits ball B, ball B rolls.

Hume Observing Causality

    If we respond to Hume, saying, "But it always happens that way, and will do so in the future, which is why we talk about laws of cause and effect," Hume responds that we do *not* know that it has always happened in the past, and we certainly do not know that it will always do so in the future, because we never have a sense datum of "the future"; all sense data are of the present, the immediate here and now. The so-called laws of nature are simply objects of belief; we "feign" them, as Hume says, the way we feign gods and angels. Hume concludes (who knows how seriously) that philosophy seems to lead us to a dead end, and that therefore perhaps we should give up the study of philosophy and get a job tending sheep instead.

David Hume—Shepherd

To his chagrin, Kant was unable to find any technical flaws in Hume's skeptical argument. Are you surprised that this blow "awakened Kant from his dogmatic slumber"? At this point, Kant began to rethink philosophy, and the product of his reevaluation is the massive *Critique of Pure Reason* (1781). There, and in its shorter, more accessible version, *Prolegomena to any Future Metaphysics* (1783), Kant chooses a different approach from Hume's. Hume asked the question Is knowledge possible? and he came up with the answer Not a whole heck of a lot. Kant, on the contrary, starts with the assumption that we do have some knowledge, and he asks the question How is knowledge possible? Unlike Hume, Kant accepts a certain kind of commonsensical position as the beginning point: I do know that this is my hand, that my window is closer to me than the house across the street, that holding a flame to my flesh causes pain. How can I know these things? What must be the case before such knowledge would be possible?

The answer is that each true synthetic proposition, such as "The cat is on the mat," presupposes the truth of certain other propositions, such as

1. "Material objects exist in space and time," and
2. "Material objects stand in causal relations with each other."

But it was precisely these two kinds of truths that Hume's skepticism challenged. Kant agrees with Hume's main claim: These sentences are not analytic—their negation does not produce a self-contradiction—and they are not a posteriori—

there are no sense data from which they can be derived. So Kant conceived of a new logical category to cover these kinds of truths; he called it **synthetic a priori.** Sentences (1) and (2) above are synthetic because they say something about reality, and they are a priori because we do not learn their truth by observation. How are they possible? Hang on to your chair. Here comes Kant's most radical claim! Sentences (1) and (2) are known to be true not because the human mind derives them from reality, but because the human mind imposes them on reality. These categories are built into the very structure of the mind. (At one point Kant calls them the "irremovable goggles" through which we must view the world.) For human beings, to think at all is to think in terms of time, space, and causality. The

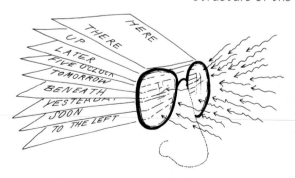

The Irremovable Goggles

structures of the mind impose order on the inchoate data they receive. Even though the content of our minds is subjective (only I can have my thoughts), the form this content takes is objective, because every mind processes the data filtered through its own screen in exactly the same way. The human mind is not a passive receptacle of sense data, as Hume thought; it is an active constructor.

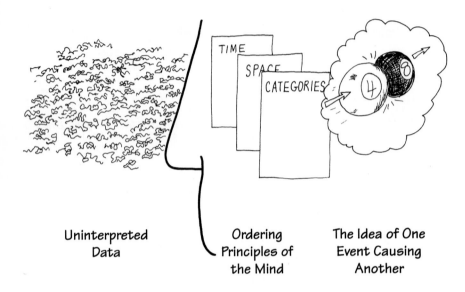

Uninterpreted
Data

Ordering
Principles of
the Mind

The Idea of One
Event Causing
Another

Kant's amazing reversal of direction—we do not derive space, time, and reality from the world; rather we impose them on the world—was soon called the Copernican Revolution in philosophy. (Recall that the Polish astronomer Copernicus [1473–1543] said that the sun does not orbit the earth; rather the earth orbits the sun.) The implication of this revolution is that the human mind is only capable of knowing the world through the lenses of these categories of the mind, hence it can never know ultimate reality (what the world is like prior to the intervention of the human mind). Kant calls the reality we can know the "**phenomenal world,**" and he calls the unknown reality the "**noumenal world,**" or the "thing-in-itself" (*das Ding-an-sich*). The good news for Kant is that the objectivity created by the universality of the structure of the human mind is firm enough to justify both our commonsense beliefs about the world (the cat is

distancing themselves from his theories, both metaphysical and moral (which is not to say that he has not made a big impression on the work of most philosophers that have studied him, nor is it to say that he has had no disciples). This judgment applies to all the fields in which he worked. As we concentrate on his ethical theory, you will quickly realize that it cannot be grasped without some hard work. However, if you do apply yourself attentively, I predict that you will achieve a feeling of self-satisfaction at having understood the meaning of an important theory conceived by a mind of great genius. You will also find much that is worth thinking about and, probably, some ideas that you will find to be quite puzzling.

The bulk of Kant's moral theory can be found in three works: *The Foundations of the Metaphysics of Morals*, written in 1785,[2] *Critique of Practical Reason*, written in 1788, and *The Metaphysics of Morals*, written in 1797–1798.[3] We will be moving among the ideas in these three works, concentrating on *Foundations*, to try to reconstruct Kant's theory in a manner that is understandable.

A Good Will

The first sentence of *Foundations* tells us in no uncertain terms, "Nothing in the world—indeed nothing even beyond the world—can possibly be conceived which could be called good without qualification except a *good will*" (9). Therefore, the first rather jarring message that Kant wants to communicate to us is that no action and no object in reality or in our imagination can be called good in and of itself without qualification except a certain *volitional attitude* toward acts and objects. This is an amazing thing to say. The only absolutely good thing is a specific mental attitude; everything else is good or bad only *relative* to that attitude. How can this be possible? Indeed, it becomes clear quite soon that Kant is overstating his case. For example, as we will see shortly, it turns out that what Kant calls "human dignity" is good in and of itself and that human dignity plays a bigger part in Kant's ethics than does the idea of a "good

will." Nevertheless, it is obvious that we had better try to understand what Kant means by a "good will" if we hope to have any grasp of his theory.

We will find that Kant has concocted a rather special definition for the word "will," one that automatically links it to other parts of his theory. (In fact, it will prove to be the case that these "other parts" constitute the essence of his theory, and this is why it is a mistake to overemphasize Kant's rather bombastic claim about a good will being the only truly good thing in the universe.[4]) To *will* is to seek a goal. Such willing is *rational* when it is governed by a **maxim,** that is, when it is guided by a policy or is rule guided. Indeed, *every true action*—as opposed to haphazard behavior or to mere reflex or habitual response to stimuli—is governed by a maxim, according to Kant—at least, every action undertaken by a *rational agent* is so governed. That is to say, rational agents can justify their actions because they have personal reasons that could be shown to be logical. But, an action does not become morally correct just because it is rational. For an action to become morally correct, it must be guided not only by a maxim, but by good will. Good will, then, is not only to will a rational act (one determined by a maxim), but to will an act that does the right thing. For an act to be moral, it must be willed as a moral act. When Kant asserts that the only truly good thing in the universe is a good will, he means that actions in and of themselves are not morally good or bad. A truly good act is one that is motivated by a personal decision to act out of goodness according to a rule that is rationally defensible.

Again, notice that a maxim is not necessarily moral in and of itself. For example, "Take a canteen of water with you whenever you travel in the desert" is a maxim. It is a rational principle that individuals can choose in order to guide certain of their actions, or can appeal to in order to explain their actions. But, as I just said, although acting rational is a necessary condition of morality, it is not a sufficient condition. For an act to have moral worth, it must not only be rational, but it must be motivated by the will to do the right thing.

Two identical acts—for example, the building of dams in two similar locations—might be evaluated very differently in terms of their moral worth. If the maxim that motivates the construction of the first dam is one that transcends the desire for individual gain, and it is motivated by the idea of moral duty, then that act of construction has moral value. On the other hand, if the simple desire for profit motivates the construction, the act has no moral worth, and it would have none even if the dam was constructed according to rational principles and produced great benefits and exceeding happiness for millions of people. Kant is not saying that the second act is wrong or bad; he is saying that it is morally indifferent.

Let's pause to take note of certain features of Kant's theory as presented so far. First, notice the striking claim that if there were no rational beings in the universe, neither would there be any moral value in the universe. There can be morality only in a world that includes rational agents.[5] This part of Kant's theory will offend the views of many ecologically minded ethical theorists who argue that nature itself has moral worth irrespective of any features of rationality.

Still, moral indifference can be lucrative.

FUTURE SITE OF HERBERT'S DAM
Serving YOU!
(unless, of course, you like wild rivers.)

Another important aspect of Kant's theory as we have seen it so far is that the moral worth of an act cannot be determined by the consequences of the act. In the dam-construction examples, the consequences of both the morally valuable case and of the morally neutral case might be identical. Similarly, if an unforeseeable natural disaster like an earthquake destroyed the morally valuable dam but not the morally neutral dam, the first act of construction would retain its moral worth even if whole cities had been destroyed in the wake of the flooding caused by the building of the dam. The same could not be said for the act that produced a shoddily constructed dam. The construction of such a dam might be under the guidance of a maxim, such as "If I want to maximize short-term profit, I will construct shoddily." Such a maxim is rational—its logic is impeccable—but it is irresponsible; it is not motivated by a good will, hence it could not be accepted by an architect who possesses a good will. Similarly, one might construct a shoddy dam if one simply had "good intentions," but did not apply those intentions to a rational program of action. This is why it would be incorrect to say that according to Kant any act motivated by good intentions is a good act. Kant knows very well that—as the old saying has it—the road to hell is paved with good intentions.

This last feature of Kant's moral theory explains why he is called a **nonconsequentialist.** Of course, **consequentialists**—theorists who hold that the moral worth of any act depends on the benefits that act provides—are at complete odds with Kant's approach. This stance will be perhaps most evident in the case of the utilitarians we will study in Chapter 4. They argue that for any act to be deemed good, it must produce social happiness. But for Kant, it is not the result of the act that is evaluated as either morally good or bad, but the motivation and rationality of the act. The kind of moral theory that Kant will develop is often called **deontology** by modern ethicists, from the

The Road to Hell Is Paved with Good Intentions

Greek *deon*, meaning that which is binding, because Kant believes that we are always bound by duty. A rational act that is motivated by a good will, hence by duty, is a morally good act.

Duty

In Kant's philosophy, the concept of "duty" is closely related to the concept of a good will. The two are not identical, but they are logically linked, because a good will necessarily submits to what it discovers to be its duty. Kant says, "Duty is the necessity of an action executed from respect for law" (16). Duty is the obligation that the agent recognizes as following from the authority of one's rational nature and of good will. Kant obviously assumes that what distinguishes human beings from most other objects in the world is their rationality, and this uniqueness—which is that of being able to choose to live according to the law that their rational nature reveals to them—bestows a certain kind of dignity on them. The duty that rationality imposes upon humans is an obligation to honor this dignity. If individuals do not acknowledge the authority of this obligation, they betray their dignity and find themselves in opposition to their own nature. By refusing to accept the authority of the law imposed by rationality, they literally become outlaws to themselves; they enter into a form of self-alienation.

Rational Nature

According to Kant, among natural beings only humans have the ability to represent law and to choose to live by it. He says, "Everything in nature works according to laws. Only a rational being has the capacity of acting according to the conception of laws, i.e., according to principles" (29). Immorality, for Kant, is the failure to choose to be guided by the reason that is part of one's essence. It is a failure of reason. Kant divides reason into a number of components. There is "pure reason" (the capacity of envisaging concepts that are free of empirical input—concepts like freedom, immortality, and God); there is "prudential" or "instrumental reason" (the capacity of envisaging what actions one must take to achieve the objects of one's desire); and there is "practical reason" (the capacity of envisaging what one ought to do in the name of goodness). When I say that for Kant, immorality is a failure of reason, I mean a failure of *practical reason*. Kant knows full well that much evil has been brought about by people who are following instrumental reason. His point is that we should not become disillusioned by reason just because we observe that many deeply immoral people are very clever. It is quite possible to be a great practitioner of instrumental reason while ignoring the demands of practical reason.

Kant seems to think that the value of the human capacity for representing rational law and choosing to be governed by the law that one envisages is that in this case the rational will surpasses nature and creates a transcendental world of its own. Kant is in awe of reason because it is the only force that can counteract our natural passions—passions that Kant sees as primarily negative, namely, our propensity for greed, ambition, haughtiness, jealousy, envy, gloating, delusion, and our desire to tyrannize over others. Kant's conception of our natural desires reveals his pessimism. His optimism is seen in his belief that all antagonism, conflict, and competition among human beings would end if each of us honored our own rational nature and that of others.

The Worst of All Animals Pushed by His Motives

How Duty Commands and Motivates Us

"Rational nature," says Kant, "exists as an end in itself" (47). It has "absolute worth" (46), and, as such, only it "could be the ground of absolute laws" (46). We see, then, that the motive behind duty is the dignity of humanity as an end in itself. In other words, value itself is derived from rationality (once again, if there were no rational beings in the universe, there would be no [moral] values), and therefore as the source of values, rational nature has absolute value. From this purported fact, Kant deduces that there are rules of rationality that tell us how we ought to act.

This is an important move in Kant's argument, but one that is difficult to state in a simple and compelling fashion. Perhaps it can be put like this:

a) If there were no rational nature, there would be no moral value. (There might be instrumental value—worms might "value" dirt, and birds might "value" worms—but there would be no moral obligations; i.e., we might say that worms desire dirt or that worms need dirt, and that birds desire or need worms, but we could not say that worms *ought* to desire dirt or that birds *ought* to desire worms.)

The John Wayne of the Worm World

b) Because moral values exist only where there is rational nature, rational nature is the ground of moral value. (That is to say, the idea of moral value presupposes the idea of rational nature.)

c) Therefore only rational nature is absolutely (morally) valuable, and all other moral values are relative to rational nature.

d) Therefore the idea of a rational nature can itself dictate the rules/laws informing us how we ought to comport ourselves (i.e., telling us what acts we ought to undertake).

The Is/Ought Problem

This is a good place to pause and remind you of the is/ought problem that you have already encountered several times in the preceding chapters. It certainly appears that Kant runs afoul of it when he tries to derive moral duty ("ought") from human rationality and dignity ("is"). He might respond to this criticism by claiming that the is/ought problem is misconstrued. All human discourse, all human community, and, indeed, human life itself, is premised upon the possibility of rationality; therefore *everything* in the human world is derived from that momentous "is" (i.e., the fact that human rationality exists). Because rational nature is itself the source of all (moral) values, it would be absurd to deny that in this case "is" implies "ought." *This* "is" (but no other) *must* imply an "ought."

The validity of this response depends upon whether Kant has correctly characterized rational nature and whether it has the ontological status (status in reality) that Kant assigns it. Is there a natural being which by its very **essence** has intrinsic value, and, if so, is this being rational nature? David Hume certainly would have denied both of these attributions, and, as you will see in Chapter 5, so will Charles Darwin.

Perfect and Imperfect Duties

We have, then, certain duties that are prescribed to us by our rational nature. Kant draws a distinction between perfect duties (some-

times called "strict" or "narrow" duties) and imperfect duties (sometimes called "wide" duties). Perfect duties set strict and specific
goals in such a way that in cases where they apply, one will know
exactly what one must do, and failure to perform that act is always
blameworthy. For example, as you will see later, according to Kant, we
must always refrain from telling lies. This is a perfect duty. Imperfect
duties set general goals but give us leeway in determining which acts
will honor those goals. For example, the happiness of others must be
a goal, but there are many different ways in which we can achieve
that goal. Both of these duties, by the way, have as *their* goal the
honoring of human dignity.

PERFECT DUTY

Do not lie

exceptions:

NONE

ways of
fulfilling duty:

ALWAYS TELL
THE TRUTH
(PERIOD!)

IMPERFECT DUTY

Be nice

exceptions:

CERTAIN
BORDERLINE
CASES

ways of
fulfilling duty:

SMILE A LOT
SHARE YOUR ICECREAM
BE A GOOD LISTENER
HELP CHANGE FLAT TIRES
GIVE TO CHARITIES
BE POLITE TO PETS*

*P.S. Not all acts
are required, but
agent must select
several from this
list.

When Kant says that the only acts that are morally worthy are those acts motivated by duty, he means that the idea of morality only applies to acts motivated by the recognition of demands made on us by human dignity itself (or, more accurately, by "rational nature" itself, because it is our rational nature that bestows dignity on us). For one's acts to be morally valuable, one must acknowledge the authority of these demands willingly and not grudgingly. (That's part of what the idea of a good will signifies.) This means that love and sympathy are not morally adequate motives for action. If I come to your aid out of love or sympathy for you, my act might be approved of by Kant, but it would have no *moral* worth. (This part of Kant's theory gets him in trouble with lots of critics, as you will see.) Such an act would have no moral worth because love and sympathy are not reliable guides to action. In extreme situations, they can be coopted by evil. For example, the "love of God" and "sympathy for oppressed peoples" have motivated terrorist acts that Kant would find evil. Mrs. Hitler (aka Frau Schicklgruber) had love for her son, Adolf, and this love might have motivated her to help him round up Jews for extermination. (It didn't, by the way. She died before he embarked on his evil program.)

He's **such a** darling.

To explain how duty motivates us, in *The Foundations of the Metaphysics of Morals,* Kant gives us four exemplary cases. I suspect you will find some of his commentary on these cases to be clear and helpful and some of it to be odd and troubling. The first one is, I believe, the easiest. It concerns a merchant who charges an inexperienced customer a fair price for the goods and does not take advantage of the customer's naïveté. Duty requires just such behavior, so the merchant's act is at least "in accord with duty" (13). But is it "performed from duty" (13)? In this case, says Kant, it is not; rather it is motivated by self-interest, because the merchant knows that if he gets the reputation of duping vulnerable customers, he will lose his regular customers. Kant says that the merchant deserves "praise and encouragement but no esteem" (14). That is, his act, though correct, is morally worthless.

Kant's second example concerns suicide. He states that "it is a duty to preserve one's life" (14). (We have not yet seen why Kant makes this claim, but later in the chapter, we will observe how that obligation is imposed on us by the authority of rationality.) Luckily, we not only have a duty to preserve our lives, but a "direct inclination" to do so. We desire—unthinkingly—to stay alive. But if a despondent man who has suffered enormous defeats in life and longs for death "and yet preserves his life without loving it and from neither inclination nor fear but from duty" (14), then his act has moral worth. Recall that the suicidal Hamlet chooses not to end his life because he fears the pains of hell (act III, scene 1).

Kant would have approved of Hamlet's decision, but would have found it to be morally worthless.

Both of these examples are, in my opinion, perfectly understandable. The third one, which we are about to inspect, is more troubling, and the fourth one is difficult to comprehend. The third example states, "To be kind where one can is duty" (14). Some people follow this principle, not out of duty, but rather out of vanity (it pleases them to think of themselves as kindly) or out of egoism (they find personal advantages derive from a kindly disposition). It is easy enough to see why Kant thinks that these types should not get moral praise. But he also says that some people "find an inner satisfaction in spreading joy, and rejoice in the contentment of others which they have made possible." In other words, they are naturally kind people. About the acts of such people Kant states that "however dutiful and amiable it may be, that kind of action has no true moral worth." He imagines a man whose mind was so clouded with sorrow that it "extinguished all sympathy for the lot of others . . . their need left him untouched because he was pre-occupied with his own need," yet he was moved "to tear himself . . . out of this dead sensibility . . . to perform this [helpful] action only from duty and without any inclination." In that case, says Kant, "[F]or the first time his action has moral worth." From the moral point of view Kant prefers the kind acts of a man who "is by tem-perament cold and indifferent to the suffering of others" (14) to the acts of the naturally philanthropic man. Kant says that "it is just here that the worth of the character is brought out, which is morally and incomparably the highest of all: he is beneficent not from inclination but from duty." (14–15). Many critics of Kant find that the coldness of this unsympathetic, unloving, but dutiful man reveals a coldness in the heart of the Kantian ethic.

According to the fourth example, we have an indirect (and imperfect) duty to seek our own happiness. (It is "indirect" because if we are miserable, we will have great temptations to ignore our more direct duties—those of preserving our own lives and of treating other people well.) Now, in fact, most of us have a strong inclination to seek our own happiness. Yet, says Kant, those of our acts that

A Kantian Hero?

are intended to promote our happiness have no moral worth if they are motivated by this natural inclination. Only such acts that are motivated by duty have moral value. What does it mean to say that

I have a natural desire to eat this ice cream cone, but I'm not doing it from desire, rather from an imperfect duty to seek happiness. Then, after that, I'll have some cake, ... and then a double martini

we ought to seek not by inclination (desire) but by duty (will)? Kant apparently recognizes that this is an odd-sounding requirement, but he explains it by comparing it to Jesus's paradoxical command to love your enemies. If you can be commanded to love someone dutifully whom you are inclined to hate, surely you can be commanded to seek happiness dutifully rather than by inclination. Still, it is not perfectly clear how in specific instances one can tell the difference between the two acts.

Perhaps we can approach Kant's point more sympathetically if we notice that for Kant, moral praise must be reserved for acts that are the result of **agency,** that is, willfully chosen, and rationally chosen, not out of impulse, inclination, or bodily function. (We applaud babies when they manage to urinate in a timely fashion at a proper place, but we don't applaud adults for doing so.)

In ethics, as elsewhere in life, we praise actions only if they have taken some effort.

What?!

No applause?

Whoosh

Moral Law: The Categorical Imperative

In the preface to *Foundations*, Kant states that the goal of his book is "the search for and establishment of the supreme principle of morality" (8). This law will be called the **categorical imperative**—"categorical," meaning absolute, and "imperative," meaning command. He is looking for an absolute command that holds sway always, everywhere, and admits of no exceptions.

Kant contrasts the categorical imperative with what he calls a **hypothetical imperative**, which is conditioned by desire and context. All hypothetical imperatives are versions of one model, which we can call *the* hypothetical imperative. It is set forth as a general formula: "Whoever wills the end, so far as reason has decisive influence on his action, wills also the indispensably necessary means to it that lie in his power" (34). So hypothetical imperatives are rational, but they address what Kant called earlier "instrumental rationality," where the act in question is an instrument for achieving another end—it is a means to that end. These kinds of imperatives are called "hypothetical" imperatives because they can be framed in terms of hypotheses: "*If* you want X, *then* you should do Y." (*If* you want to succeed in life, *then* you should work hard.) In this kind of hypothesis, the then-clause (the one containing the word "should," which is what makes this an imperative) can always be defeated by denying the if-clause.

Hypothetical Imperative

A categorical imperative, on the other hand, cannot be defeated. There is no if-clause, because it is not relative to any goal. It is, as I said, absolute. The categorical imperative will be an expression of law itself, derived from practical reason, which exemplifies rational nature, the highest value in Kant's system. Only rational nature is capable of representing or envisaging law and choosing to live by it. Therefore the categorical imperative is not simply rational, it is the expression of rational nature itself. What is this law?

In *Foundations*, Kant formulates five versions of the categorical imperative.[6] Kant says that these different "ways of presenting the principle of morality are fundamentally only so many formulas of the very same law, and each of them unites the others in itself" (54). I will now quote each of the variant versions of the categorical imperative, and we will inspect them all.

1. *The Formula of Universal Law* (FUL).[7] "Act only according to that maxim by which you can at the same time will that it should become a universal law" (39).
2. *The Formula of the Law of Nature* (FLN). "Act as though the maxim of your action were by your will to become a universal law of nature" (39).
3. *The Formula of Humanity as an End in Itself* (FH). "Act so that you treat humanity, whether in your own person or in that of another, always as an end and never as a means only" (47).
4. *The Formula of Autonomy* (FA). "Never choose except in such a way that the maxims of the choice are comprehended in the same volition as a universal law" (59).
5. *The Formula of the Realm of Ends* (FRE). "Every rational being must act as if he, by his maxims, were at all times a legislative member in the universal realm of ends" (57).

We will now look at each of these five versions in order to try to understand their meaning and how they relate to each other.

Number 1: *The Formula of Universal Law (FUL)*

Act only according to that maxim by which you can at the same time will that it should become a universal law.

Remember that a maxim is a personally chosen rule that governs and justifies one's act in a particular situation. Maxims are subjective in the sense that they are personally chosen rather than being imposed objectively upon the subject by the sheriff, the school principal, or "the Man."

Recall that, according to Kant, behind every rational act is a maxim—whether articulated or not, or even whether made conscious or not—that is, a privately chosen rule that when stated would explain the general reason for our action.

Now, when Kant says that you should act only by a maxim that you could will to be a universal law, he is asking you to conceive of a world in which the maxim of your action could serve as a law governing everybody's behavior all the time. A maxim is universalizable if it can be a rule that anyone could follow. **Universalizability** is roughly the idea behind the moral instruction provided by parents when they admonish a selfish child, asking the child, "What would happen if *everybody* did that?"

If the idea of willing a world governed by the maxim of your act contains no self-contradiction, then the act you are about to undertake is consistent with duty. If, however, the idea involves a self-contradiction, then your maxim is irrational, and the act governed by that maxim is not consistent with duty; it is immoral, and you have a strict obligation not to perform it. Notice, it follows that for Kant, we only know what we *must do* by inverting what we *must not do*. If we *must not lie*, then we *must tell the truth*.

So, are there any situations in which it would not be immoral to lie, steal, or murder? Imagine that I owe a considerable sum of money to an old woman who has befriended me. The time has come to repay her, but doing so would make things very difficult for me. It occurs to me that I could lie to her, saying that she must have forgotten that I paid her back long ago. In that case, the maxim of my action might be "Lie if doing so will extricate you from difficulty." Can I will this maxim as a universal law?

Imagine a world in which everyone is commanded to lie in certain circumstances. Such a world is a logically impossible world. The concept of lying is parasitic upon the concept of truth telling. That is, there can be lying only against a general backdrop of honesty. In a world in which everyone is commanded to lie, no such backdrop can exist. In fact, if a visitor to that world asks a police officer what the law of the land is, that visitor cannot know whether the officer is lying when he communicates the law.

Where Lying Is the Law of the Land

A world in which one cannot state the law without breaking it is an impossible world. It is a world that cannot even be described without contradiction. Therefore, according to Kant, lying is *always* wrong.

Similar results follow from an analysis of stealing (appropriating the belongings of others without permission). I cannot solve my problem by returning the money to my neighbor and then stealing it back. The maxim of such an act cannot be universalized without contradiction. The concept of stealing can only exist in a world where the concept of legal (or moral) ownership exists. But a law requiring that everyone steal would undermine the concept of property. Such a law would be yet another self-contradictory law, and a world governed by that law would be an impossible world. There would be no property and no stealing of property. There would just be stuff passing through people's hands. Therefore, according to Kant, stealing is *always* wrong.

Where Theft Is the Law of the Land

I cannot solve my problem by killing my neighbor either. A world in which everyone was commanded to kill someone sometime would similarly be an impossible world, because if the law were obeyed, there would be nobody to obey it.

Therefore, according to Kant, murder (or taking the life of another when not under military orders or when not acting as a legit-imate agent of the law) is *always* wrong. Kant does not even allow self-defense as an excuse.[8]

So we see that the first formulation of Kant's categorical imperative (FUL) demon-strates that if the maxim of an action produces a logical self-contradiction when universalized (i.e., when applied to every human agent in all identical cases), then there is something wrong with that action. There is something wrong with it because it fails a test of reason. The perpetrator of such an act is immoral because he fails to honor that rational nature which is the source of all moral values, and he is also a fool or a hypocrite because he tries to make himself a "privileged exception to universal moral laws that everyone else is rightly expected to follow."[9]

Number 2: *The Formula of the Law of Nature (FLN)*

Act as though the maxim of your action were by your will to become a universal law of nature.

The difference between FUL and this version is that in the former case the agent wills that her maxim should become a universal *moral* or *legal* law. The way to test that version is to see whether the universal-ization of the maxim leads to a logical contradiction. In the case of FLN, the agent wills her maxim to be a *natural* law, so the test will be different. Rather than looking for logical impossibility, one looks for causal impossibility. If I will the maxim of my action as a law of nature, and if doing so produces a physical impossibility (given the actual laws of nature), then I cannot consistently justify my action. For example, if I choose not to help my neighbor change her flat tire, the maxim of my action is, perhaps, "I do not need to help my fellow human beings when they are in need of aid." If we apply FUL to this case, it seems that the maxim here can be universalized without logical contradiction. (A world in which no one helped his or her needy fellow human would not be a logically impossible world.) But, according to Kant, it is an empirical fact that no human can survive without help from others. Therefore, to will the universalization of such a maxim would be to will a physically impossible world. Therefore, according to Kant, there is a moral duty to help other humans in need, and this duty is revealed by FLN.

Another (perhaps less compelling) of Kant's examples to be analyzed by FLN is that of a well-off man who chooses to while away his life in laziness and uselessness, seeking merely idle pleasures. But, says Kant, such a man cannot will the maxim of his actions as a natural law because, "as a rational being, he necessarily wills that all his faculties should be developed, inasmuch as they are given to him for all sorts of possible purposes" (41). In other words, according to Kant, it is an empirical fact about human nature that humans want to develop their talents and make use of them. Willing a world of idleness would contradict the facts about human nature, hence is impossible, according to FLN.

Expectation of Reward

Pity

Duty

Three Different Motives for Helping Your Neighbor Fix Her Flat

Allen Wood points out that the application of FLN to moral problems proves the error of those critics of Kant who complain that Kant's system is merely an *a priori* structure, ignoring empirical facts about human nature and the human condition. To the contrary, as we see, FLN assumes certain empirical facts about humans to be true and tailors its standards to those facts. (This move may not be completely successful, however, because some of Kant's claims about the facts of human nature are quite dubious.) Wood makes another interesting observation about FLN. The first version of the categorical imperative (FUL) generates "perfect duties"—that is, it reveals specific acts that must be performed (e.g., truth telling) or specific acts that must be avoided (e.g., stealing, killing)—while the second version (FLN) generates "imperfect duties"—that is, these duties demand certain goals, such as aiding one's fellow human in need, but they allow the agents leeway in deciding how to bring about these goals.

Ever since Kant published *Foundations*, his moral system has been accused of what some critics call an "empty formalism"—that is, it has no content, only form; it has no object. According to these critics, Kant gives us a law that instructs one to obey the law, and if we ask why we should obey the law, he says because it's there. My view is that, indeed, Kant is somewhat guilty of wording his theory—at least as we've seen it so far—in such a way that it is vulnerable to such an attack. However, Kant seems to have believed that all versions of the categorical imperative are expressions of the same principle or, more accurately, that each expression reveals an aspect of that principle, perhaps just as views of the Grand Canyon from different vantage points reveal different features of that immense space. To prove that some aspects of Kant's principle reveal some genuine content in his otherwise empty formalism, we will look next at his third version of the categorical imperative.

Number 3:
The Formula of Humanity as an End in Itself (FH)

Act so that you treat humanity, whether in your own person or in that of another, always as an end and never as a means only.

In fact, we have already reviewed Kant's claim that the highest value in the world (highest because all other values derive from it) is rational nature, and that rational nature is manifested in each human being. This new version of the categorical imperative honors just that conception of humanity. It is this principle that, when linked up with FUL and FLN, gives substance to Kant's ethics, thereby saving it from emptiness. The requirement to treat ourselves and others as ends in themselves and not merely as means to other ends is the requirement that, to put it in everyday language, we not use other people—at least, we may not use them merely to fulfill other, selfish, goals.

Therefore, treating others merely as a means of earning profit, or achieving power, or acquiring revenge, or getting out of trouble, or saving one's own skin, or for the glory of the homeland, or the glory of the king or of the gods, is *always wrong.* This point raises an important question. Are my students reducing me to

Using People as Pawns

a means to their own ends when they take my classes? Are they using me to get their degrees, leading to jobs, success, and wealth? Am I using them when I accept my paycheck?

In other words, don't we use each other all the time? Hasn't Kant's demand made human interaction as we know it pretty much

impossible? Well, notice that Kant's formulation says we must treat people "always as an end and never as a means only." It does not prevent us from using people as means to our own ends as long as we treat them as ends as well. That is, in my dealings with you, I can use you as part of a plan to achieve my own goals only if I can do so without denying or ignoring your dignity as a rational being. If in the process of using you, I cheat you, mislead you, lie to you, convince you to buy a product that is not good for you or that you don't need —if I do any of these things, I turn myself into a hypocrite or an evil being because I cannot universalize the maxim behind my actions. I certainly would not accept that maxim if it were directed against me.

In my view, this aspect of Kant's ethics has a strong plausibility. Furthermore, his argument, using as it does the principle of universalizability, links FH with the other formulations of the categorical imperative and strengthens their plausibility as well. But Kant is not done yet. There are two more versions of the categorical imperative remaining to be inspected.

Number 4: *The Formula of Autonomy (FA)*

> Never choose except in such a way that the maxims of the choice are comprehended in the same volition as a universal law.

At first glance, this version may appear to be identical to the first version, FUL, but in explaining it Kant says, "Autonomy of the will is that property of it by which it is a law unto itself independently of any property of objects of volition" (59). What Kant stresses here is the fact that the human will is autonomous. It transcends nature because it can represent the law to itself, and because it can formulate the law and recognize its duty to be bound by that law, and because it can choose to accept that duty. According to Kant, nothing else in nature has such capabilities. We once again see Kant's reason for believing that rational nature is both the source of all moral values and is itself of the highest worth. The fourth version of the categorical imperative tells us that in choosing maxims for our actions, we must always hold this fact before us.

The fifth version of the categorical imperative is a different expression of this same idea, according to Kant. Wood calls it the Formula of the Realm of Ends (FRE).

Number 5: *The Formula of the Realm of Ends (FRE)*

Every rational being must act as if he, by his maxims, were at all times a legislative member in the universal realm of ends.

What does Kant mean by the "realm of ends"? If rational nature has a dignity higher than any other value, and if the dignity of humanity is an end in itself, then the hypothetical community of rational beings transcends mere nature. In rational beings nature surpasses itself, creating a distinct world of law and rationality— a world in which, if it followed its own principles, all conflict would be overcome, and perfect justice would reign.

A Transcendental World of Harmony and Justice Achievable If We All Follow Our Own Rational Nature

Such a transcendent world is, in Kant's eyes, the end, the goal, the **telos,** of nature, and ultimately gives nature its meaning. The fifth version of the categorical imperative, namely, the Formula of the Realm of Ends (FRE), tells us that our maxims for all our actions must be capable of being universalized into the laws governing such an ideal rational world. If not, our actions attack our own human dignity and the dignity of all others.

Recall that the traditional criticism of Kant's theory holds that Kant's moral theory is one of pure formalism and as such empty because it ignores any empirical (*a posteriori*) truths about human nature. Wood has virtually refuted this criticism by showing how the different versions of the categorical imperative are related to each other, how they are all guided by a vision of a hypothetical community that is the realm of ends, and by showing us how Kant, in his later works, developed this idea around his conception of the empirical facts about human nature. The problem is—as Wood knows very well—that the alleged empirical facts Kant attributes to human nature are now highly questionable. The natural teleology that Kant imagines to be in place, wherein nature has goals, and the human being is the true end of nature, was soundly refuted by Charles Darwin some fifty-five years after Kant's death (more about this in Chapter 5). Without denying that Darwin has rendered obsolete Kant's theory of natural teleology, Wood defends Kant. He believes that it is possible to reformulate Kant's insight without using the outmoded idea of goals within nature. We should think of the realm of ends as the ideal world that would be brought about if each person follows his or her naturally given powers of reason. The fact that such a world will never exist does not prevent it from being an ideal toward which we should strive.

Furthermore, Wood likes what he takes to be Kant's project. Kant, who is seen by some as a stuffy old conservative, is applauded as a radical by Wood:

> Kantian principles require treating all human beings as ends in themselves with absolute, hence equal worth. They demand that human

beings unite their ends into a single, reciprocally supporting teleological system, or "realm." The ideals of Kantian ethics are *autonomy*, *equality*, and *community*. Or, to put these ideals in the political language of his own time: *Liberté, égalité, fraternité*. (335)

Immanuel Kant—Revolutionary Hero?

By showing Kant's affiliation with the ideas of the French Revolution, Wood demonstrates at least that in Kant's own day he was a radical. Wood also demonstrates that the correct understanding of Kant places him in the Western liberal democratic tradition that opposed tyranny and oppression, and supported freedom and self-governance.

Wood's support for Kant does not blind him to Kant's many weaknesses and excesses. Hardly any contemporary defender of Kant will accept some of Kant's most egregious assertions, such as his claim that the death penalty must be obligatory for murder (he believes that as long as one murderer remains alive in prison, the citizens of the host society are in danger of "blood guilt"[10]), Kant's defense of racism,[11] his antiquated attitudes toward women,[12] and his views about sex.[13]

Perceived Strengths and Weaknesses
Strengths

- Kant's philosophy provides the articulate formalization of an intuition of morality as fairness, justice, and equality.
- It gives voice and justification to a widely shared moral intuition that it is immoral to use other people for one's own ends.
- A logical test for moral hypocrisy, egoism, and irrationality is provided in the form of a theory of the universalizability of the principles governing our behavior.
- Kant generated a moral vision related to the historical struggle against tyranny and to the rise of democracy.

Weaknesses

- The theory's tendency toward empty formalism can be dissolved only by a careful and detailed **apologetic** (of the type prepared by Wood).
- The theory also exhibits a tendency toward absolutism.
- There appears to be a coldness of heart at the center of Kant's moral vision.
- Kant's views about human dignity participate in **speciesism** and **anthropocentrism,** which do not fit with today's concern for the natural world.
- Much of Kant's moral philosophy rests tenuously on his questionable ideas about freedom, and it presupposes an outmoded pre-Darwinian metaphysics.

Questions for Consideration

1. What features of Kant's overall philosophy are referred to in the phrase "the Copernican revolution in philosophy"?

2. What does it mean to say that Kant suggests that we treat sentences such as "God exists" and "Human beings are constitutionally free" as if they were synthetic *a priori* truths, even though they are not?

3. The terms "good will" and "maxim" appear early in Kant's ethics. Explain what they mean and how they are related to "duty."

4. What is the role played by human dignity in Kant's ethics? According to you, is there such a thing as "human dignity"?

5. If Kant successfully makes the close connection between rationality and morality, how can he explain the existence of smart criminals who plan their crimes rationally?

6. If you saw that your neighbor's house was in flames, and, out of natural sympathy, you rushed over to help her extinguish the fire, what would Kant say about the moral worth of your act?

7. According to Kant, "to be kind where one can is a duty." In Kant's system, is this duty "perfect" or "imperfect"? Say why.

8. Explain the difference between a "categorical imperative" and a "hypothetical imperative."

9. Compare and contrast Kant's first version of the categorical imperative, "Act only according to that maxim by which you can at the same time will that it should become a universal law," and Jesus's Golden Rule, "Do unto others as you would have them do unto you."

10. Explain in your own words why Kant believes that killing another human being is always wrong. Based on what you've learned about Kant in this chapter, can you find a way to make this claim consistent with Kant's belief that killing an enemy in a just war is allowable, as is capital punishment in the case of convicted murderers?

11. Explain the difference between a "legislated" law (moral or legal) as it appears in the first version of the categorical imperative, the Formula of Universal Law (FUL), and a "natural law" (a law of nature) as it appears in the second version of the categorical imperative, the Formula of the Law of Nature (FLN).

12. Defend or criticize Kant's claim that it is a scientific fact about each human being that "as a rational being, he necessarily wills that all his

faculties should be developed, inasmuch as they are given to him for all sorts of possible purposes."

13. Kant claims that all formulations of the categorical imperative are really versions of the same principle. With this claim in mind, inspect what is called here the Formula of Universal Law (FUL) and the Formula of Humanity as an End in Itself (FH), and defend or criticize Kant's assertion that these two formulas express the same idea.

14. In his final version of the categorical imperative, Kant says, "Every rational being must act as if he, by his maxims, were at all times a legislative member in the universal realm of ends." What does Kant mean here by the phrase "realm of ends"?

Study Guide: Outline of Chapter Three

I. Hume and Kant on Epistemology.

  A. Hume's view.

    1. All propositions are either analytic (*a priori* tautologies that represent relations among ideas) or synthetic (*a posteriori* representations of sense data).

      a. Analytic propositions provide no factual information about reality.

      b. Synthetic propositions only provide information about sense data.

      c. Neither provide enough information to justify our beliefs about substantiality or causation.

    2. Therefore skepticism is the only rational posture.

  B. Kant's response to Hume's skepticism.

    1. The Copernican revolution in philosophy.

      a. Hume cannot find time, space, and causality through observation because they are not "in" the perceived world; rather they are imposed upon the world by the structures of the mind.

      b. Statements about time, space, and causality are synthetic *a priori* truths.

2. Hume was right about the propositions of metaphysics (e.g., God, immortality, freedom).

   a. They are not empirical.

   b. They are not synthetic *a priori* truths.

3. Nevertheless, on pragmatic grounds, we have the right to posit certain of these metaphysical propositions as if they were synthetic *a priori* truths.

4. Kant's whole moral system seems to be premised on the hope that humans are free.

   a. Without freedom, Kant's kind of moral system fails.

   b. We cannot know for certain that we are free.

   c. We have the right to posit freedom as if it were a synthetic *a priori* truth.

II. "Good will": Only a good will "could be called good without qualification."

   A. Implication: Moral value adheres not to acts, nor to the consequences of acts, nor to principles, but to a certain volitional attitude.

   B. Overstatement of Kant's thesis? Don't other factors have an even higher moral value for Kant?

      1. E.g., human reason?

      2. E.g., human dignity?

      3. E.g., law?

III. A good will seeks to be guided by rational maxims.

   A. A maxim is a "subjective principle" that guides and rationalizes one's instrumental or one's practical (moral) actions.

   B. Maxims can guide either instrumental reason or practical reason.

IV. Reason (rationality) imposes a duty upon us.

   A. Reason is the defining characteristic of humanity.

      1. Reason gives us the capacity of representing the idea of law to ourselves.

      2. Reason allows us to oppose desire and choose law.

B. Reason itself is what gives us our dignity.

C. A good will is a will committed to reason and to the dignity that rational nature bestows upon individuals.

V. The divisions of reason.

   A. Pure reason: the source of metaphysical concepts.

   B. Instrumental reason: the source of prudence (watching out for oneself).

   C. Practical reason: the source of morality.

VI. Duty: A good will wills duty.

   A. Duty (moral obligation) is dictated by reason.

   B. Reason implies dignity; dignity implies duty.

      1. The is/ought problem? How can one derive "ought" (duty) from "is" (reason)?

      2. Kant's response:

         a. Reason and only reason creates values.

         b. Therefore, in this unique case, "is" (reason) implies "ought" (duty).

   C. Kinds of duties.

      1. Perfect duties: specific duties that must be directly assumed.

      2. Imperfect duties: general duties where some leeway is afforded in trying to meet them.

   D. The only morally worthy acts are those motivated by duty.

VII. The moral law.

   A. How can I know my duty?

      1. The hypothetical imperative: rules for instrumental reason (if . . . then . . .).

      2. The categorical imperative: rules for practical reason.

      3. The categorical imperative is absolute.

         a. It employs no hypothesis (if . . . then . . .).

         b. It is absolute, binding everybody always.

   B. Five versions of the categorical imperative each provide a different perspective on the moral law (duty).

1. The Formula of Universal Law (FUL).

2. The Formula of the Law of Nature (FLN).

3. The Formula of Humanity as an End in Itself (FH).

4. The Formula of Autonomy (FA).

5. The Formula of the Realm of Ends (FRE).

C. The relation between Kant's moral law and the ideals of the Enlightenment and the French Revolution.

For Further Reading

General Philosophical Works by Kant

Critique of Pure Reason, trans. J. M. D. Meiklejohn. London: Dent [Everyman's Library], 1991.

Prolegomena to Any Future Metaphysics. Indianapolis: Bobbs-Merrill [Library of Liberal Arts], 1950.

Ethical Works by Immanuel Kant

The Foundations of the Metaphysics of Morals, trans. Lewis White Beck. Indianapolis: Bobbs-Merrill Publishing, 1976.

Critique of Practical Reason, trans. Mary Gregor and Andrews Reath. Cambridge and New York: Cambridge University Press, 1997.

Metaphysics of Morals, trans. and ed. Mary Gregor. New York: Cambridge University Press, 1998.

Secondary Sources on Kant's Moral Philosophy

Baron, Marcia W. *Kantian Ethics Almost Without Apology*. Ithaca, NY: Cornell University Press, 1999.

Guyer, Paul. *Kant on Freedom, Law, and Happiness*. Cambridge and New York: Cambridge University Press, 2000.

Hill, Thomas E. *Dignity and Practical Reason in Kant's Moral Theory*. Ithaca and London: Cornell University Press, 1992.

Sullivan, Roger J. *An Introduction to Kant's Ethics*. Cambridge and New York: Cambridge University Press, 1994.

Wood, Allen W. *Kant's Ethical Philosophy*. Cambridge and New York: Cambridge University Press, 1999.

Notes

1. Though there can be no empirical evidence of the nature of the noumenal world, Kant does seem to believe that there may be hints about it in certain of our

experiences. He wrote, "Two things fill the mind with ever new and increasing admiration and reverence . . . the starry heavens above me and the moral law within me." Immanuel Kant, *Critique of Practical Reason*, trans. Mary Gregor and Andrews Reath (Cambridge and New York: Cambridge University Press, 1997), 133.

2. Immanuel Kant, *The Foundations of the Metaphysics of Morals*, trans. Lewis White Beck (Indianapolis: Bobbs-Merrill Publishing, 1976). Unless otherwise indicated, all quotations from Kant in this chapter are taken from this book. I will refer to it as *Foundations*, and page numbers will be cited parenthetically in the text.

3. Immanuel Kant, *The Metaphysics of Morals*, trans. and ed. Mary Gregor (New York: Cambridge University Press, 1998).

4. In warning against overemphasizing the idea of a good will in Kant's theory, I am following the lead of Allen W. Wood of Stanford University in his book *Kant's Ethical Philosophy* (Cambridge and New York: Cambridge University Press, 1999). See p. 20 and p. 120. Future references to this book will be included parenthetically in the body of the text.

5. Notice, however, that, strictly speaking, it would be incorrect to say that there can be moral values only where there are human beings. Kant's term "rational agent" would include gods, angels, intelligent extraterrestrials, if any of these exist; and it could include certain other species of animals (in Chapter 5 you will see Darwin arguing that some nonhuman mammals have significant amounts of rationality), and possibly certain robots in the future.

6. Kant himself purports to be putting forth three distinct formulas, two of which have separate expressions (total, five). But each of these five versions stands on its own; so, for simplicity's sake, rather than using Kant's complicated system of divisions, I will treat them as five distinct versions of the categorical imperative.

7. In all five cases I will be using the titles and abbreviations provided by Allen W. Wood, pp. 17–18 of *Kant's Ethical Thought*, both because they are convenient and because they have already entered into the literature of Kantian studies as accepted notation. The quotations themselves are from *Foundations*.

8. There are other possible interpretations of Kant's theory. For example, there is a debate concerning the generality or specificity of the maxim to be universalized. Some Kantian scholars believe that the correct rendition of the categorical imperative requires adding the phrase "similarly circumstanced" to each of the laws suggested. For instance, when you think about killing your friend to avoid paying your debt, rather than testing the morality of your action by suggesting a law that states, "Everyone ought to kill someone," you should propose the maxim "Everyone desiring to escape an onerous obligation should kill the person to whom he or she is obligated." (There would be similarly circumstanced maxims in the case of lying to the lender or stealing from her.) These formulations stressing circumstance would make it harder for Kant to demonstrate the self-contradictoriness of these maxims, but they would perhaps protect Kant against the charge of inconsistency sometimes leveled against him for his support of capital punishment and the killing of enemies in "just" wars.

9. Allen W. Wood, *Kant's Ethical Thought*, 108.

10. According to Kant's *Metaphysik der Sitten*, "even if a civil society were to be dissolved by the consent of all its members . . . , the last murderer remaining in prison would first have to be executed, so that . . . blood guilt does not cling to the people." Quoted by Wood, p. 2.

11. Wood quotes Kant as saying of Africans in *Anthropologie in pragmatischer Hinsicht*, that they are "excessive in feelings; they have a strong sense of honor, and can be educated, but chiefly for servitude. . . . The Negroes are not susceptible of further civilization" (p. 339).

12. Wood says that according to Kant "although women are rational beings, they are not suited by temperament or intellectual endowment to be treated as full adults in the public sphere" (p. 3).

13. Kant writes in *Metaphysik der Sitten* that sexual intercourse is a "degradation of humanity," and that "unnatural" practices such as masturbation "are still viler than suicide" and turn the human being into "a loathsome object." Quoted by Wood, p. 2.

4
Utilitarian Ethics

The moral doctrine of utilitarianism that you are about to study has the advantage from the perspective of the student of philosophy of being easy to characterize at first glance. It has the disadvantage of becoming increasingly difficult the more one tries to give it a precise formulation—this despite the fact that one of its main virtues is supposed to be its simplicity. At the heart of the theory is the **principle of utility,** according to which actions should be chosen that bring about the greatest amount of happiness for the greatest number of people. John Stuart Mill, one of utilitarianism's main architects and defenders, put the issue this way:

> The creed which accepts as the foundation of morals, Utility, or the Greatest Happiness Principle, holds that actions are right in proportion as they tend to promote happiness, wrong as they tend to promote the reverse of happiness.[1]

Well, what could be easier to understand? How can you be against an ethical system that promotes everybody's happiness and tries to minimize their unhappiness? Its defenders say that this theory has the virtues of being easy to comprehend, being down to earth, being democratic and scornful of elitism, and of opening all moral problems to empirical resolutions. Yet, as you will soon see, there is a very real question concerning exactly what this principle means, how to apply it, and why it should be accepted in the first place. But before attempting to get a clearer grasp of utilitarianism's main ideas, as well as its strengths and weaknesses, let me say a few words about its ancestry.

Background of Utilitarianism

There are, after all, hardly any brand-new moral theories, and this is not a surprising fact. Most current moral theories are variations on themes provoked by moral feelings and intuitions, many of which are fairly universal and most of which have been around for a long time. This characterization certainly holds for utilitarianism. General happiness as a philosophical theme appears at least as early as the fifth century B.C.E. in China, in the writings of Mo Tzû, and people have claimed to detect a similar concern in Plato, Aristotle, Epicurus, and Jesus. But utilitarianism as we will study it has its most immediate roots in seventeenth-century Britain. The Englishman Jeremy Bentham coined the term "utilitarianism" in 1789, and he is usually presented as pulling the theory whole out of his hat.

Therefore, philosopher Geoffrey Scarre performs a worthwhile service when he reminds us how much of the doctrine of utilitarianism had already been laid out before Bentham

The Birth of Utilitarianism?

put pen to paper.[2] The Scottish philosopher Francis Hutcheson (1694–1746) was the first to state what Bentham and Mill would later call the Greatest Happiness principle when he wrote, "That Action is best, which procures the greatest Happiness for the greatest Numbers; and that, worst, which, in like manner, occasions Misery."[3] Hutcheson shows himself not to be fully committed to all tenets of what would soon be called utilitarianism when he justifies the Greatest Happiness principle by appealing to intuitions derived from an innate "moral sense." Later utilitarians would unanimously reject the idea of a moral sense, claiming that such an idea is a mystification. For them, all utilitarian principles would have to be empirical, that is, derived from observable fact. Scarre also calls Hutcheson's countryman David Hume (1711–1777) a utilitarian, pointing out that it was he who contributed the word "utility" to the theory when he asserted that "the circumstance of *utility*, in all subjects, is a source of praise and approbation"[4] It is clear that Hume used the word "utility" in its ordinary sense of "usefulness," unlike Bentham, who meant "capable of promoting pleasure." (Hume says, "In common life . . . the circumstance of *utility* is always appealed to; nor is it supposed that a greater eulogy can be given to any man, than to display his *usefulness* to the public, and enumerate the services, which he has performed to mankind and society"[5]). Nevertheless, Hume does indeed associate this usefulness with general "happiness and welfare."

Jeremy Bentham

Not only did Jeremy Bentham (1748–1832) give utilitarianism its name, but he also brought it to the attention of a wide audience and, for better or for worse, put his personal stamp upon it. In fact, as you will see, many of utilitarianism's later defenders have had to compromise Bentham's vision of utilitarianism in order to meet some of the objections against it. Bentham did not think of himself as a philosopher, rather primarily as a legal reformer.

Young Jeremy's Optimism

He was born in Houndsditch, a part of London. He entered Oxford University at age twelve and graduated at fifteen. He went on to study law and was called to the bar at age nineteen. (In eighteenth-century England being "called to the bar" meant being allowed to take one's seat on the other side of the barrier separating the desks of aspiring lawyers from those of the senior lawyers who were already established in the profession.) Despite his lifelong dedication to law, Bentham never actually worked as a barrister; rather he was a theorist, attacking British jurisprudence as an outdated, cumbersome, oppressive system based on privilege and obfuscation. He thought that the doctrine of utilitarianism offered the foundations of a truly efficient, humane, and fair system. To that end he wrote thousands of pages but published only a small part of his writings in book form. He did produce many pamphlets and tracts on such topics as the revision of the penal institutions and the deletion from the legal code of laws that were unenforceable, or enforced selectively. According to Bentham, those "crimes" in which no one suffered (particularly a long list of sexual "crimes") would be decriminalized, and those crimes that did cause great suffering (and this included crimes committed by jurists themselves in the courtroom) would be punished severely, but only if such punishment was likely to prevent suffering and promote well-being. Bentham even drew up a blueprint for a rationally based prison, with cells open to a central court that would have a high tower in its center, called a "panopticon," from which invisible authorities could

Bentham's Panopticon

monitor the activities of the prisoners twenty-four hours a day.

Bentham's main book—the one that should be studied for his utilitarianism—is the *Introduction to the Principles of Morals and Legislation*, published in 1789.[6]

Bentham remained a bachelor until the end of his life, and derived most of his social life from his association with like-minded gentlemen radicals. Bentham was tremendously influential during his lifetime and after, successfully lobbying to overturn archaic laws and legal traditions, and leaving in his wake a number of important followers who continued his work. The movement that he established even managed to found a university—University College, in London. His fully dressed, mummified body with a wax head still presides over the trustees' meetings because his fortune was left to them with the provision that he be able to attend all their meetings. His mummified head is also on display. There is no empirical evidence as to the effect that his stolid presence has had on the votes of the living members of the board of trustees.

The Mummy's Veto Power

Bentham's Hedonism

Despite the lengthy agonizing over the definition of happiness that we find in philosophies such as those of Plato and Aristotle, Bentham has little trouble defining it quite simply as pleasure, as did Epicurus before him. Therefore, we say that the foundation of Bentham's ethics is hedonism, with which you are now familiar. In fact, there are serious problems with this equation, as you will see, but it does have the advantage of finding the criterion of morality to be something we all recognize with relative clarity, certainly in ourselves and probably in others. We may struggle with the question Am I happy? but the question Is there more pleasure in my life than there is misery? will probably draw a fairly quick response.

Is there pain in your life?

Yes!

Are you happy?

I don't have the slightest idea.

However, under Bentham's scrutiny, the idea of pleasure appears to be more complicated than it might seem at first glance. There are, according to him, *simple* and *complex* pleasures, complex pleasures being combinations of simple pleasures. There are fourteen types of simple pleasure. The first one, sensual pleasure, is quite obvious, but it too is subdivided. There are the pleasures of taste, of smell, of touch, of sound, and of sight. Of course, Bentham does not fail to include sexual pleasure in this list of the delights of the senses. He also includes drunken pleasure, as well as the pleasures of health and of novelty. The remaining twelve types of simple pleasure include pleasures of friendship, of wealth, of skill, of a good name, of religious sentiment, of power, of imagination,

Religious Pleasure
Saint Teresa in Ecstasy
(after Gianlorenzo Bernini, 1652)

of expectation, of relief, of intellectual activity, of benevolence, and of malevolence. (This last pleasure seems strikingly out of place, but Bentham does not shy away from admitting that there is a side of human nature that enjoys causing others to be miserable; therefore, this pleasure too needs listing.) As with sensual pleasure, Bentham finds that many of the other simple pleasures also have numerous subdivisions. Complex pleasures are those provided by activities that combine various simple pleasures. (Bentham does not say whether there is any one activity that combines all fourteen of the simple pleasures and their subcategories into one great pleasure.) You will probably not be surprised to hear that Bentham also provides a catalogue of all the possible forms of pain and their many subdivisions. (One gets the impression that Bentham left one pleasure off his list—the pleasure taken in compiling long, tedious lists.)

Now, if there are this many pleasures and pains, how do we evaluate them? Are they all of equal value? In fact, says Bentham, pleasures are all of equal value—in the sense that there is no natural hierarchy of value. According to Bentham,

> Prejudice apart, the game of push-pin is of equal value with the arts and sciences of music and poetry. If the game of push-pin furnishes more pleasure, it is more valuable than either.[7]

Two questions come to mind. First, what is push-pin, and how do we get in on the game? Second, how can Bentham say something this outrageous? I can't answer the first question. (My dictionary says only that it's an early children's game.) The second question I'll address by pointing out that Ben-

Young Jeremy at Work

tham doesn't say push-pin *is* better than poetry or music; rather he says that it is better *if* it furnishes more pleasure. Well, *does* it?

The Calculus of Felicity

To answer questions such as whether one pastime furnishes more pleasure than another, Bentham provides us with a mathematical test called the **Calculus of Felicity** (or the "Felicific Calculus"). It is yet another list—this one of seven characteristics that any pleasure may have. We are to apply this list as a guide to choosing not among different pleasures, but among different *activities*. If two (or more) ideas presented themselves to you as possible activities, acts, or projects, how would you choose between them in the most rational and moral manner? According to Bentham, you would consider the pleasures that each of them were likely to produce, and analyze them in terms of the seven categories of the Calculus of Felicity:

1. Intensity —— (How intense are the pleasures likely to be?)
2. Duration——— (How long are the pleasures likely to last?)
3. Certainty —— (How certain are the pleasures?)
4. Propinquity—— (How soon will the pleasures be available?)
5. Fecundity —— (How many more pleasures are likely to follow in their wake?)
6. Purity——— (How free from pain are the pleasures?)
7. Extent ——— (The pleasure of how many people will be affected by your acts?)

For example, say you need to study for tomorrow's chemistry examination, but it turns out that today promises to be the most glorious day of the year. The beach positively beckons. Try out the Calculus on such a decision—

On a scale of one to ten, this is a "ten" in all categories.

studying for a chemistry midterm or going to the beach with some friends. Obviously, the beach party will be strong in some categories (1, 3, 4, 6) and weaker in others (2, 5). Studying will be weak in most categories but strong in a few (2 and 5, and 7 also, if others have an interest in your succeeding in college). Are the assets of studying strong enough to overcome its deficits in the face of the fun enticing you to the beach? (Of course, the guilt you would experience at the beach has to be taken into consideration too.)

Beach Guilt

We can imagine that if Bentham had lived in today's world of inexpensive calculators, he would have invented a pocket "calculator of felicity." The image of someone punching the values of various acts into a calculator seems a bit ridiculous, but Bentham thought that his Calculus of Felicity was actually the schematization of something we do semiconsciously (hence often poorly) anyway and that once we became experienced in manipulating these figures, we would be able to do it intuitively.

Looking back at the Calculus, take note of category 7, "extent." It is this category that makes Bentham's utilitarianism a form of social hedonism, as opposed to the individualistic hedonism that you have already seen in the cases of Epicurus, Hobbes, and Rand. One must consider the pleasures and pains of others and not only one's own. In fact, what Bentham and Mill called the "principle of utility" stresses precisely this aspect, which shows that altruism is required as a component of utilitarianism: "the greatest amount of happiness for the greatest number of people." If an act I am about to perform will bring much happiness to a large number of people, then I should perform it even if it brings mostly discomfort to me. But, how is altruism possible? First, recall that, for Bentham, one of the simple pleasures is the pleasure of benevolence. We take pleasure in promoting the happiness of others, and we are often willing to forgo certain pleasures of the senses to be of service to others. Furthermore, if pleasure is the key value in Bentham's theory of motivation, then it takes precedence over the value of selfhood (or me-first-ism). The idea of pleasure is more basic than the idea of selfhood. Of course, I want pleasure for myself, but I am motivated to produce pleasure at large as well. (Notice that neither of these justifications really talks about altruism in its strictest sense, where I sacrifice my own interests for the interests of others. In the first case, I take pleasure in my benevolence toward others. In the second case, selfhood ["I"/"they"] evanesces, or fades away, and only pleasure remains. But perhaps Bentham's idea is compatible with a weaker definition of altruism, according to which altruism would be the claim that it is sometimes possible to prioritize the interests of others over your own.)

One Person, One Vote

Besides this social aspect of Bentham's utilitarianism, there is also a democratic bias built into it. When it comes to evaluating acts in terms of the pleasure they will produce, Bentham firmly believed in the "one person, one vote" principle or as he stated it, "everybody to count for one, nobody for more than one."[8] Each person's judgment is as important as every other person's. No one—be she your parent or the state—has the right to *inform* you that you are or are not having fun.

If push-pin is your thing, vote for it! If it provides a greater amount of happiness for a greater number of people than its alternatives, then push-pin it is!

You are now enjoying yourselves! This is an official proclamation!

Facts and Values

There are some serious problems with Bentham's rather facile equation of happiness with pleasure. Indeed, shortly you will see Mill and other later utilitarians trying to do damage control. But here, I want to mention briefly another difficulty with Bentham's view, namely, its collision with the is/ought problem, a

Fascistic Hedonism

topic you have already read about in each of the preceding chapters. Bentham begins his *Introduction to the Principles of Morals and Legislation* with this claim about pleasure and pain:

They govern us in all we do, in all we say, in all we think: every effort we can make to throw off our subjection, will serve but to demonstrate and confirm it. In words a man may pretend to abjure their empire: but in reality he will remain subject to it all the while. (1)

Even if you did accept Bentham's deterministic claim that every thought and action is motivated by the pursuit of pleasure and the flight from pain, it certainly wouldn't follow logically that you have a moral obligation to seek pleasure. First, it only makes sense to say that you are morally obligated to do X if it is possible to do not-X. (You are not morally obligated to obey the laws of gravity, even though you are certainly physically constrained by those onerous laws.) But Bentham's wording here commits us to a determinism from which we cannot escape. Even if we reword his statement to eliminate the determinism (e.g., if we say there is a strong tendency to be motivated by the pursuit of pleasure), there is no legitimate logical jump from that assertion to the claim that we are morally obligated to pursue pleasure. Once again, "is" does not imply "ought." As we proceed through this chapter, we will see if later utilitarians manage to support the principle of utility without committing the naturalistic fallacy.

John Stuart Mill

John Stuart Mill (1806–1873) was probably the most influential British intellectual of his day. As a philosopher, his interests and writings ranged over the fields of logic, metaphysics, social philosophy, and moral philosophy. He was also known as an economist and as a feminist. His works were written not only for philosophers and professionals but for a general public, and they were widely read. He was born in London into a well-known middle-class family. He was the son of Harriet Burrow Mill and James Mill, whose own father had been a shoemaker in Scotland. James Mill had achieved his education thanks to the patronage of a Scottish aristocrat, Sir John Stuart (after whom John Stuart Mill was named), and, before his son's birth, James had already developed a reputation as a philosopher and an economist and had become a disciple of Jeremy Bentham. All of this, his son would also do later. He would also work as an administrator in the same company as his father.

**John Stuart Mill with the
Mummified Head of Jeremy Bentham**

James Mill homeschooled his son, giving him one of the most rigorous educations on record. Little John Stuart started studying Greek at three and Latin at eight. By his early teens he had read the classical literature of Greece and Rome in the original languages, as well as having made a broad study of mathematics, logic, and history. He also read the philosophy of Jeremy Bentham (in French!) and became a dedicated disciple. However, in his twentieth year he had a nervous breakdown from which he suffered for months. In his auto-biography he blamed his sudden fall into chronic depression on the strictness, narrowness, and intensity of the education to which his father had submitted him. After he slowly emerged from under his dark cloud, he began to question many of the ideas into which he had been indoctrinated, including the utilitarianism of his father's good friend and mentor, Jeremy Bentham. To cure himself, he read Wordsworth.

In the meantime, John Stuart's father, an important functionary in the East India Company, had arranged for his son to work as a clerk in that enterprise, which was one of the strong arms of British capitalism, imperialism, and colonialism. John Stuart remained with the company for thirty-five years, working his way up to high office, all the while writing and publishing his philosophical, moral, social, and economic theories. Though his life seems to have been rather uneventful, it did have its rewards. One such reward was his long Platonic friendship with Harriet Taylor, whom he had met in 1823. She was a highly intelligent woman, and about Mill's age, but unfortunately she was already the wife of an acquaintance and the mother of a number of children. He admired her wit, insight, and critical ability, and he clearly fell in love with her. Their chaste relationship lasted for years. When her husband died in 1849, after waiting a respectable three years, Mill and Mrs. Taylor married.

Harriet Taylor was a great influence on Mill's thinking, especially on his feminism as expressed in *On the Subjection of Women*. Nine years later, while the Mills were visiting the south of France, Harriet died in Avignon, where she is buried. Mill built a house near the cemetery to be near her final resting place, and upon retirement from the then-defunct East India Company, he spent much of his time in Avignon. Harriet's daughter, Helen, took care of Mill for fifteen years after Harriet's death, and she was in attendance when Mill died at sixty-seven in 1873.

Mill's Rejection of the Calculus

You saw that Mill's adolescence was a period of unquestioning dedication to Bentham's philosophy; then, after his nervous breakdown, he backed away from Benthamite views, and when he did return to them, he had revised them considerably. By the time he wrote *Utilitarianism* in 1861, he was still willing to define happiness using Bentham's terms: "By happiness is intended pleasure, and the absence of pain; by unhappiness, pain, and the privation of pleasure"[9].

But the reason he now accepted Bentham's language is that in the meantime he had expanded the meaning of Bentham's term "pleasure." Bentham had understood this sensation to be *quantitative*—the Calculus of Felicity involved a numerical analysis: How intense? How long? How soon? etc.—but Mill had decided that the idea of pleasure also admits of *qualitative* analysis.

Mill felt that an adherent of Bentham's Calculus might indeed conclude that push-pin (or watching football on TV) is better than the arts and sciences, and Mill felt in his heart that such a conclusion is not true. Utilitarianism would have to be rewritten in such a way as to demonstrate that the reading of Shakespearean sonnets is of more value than some of its alternatives. The absence of qualitative distinctions in the Calculus entailed the erosion of culture over a number of generations.

In order to bring Mill's concern into our own time, imagine offering the following proposition to the electorate of a particular state: "It has been determined that the teaching of Shakespeare in the schools, colleges, and universities of this state costs each taxpayer $25 every three years. Now, the state would like to know if you taxpayers would prefer to continue paying $25 each to cover the next three years of instruction of Shakespeare, or would you prefer a rebate of $25 in the form of two cases of beer per taxpayer?" Mill was afraid that, given the tenuous foothold that culture has among the masses and given Bentham's "one person, one vote" principle, people would go for the beer. In a number of generations, no one would even remember who Shakespeare was.

In order to counteract the possibility of this dumbing down of culture, Mill insisted that it was part of our human heritage to have desires higher than those that lent themselves exclusively to analysis in terms of the Calculus of Felicity. In *Utilitarianism*, he expressed it this way:

> Few human creatures would consent to be changed into any of the lower animals, for a promise of the fullest allowance of a beast's pleasures; no intelligent human being would consent to be a fool, no instructed person would be an ignoramus, no person of feeling and conscience would be selfish and base, even though they should be persuaded the fool, the dunce, or the rascal is better satisfied with his lot than they are with theirs. (10)

Apparently, Mill felt that the "lower" desires (those of animals and perhaps the most biologically basic human desires) could be adequately dealt with in terms of the quantitative analysis provided by the Calculus of Felicity but that the "higher" desires could be talked about only in terms of quality, something that no calculus could evaluate. According to Mill in *Utilitarianism*,

It is quite compatible with the principle of utility to recognize the fact that some kinds of pleasure are more desirable and more valuable

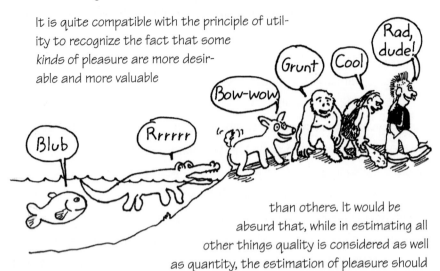

The Evolution of Pleasure

than others. It would be absurd that, while in estimating all other things quality is considered as well as quantity, the estimation of pleasure should be supposed to depend on quantity alone. If I am asked what I mean by difference of quality in pleasures, or what makes one pleasure more valuable than another, merely as pleasure, except its being greater in amount, there is but one possible answer. Of two pleasures, if there be one to which all or almost all who have experience of both give a decided preference, irrespective of any feeling of moral obligation to prefer it, that is the more desirable pleasure. If one of the two is, by those who are competently acquainted with both, placed so far above the other that they prefer it, even though knowing it to be attended with a greater amount of discontent, and would not resign it for any quantity of the other pleasure which their nature is capable of, we are justified in ascribing to the preferred enjoyment a superiority in quality so far outweighing quantity as to render it, in comparison, of small account. (10)

These passages have provoked some critics to bring a pair of related charges against Mill. The accusation is that in his attempt to preserve "culture" from the barbarians, (a) Mill has abandoned hedonism, hence abandoned utilitarianism itself, and (b) Mill has replaced utilitarianism's democratic commitment with elitism. We will look briefly at each of these charges.

Has Mill abandoned hedonism? At first glance, it does not seem so, because he still admits that the sole criterion of value is pleasure.

But he also claims that some pleasures are *better* (more valuable) than others. We must ask, more valuable according to what criterion? The criterion can't be just "pleasure" because some pleasures are *better* than others, and "better" here no longer means "more intense, purer, more lengthy, more certain, more immanent," and so on with the other quantitative categories. Rather, it means "has more quality." But what is this elusive thing called "quality" that only those who have experienced it can recognize? In an odd way, we seem to have exchanged utilitarianism for virtue ethics and the world of Plato's and Aristotle's doctrine of **areté** (virtue, excellence). Indeed, one of the English translations of *areté* is "quality."[10] (We will look into this idea more in Chapter 6.) In *Utilitarianism*, speaking of the virtues, Mill says, "They are desired and desirable in and for themselves; besides being means, they are part of the end" (44–5). There does seem to be some tension between claiming that only happiness can be an end in itself and claiming that because virtue is a *part* of happiness, it too can be willed as an end in itself. Still, most contemporary utilitarians have abandoned hedonism, and some have even spurned the term "happiness" as utilitarianism's goal, replacing it with "interests," "well-being," or "human flourishing."

One Person, One Vote?

We will now turn to the second objection that Mill's passage on quality has provoked. Has Mill abandoned utilitarianism's democratic commitment (one person, one vote) for a form of elitism? The basis of the charge can be seen in Mill's well-known line, "The uncultivated cannot be competent judges of cultivation."[11]

We are, after all, civilized.

The Uncultivated Cannot Be Competent Judges of Cultivation

Remember from above: In choosing between the value of reading Shakespearean sonnets and drinking beer in one's closet, only "those who have experience of both" are warranted in having their opinion taken seriously. If one must demonstrate "competence" before one is granted a vote, then on many issues, only a small minority will have the right to express an opinion. This minority will often turn out to be the best educated, the wealthiest, and most powerful segment of society. Indeed, we are told that Mill had been strongly influenced by Alexis de Tocqueville's critique of American democracy and by Samuel Taylor Coleridge's argument that one should consider "the cultured class as the leader of opinion in a nation."[12]

On the other hand, Mill's fear for the future of culture was not motivated merely by elitism. In a populist participatory democracy where everybody is eligible to vote on all decisions, beer might very well win out over Shakespeare. (In the United States, we have accepted a compromise version of Mill's solution. We are not a "participatory democracy" but a "representative democracy." Not everyone votes on all issues; rather we elect representatives who in theory are, by virtue of their excellent education and paid staff of assistants, competent to decide certain issues concerning which we ourselves have no competence. However, in some states the citizens reserve the right, through the initiative process, to bypass those representatives on certain matters. In California, in 1978, Proposition 13 gave the voters such an opportunity. As I see it, they went for the beer.)

Tough Benthamite Decisions

Why Should We Do It?

Finally, in our discussion of Mill's version of utilitarianism, I will ask whether his justification of its foundation is satisfactory. Ultimately, why *should* we desire happiness? As Mill wrote in *Utilitarianism*,

> The only proof capable of being given that an object is visible, is that people actually see it. The only proof that a sound is audible, is that people hear it: and so of the other sources of our experi-

ence. In like manner, I apprehend, the sole evidence it is possible to produce that anything is desirable, is that people do actually desire it. (43)

Virtually all commentators on this passage dwell on its flaws. Saying, "X is visible" may indeed mean "X can be seen," and saying, "X is audible" may mean "X can be heard"; but saying, "X is desirable" does not mean "X can be desired." When we say that X is desirable, we imply that X is desire-worthy—that X ought to be desired. But, as Hume said, "No 'is' implies an 'ought'." Once again, from the fact (if it is a fact) that everyone does desire happiness, it does not follow that everyone should desire happiness. So it looks to me as though Mill's defense of utilitarianism's foundation has not advanced over Bentham's. You will see shortly what more contemporary utilitarians have said about this problem.

Utilitarianism: A More Precise Characterization

We have taken a brief look at utilitarianism's origins in a moral intuition concerning the supreme value of human welfare, an intuition that has been shared by many individuals and schools in a number of cultures throughout history. Then, by looking at utilitarianism's two most famous defenders, Jeremy Bentham and John Stuart Mill, we have seen how these historical philosophers each in his own way tried to build an ethical and legal system around that intuition. At this point, we will try to formulate a more precise characterization of this moral theory than has been presented so far. It is necessary to attempt this because of contradictions and discrepancies among the various philosophers who are thought of as utilitarians and who called themselves by that name. Unlike the adherents of one or another particular religious tradition, those moral philosophers who have been attracted to utilitarianism do not feel the need to create a system that is true to the "holy scriptures" of the "prophets" (in this case, Bentham and Mill).

Two Prophets of Pleasure

Rather, they want to develop a consistent moral theory that is based on the fundamental vision of Bentham and Mill (and their fore-runners) concerning the relation between moral action and human well-being; but they do not feel obliged to become merely interpreters of the pioneers, nor even to agree with those pioneers, much less to agree among themselves. The result is that utilitarianism has become a kind of "baggy monster" that is hard to define. To this end, I will use a helpful categorization scheme that I am borrowing from the British philosopher Geoffrey Scarre.

Utilitarianism can be conceived in terms of five categories. Utilitarians are (1) welfarist, (2) consequentialist, (3) aggregative,

(4) maximizing , and (5) universalist. These categories are not definitional; not every one of the five categories will necessarily be found in every philosophy calling itself utilitarianism. Scarre calls the five categories "family resemblances" (4). Like family resemblance in real families, not all of these characteristics will be present in every member, but they will wind their way throughout any sustained discussion of utilitarianism. We will look briefly at each of the five categories.

Welfarist

Utilitarian theories try to define moral value in terms of some interrelated categories having to do with welfare—usually the welfare of human beings, but sometimes extended to the welfare of all sentient beings.

Utilitarians do not always agree on the terms appropriate for naming the constituent components of welfare. We have seen attempts to do so in terms of "pleasure" and "happiness," but one sometimes sees prioritizing in terms of "well-being," "interests," "desires," and "flourishing" in addition.

Consequentialist

Utilitarian ethics concentrate on the results or consequences of acts rather than on, say, the authority behind the commandments (as in some religiously grounded moral theories) or on the intentions behind the acts (as in Immanuel Kant's ethics, studied in Chapter 3). An act, or the rule governing acts—this distinction will be clarified shortly—is morally correct if the consequences of the act (or of obeying the rule) are better—or no worse—than those of following its alternatives. The word "better" in the foregoing sentence is, of course, defined in terms of welfare, as treated in the previous paragraph.

Aggregative

Utilitarian ethics assumes that the good—welfare in any of its multiple guises—can be quantified. (Oddly enough, this means that in Mill's case, quality can be quantified.) That is, there can be more or less of the good in such a way that different cases can be compared and contrasted with each other. For utilitarians, this aggregative feature of goodness means that any one of two alternative acts or situations consequentially involves either more, less, or the same amount of welfare (pleasure, happiness, well-being, flourishing) as the other alternative, and that we can make rational comparisons of these different alternatives. Notice that this last point assumes that all humans (or in the case of some utilitarian theories, humans and animals) have enough in common that we as individuals can make these comparisons. This probably means that we are able to "put ourselves in the other's shoes," and are capable of imagining the suffering and joy of other beings.

Maximizing

Utilitarian ethics seems committed to the moral project of the maximization of welfare, or, as the principle of utility has it, seeking "*the greatest amount of good* for the greatest number of people." We are required to be in a state of constant moral vigilance. There are no morally neutral situations. We must always try to increase well-being.

Universalist

Utilitarian ethics seems committed to the moral project of the universalizing of welfare or, as the principle of utility has it, seeking "the greatest amount of good *for the greatest number of people.*" Welfare (or happiness, etc.) must not only be maximized—as much of it as possible—but it must be distributed as broadly as possible. This is the side of utilitarianism that, as philosopher Samuel Scheffler has said, holds that "any person, no matter how poor, or powerless, or socially marginal, no matter how remote from the centers of influence and privilege, may, by invoking moral principles, assert a claim or express a grievance in the language of a system to which nobody, however rich, powerful, or well-bred, may claim immunity."[13]

Attacks on Utilitarianism and Utilitarian Defenses

On the face of it, utilitarianism is plausible. It does indeed appear that morality must essentially have something to do with promoting happiness and well-being and with minimizing unhappiness and misery. It would be odd to claim that some act was good even though it brought nothing but unhappiness and misery to absolutely everybody. Therefore, there must be something right about the view that an act is good if it brings happiness and well-being to everyone, and this just happens to be utilitarianism's view. Still, some serious problems arise with utilitarianism. We will review some of the more salient difficulties next.

The Problem of Meritoriousness and Fairness

The essence of the problem of meritoriousness and fairness can be revealed in a fictitious example. Suppose you had to go to court for failing to pay a few parking fines. You are alone in a small courtroom with the judge, the bailiff, and the court reporter. After the bailiff reads the charge ("failure to pay three fines for expired parking meters"), you respond ("Guilty, your Honor"), and she announces her judgment: "I find you guilty on all charges. The punishment will be that you shall suffer death at the hands of a firing squad." "What?!!" you scream. "Death for three lousy parking tickets??" The judge leans forward and whispers, "I know you don't deserve this punishment, but there has been a rash of murders in our community, and a study has just been released demonstrating that immediately after an execution, the crime rate drops substantially. Unfortunately, we don't have any convicted murderers on our hands right now. But we do have you, and there is good reason to believe that if we execute you, the public good will be served. Hence, even though my decision may seem unfair to you personally, it will certainly promote the greatest amount of happiness for the greatest number of people. So it is the only judgment I can really reach in good conscience."

Take another example, one that appears in almost every critical discussion of utilitarianism

Please! I promise not to overpark again!

and that even has a name: the "case of Sam." Sam, a basically normal, rather nondescript, but "nice" human being, goes to the hospital to visit his only living relative, his senile, sick aunt. His visit coincides with five medical emergencies at the hospital. One person needs a liver transplant, another a spleen transplant, another a lung transplant, another a new heart, and a fifth a new pineal gland. Each of the five patients is a tremendously important, much-loved person whose death would bring a great deal of grief and actual physical discomfort to a great number of people. Sam's death, however, would be mourned by no one (except possibly by his aunt in her rare lucid moments). The top members of the hospital administration, all strict utilitarians, lure Sam into an operating room, remove all his vital organs, and distribute them to the other needy patients, thereby operating (literally) in accordance with the principle of utility: the greatest amount of happiness for the greatest number of people.

Sam Visiting His Sick Aunt

The reason that these fictitious cases are so jarring is that they go so radically against our intuitive sense of justice and meritoriousness. Neither the parking meter violator nor Sam deserves the fate dished out by the executing judge and the hospital staff. Because these cases are compatible with utilitarianism, either something is wrong with our intuitive sense of justice or something is wrong with utilitarianism. Well, could there be something wrong with our so-called intuitive sense of justice? Certainly philosophical minds should be prepared to challenge the trustworthiness of all intuitions. Intuitions may, after all, be the flawed product of historical bias and prejudice. Apparently one of the most radical of the utilitarians, William Godwin (1756–1836), thought such was the case with traditional moral feelings. Godwin was the husband of Mary Wollstonecraft, the feminist author of *A Vindication of the Rights of Woman*, and he was the father of Mary Shelley, who as a teenager penned *Frankenstein*. Godwin believed that any moral obligation not derived from the principle of utility is unjustifiable—for example, the supposed obligation to make more of an effort to protect one's family than to protect strangers—and he believed that *all* of the consequences of the principle of utility should be rigorously accepted. Innocent individuals *could* be executed if doing so promoted public welfare, and people being saved from a burning building should be selected in the order of their likely public usefulness. Still, despite Godwin's advice, most people are more likely to jettison a theory like utilitarianism than to go against their sense of justice if the two conflict.

Act Utilitarianism and Rule Utilitarianism

Even though no utilitarian wants to base moral theory on intuition, many contemporary utilitarians have recognized the power of the sense of justice and meritoriousness and have tried to adjust utilitarian theory to correspond more with our intuitions. To this end, they have drawn a distinction between act utilitarianism and rule utilitarianism. The term "act utilitarianism" designates the traditional form. According to it, one must perform the specific *act* that will produce the greatest amount of happiness for the greatest number of people. To the contrary, "rule utilitarianism" says—in a formulation reminiscent of Kant— that in contemplating which of two acts to perform, a person should choose that act governed by a (hypothetical) rule whose general obedience would produce the greatest amount of happiness for the greatest number of people. According to rule utilitarianism, even if a particular self-serving deceit or lie may go undetected, hence cause no one any unhappiness, I should probably not engage in it because, generally, lying and deceiving cause more unhappiness than happiness. It also means that the executing judge and the hospital administrators cannot proceed as they desire because the rule governing their acts would be something like this: "If the lives of a number of people (or even a few exceptional people) can be saved by sacrificing an innocent bystander, the sacrifice should be performed." But such a rule would not produce the greatest amount of happiness because members of a community who knew that they might be set upon by the authorities and arbitrarily killed or disemboweled would be members of a community of fear, one whose citizens would be loath to set foot on the streets in daylight.

A Community of Fear

In this case, rule utilitarianism seems to correspond better with our intuitions about justice.

But rule utilitarianism itself might lead to unpalatable consequences. One critic asks, "What about the Dutch family during World War II who hid Jews in their attic?" According to rule utilitarianism, when the Gestapo comes to their house looking for Jews, would this family be required to answer truthfully on the grounds that lying generally creates more unhappiness than does honesty and that therefore one may not lie? But perhaps the rule utilitarian can operate according to the general rule "Lying is wrong, except when directed to evildoers in order to save the lives of innocent people." The problem here is that there is no principle to govern these kinds of ad hoc adjustments to the general rule, and this invites abuse. One begins to suspect that the clever, self-serving rule utilitarian can think of a general rule to rationalize all sorts of questionable behavior. ("Shoplifting from large department stores is okay as long as the store chain continues earning large profits," or even more brazenly, "It's okay as long as one does not get caught and no one ever finds out.") Such rationalizations would surely begin to unravel rule utilitarianism.

The Consequentialist Problem

According to the view we are now studying, no act is good or bad in and of itself. Rather, an act is good or bad only in terms of its consequences.

Acts that result in happiness, well-being, and flourishing are good; acts that result in the opposite are bad. Now, there is a certain prima facie plausibility to this view, but at some point it too runs up against

the moral intuition of many people because a lot of us feel that certain acts, such as wanton cruelty, are bad in and of themselves regardless of their consequences. We also feel that some acts—such as heroic self-sacrifice to come to the aid of the needy—are right, independent of their consequences. People who are dedicated to preserving biodiversity and protecting endangered species do so not because they believe that their commitment will produce a greater amount of happiness, but because they believe that these goals have intrinsic value in themselves. If utilitarianism in its standard forms is true, then these dedicated moral agents are wrong. There are no intrinsic values except happiness.

Consequentialism: The moral worth of act X depends on the consequences of X.

Nonconsequentialism: The moral worth of act X depends exclusively on act X.

The Problem of Utilitarian Sainthood

The question here is Does utilitarianism make too heavy a demand on the individual? Utilitarianism is selfless. The principle of utility, urging us to pursue the greatest amount of happiness for the greatest number of people, is impartial; the agent has no justification for considering his or her own happiness to be in any way more important than that of any other human on the face of the earth. Breaking this rule of impartiality is always immoral. Contrast this with Jesus's Golden Rule: Do unto others as you would have them do unto you. Here, one's own happiness seems to become a kind of standard in deciding how to promote the happiness of others—but not in utilitarianism. Utilitarianism's "Do unto others . . ." seems to entail sacrificing a great part of your own happiness if doing so will be beneficial to others. (It is true that Jesus tells a rich young man to sell all of his possessions and give them to the poor, but, as Geoffrey Scarre points out, Jesus prefaces the command with the line "If thou wilt be perfect . . ." [Matt. 19:21]. Bentham's preface appears to be more like "If thou wilt be moral. . . .")

Some critics of utilitarianism think that this demand is psychologically impossible to meet, and they hold that any moral philosophy that makes impossible demands is absurd ("ought" implies "can," they say). Therefore, according to these critics, the feature of utilitarianism that demands sainthood of all constitutes what logicians call a **reductio ad absurdum** of utilitarianism (reduction to an absurdity), and therefore utilitarianism is not worthy of our serious consideration.

Utilitarians seem to have had several different kinds of response to this criticism. Some bite the bullet and agree that utilitarianism does indeed make saintly demands of us, even if we all fail to achieve the level of goodness that (utilitarian) morality requires of us. Concerning the discrepancy of poverty levels among the most affluent and least affluent nations, the Australian utilitarian Peter Singer has argued that the richer nations are morally obligated to donate to the poorer nations an amount of money that would result roughly in an equivalence of resources. Similarly, individuals are morally prohibited from "spending money on new clothes or a new car instead of giving it to famine relief."[14] In public interviews, Singer has claimed that he donates large portions of his personal income to organizations that provide for the needy, though he makes no claim to have achieved moral sainthood.

Another kind of response argues that utilitarianism is not averse to pragmatic compromise. Every moral agent simply has to do the best he or she can to uphold the principle of utility, and does not need to try to push this principle to unreasonable or absurd ends. Yet another response is to admit that it is not at all unusual nor unhealthy for human beings to pursue certain personal commitments, projects, and ambitions in a manner that is disproportionate to the level of their concern about the general interests of others; indeed, according to this argument, it would be an odd person who did not. In fact, such forms of self-interested behavior constitute a large part of what it is to be a human being, and to take it away would be to take away something of their humanity as well as their individuality. Therefore, any attempt to outlaw morally such pursuit of personal projects and concerns by demanding only an impersonal quest for utility in the abstract would thwart the very principles of utilitarianism. Geoffrey Scarre, who seems to hold this view, puts it this way:

> The basic idea behind this strategy is that a world of people who pay some special attention to their own favoured projects and aspirations is likelier to be a happier world than one in which everyone tries to be a moral saint. Allowing people scope to live their own lives and develop individual personalities not only makes them happier themselves, but enables them to become more sensitive and efficient producers of happiness for others. (190)

In other words, according to Scarre, "The fulfilment of each individual's goals is a proper part of the general good" (201). In this version of utilitarianism, there will still be constant tension in balancing one's personal goals against the great amount of misery suffered by so many people throughout the world at any given time. It appears that, even here, more self-sacrifice will be required than most people are prepared to make.

The Problem of Consistency

The preceding discussion raises this question: Are the two parts of the principle of utility consistent? Do they tend to cancel out each other? If I pursue the principle of maximization (the greatest amount of happiness . . .) and the principle of universalization (. . . for the greatest number of people), don't I level all pleasure out so that each individual has exactly the same amount? It seems that nobody would be really happy; everyone would be equally unhappy. Also, there would be even less production of goods for the needy because producers would know that the bulk of their production would go to someone else. Is it possible to pursue both maximization of happiness and universalization of happiness at the same time without betraying one for the other?

The Is/Ought Problem

Here, the question is Why should we believe utilitarianism to be true? Utilitarianism makes heavy demands on us, so it had better answer this question in a convincing manner. Ideally, when we have to make important decisions, we can appeal to certain facts in the world that help us make a reasonable choice. Are there any facts—either about human nature, human society, or the natural world—that we might find compelling enough to force us to opt for utilitarianism as a moral guide? Well, as you may remember from Chapter 1, the very wording of that question causes problems for anyone trying to justify the choice of one moral code over another. The stumbling block is the warning against the so-called naturalistic fallacy, which is the error of deducing moral claims from empirical facts about the world (similar to David Hume's "No 'is' implies an 'ought'"). We have already seen that both Bentham and Mill try to make such a leap, deducing from the fact that we *do* seek happiness the claim that we *ought* to do so. This is recognized by almost all philosophers as a false deduction—a genuine fallacy. Yet, indeed, utilitarianism does presuppose a linkage between the fact of the desire for happiness and the desirability (goodness) of happiness. Has any utilitarian managed to demonstrate such a linkage?

In my view, the closest thing to a successful attempt to demonstrate a logical connection between the moral demands of utilitarianism and empirical facts about human nature is one provided by the British philosopher Hugo Meynell in his book *Freud, Marx and Morals*. Meynell would agree that the good cannot be *defined* in terms of the desire for happiness—or in terms of any other empirical facts about human beings. There is no relation of **"strict entailment"** (as he calls a logically **necessary connection**) between happiness and any moral judgment at all. But he claims that there does exist an important logical link of another kind between them—a relationship that he calls "loose entailment." Meynell explains this concept this way:

> Statement A loosely entails statements p, q, r and s, when to assert A and at the same time to negate p (or any single one of the others) is not to contradict oneself, though to assert A and to negate p, q, r, and s all together is either to contradict oneself or to talk so eccentrically as to be unintelligible.[15]

He believes that Ludwig Wittgenstein demonstrated the meaning and significance of loose entailments in the famous analysis of the concept of "game" in his *Philosophical Investigations* (to which you were briefly introduced in Chapter 1) by showing that even though we all understand the concept quite well, no one can exhaustively define it; there are no necessary connections between the concept of "game" and any of its distinctive components. We conceive of games in terms of amusement, competition, skill, and luck. However, we can all think of games that do not involve luck, others that do not involve skill, others that are not competitive, and some that are not amusing, even if they were meant to be. The point is, as you may recall, they do not cease to be games when they stop being fun— we are still playing Monopoly even when we are sick and tired of it.

People Not Enjoying Monopoly

According to Meynell,

Wittgenstein shows in effect that the statement that some human activity is a game does not strictly entail anything about it, but loosely entails a number of things about it, the absence of no one of which would disqualify it from being a game, but the absence of all of which would presumably do so. (165)

So if you said that X was a game, but that X was not fun (which is what I say about Monopoly, and what the losers said about Mayan

jai-lai), or that it was not competitive, and involved no skill or luck (as is true of ring-around-the-rosy), it is hard to see why you would call it a game at all. You can probably see where all this is going. If someone claimed that a particular action was good—even though he admitted that it brought no pleasure and no happiness to anyone; did not help overcome the discomfort or misery of anyone; contributed absolutely nothing to the flourishing or well-being of anybody; and in fact did nothing but promote pain, unhappiness, and misery for everyone—then, according to Meynell, the person who made that claim is speaking English in such an eccentric fashion that we might suspect that he did not understand the words he is using. Meynell is arguing that, in a loose sense, sometimes "is" does imply "ought." According to him, utilitarianism is logically justified by this loose entailment.

Perceived Strengths and Weaknesses
Strengths

— Utilitarianism's basic principle—the principle of utility—is easy to state and to understand.

— The principle of utility corresponds with certain widely experienced moral intuitions (e.g., acts that promote happiness and well-being and minimize misery are good; acts that produce more misery than happiness are bad).

— Utilitarianism's democratic bias and anti-elitism fit into the modern mentality.

— Utilitarianism's attempt to resolve moral problems empirically is laudable.

Weaknesses

— Despite its initial clarity and simplicity, working out the details of utilitarianism is complex and difficult.

— Some of Mill's "improvements" over Bentham's utilitarianism tend to undermine the one person, one vote advantage and promote elitism.

— Utilitarianism goes against the widely experienced moral intuition that some values besides happiness are good in and of themselves, and some acts are good or bad regardless of their consequences.

— Utilitarianism is often formulated in ways that bog it down in the is/ought problem.

Questions for Consideration

1. What do defenders of utilitarianism mean when they say that utilitarianism is "down-to-earth, democratic, and scornful of elitism"?

2. Why does the author say on page 186 that despite Francis Hutcheson's commitment to the greatest happiness principle, his defense of

this principle is un-utilitarian insofar as it appeals to intuitions derived from an innate moral sense?

3. On page 188, you read that Jeremy Bentham wanted to decriminalize (i.e., legalize) all "victimless crimes" (acts that have been designated as criminal, even though no one but the perpetrator suffers from them). Using utilitarian philosophy, write a long paragraph defending the decriminalization of drunkenness, prostitution, and drug use.

4. Reread question 3. Using utilitarianism as your guide, write a long paragraph defending the criminalization of drunkenness, prostitution, and drug use.

5. Pick some significant kind of decision that has presented itself to you, or that might do so in the future (such as whether to pursue higher education or enter the workforce, whether to marry or remain single, whether to have children), and analyze that choice in terms of all the categories of Bentham's Calculus of Felicity.

6. Bentham insists that his hedonistic theory is compatible with altruism—even extreme altruism, where one might be asked to sacrifice one's life for others. Do you agree with Bentham on this topic?

7. What features of utilitarianism provoke critics to say that it runs afoul of the is/ought problem?

8. What major revision is made by Mill of Bentham's version of utilitarianism?

9. Explain why some critics of Mill have claimed that his revision of Bentham entails an abandonment of Bentham's hedonism (the idea that all value is ultimately based on pleasure).

10. Explain why some critics of Mill have claimed that his revision of Bentham entails an abandonment of utilitarianism's democratic commitment and replaces it with elitism.

11. The utilitarian category of maximizing is based on the idea of maximizing pleasure ("the greatest amount of pleasure . . ."), while the category of universalizing is based on the idea of universalizing pleasure ("for the greatest number"). Are there problems with trying to pursue both categories at the same time?

12. Explain the differences between act utilitarianism and rule utilitarianism.

13. Do you think that rule utilitarianism successfully addresses what the author calls "the problem of meritoriousness and fairness" in utilitarianism?

14. What is the "problem of utilitarian sainthood"? In what ways have utilitarians addressed the problem?

15. How is Hugo Meynell's idea of loose entailment meant to address the is/ought problem that utilitarianism faces?

Study Guide: Outline of Chapter Four

I. History of utilitarian thought: a long tradition of utilitarian-related thinking.

II. Jeremy Bentham's utilitarianism.

    A. The principle of utility: the greatest amount of happiness for the greatest number.

    B. Hedonism: pleasure and pain the ultimate arbiters of value.

    C. The Calculus of Felicity.

        1. Its seven categories: intensity, duration, certainty, propinquity, fecundity, purity, extent.

        2. The move from egoistic to social hedonism.

            a. The pleasure of benevolence.

            b. The priority of pleasure over selfhood.

    D. The democratic bias: one person, one vote.

    E. Bentham and the is/ought problem.

III. John Stuart Mill's utilitarianism.

    A. Mill's acceptance of the principle of utility.

    B. Mill's criticism of Bentham's Calculus of Felicity.

        1. Some pleasures are qualitatively better than others.

        2. The application of a purely quantitative criterion of pleasure eventually erodes higher cultural values.

    C. Problems with Mill's version of utilitarianism.

        1. Does Mill abandon utilitarianism's hedonism (and does it matter if he does)?

        2. Does Mill promote elitism?

        3. Does Mill solve the is/ought problem for utilitarianism, or does he run aground on it?

IV. Contemporary discussions of utilitarianism.

    A. Scarre's five categories of utilitarianism: welfarist, consequentialist, aggregative, maximizing, and universalist.

    B. Contemporary attacks on utilitarianism and its defense.

        1. The problem of meritoriousness and fairness.

            a. Does traditional utilitarianism encourage unfairness (e.g., the punishment of innocent people where such punishment has utility)?

            b. Response: act utilitarianism vs. rule utilitarianism.

        2. The consequentialist problem.

            a. Are there really no other intrinsic values besides happiness?

            b. Aren't some acts good in and of themselves, rather than because of their consequences?

        3. The problem of utilitarian sainthood: Does utilitarianism make unreasonable demands on us?

        4. The is/ought problem again, and Hugo Meynell's response.

For Further Reading

Works on Ethics by Bentham and Mill

Bentham, Jeremy. *Introduction to the Principles of Morals and Legislation.* New York: Hafner Publishing Co., 1961.

Mill, John Stuart. *Utilitarianism,* in *Utilitarianism, Liberty, and Representative Government.* New York: Dutton and Co., 1959.

Secondary Works on Utilitarianism

Crisp, Roger. *Routledge Philosophy Guidebook to Mill's Utilitarianism.* London and New York: Routledge, 1997.

Miller, Harlan B., and H. Williams, eds. *The Limits of Utilitarianism.* Minneapolis: University of Minnesota Press, 1982.

Quinton, Anthony. *Utilitarian Ethics.* London: Macmillan, 1973.

Scarre, Geoffrey. *Utilitarianism.* London and New York: Routledge, 1996.

Scheffler, Samuel, ed. *Consequentialism and its Critics.* Oxford and New York: Oxford University Press, 1988.

Sen, Amartya, and Bernard Williams, eds. *Utilitarianism and Beyond.* Cambridge and New York: Cambridge University Press, 1982.

Smart, J. J. C., and Bernard Williams, eds. *Utilitarianism, For and Against.* Cambridge and New York: Cambridge University Press, 1973.

Thomas, William. *Mill.* Oxford and New York: Oxford University Press, 1985.

Notes

1. John Stuart Mill, *Utilitarianism*, in *Utilitarianism, Liberty, and Representative Government* (New York: Dutton and Co., 1959), 8. Future references to this work will be included parenthetically in the body of the text.

2. Geoffrey Scarre, *Utilitarianism* (London and New York: Routledge, 1996). Future references to this book will be included parenthetically in the body of the text.

3. Francis Hutcheson, *A System of Moral Philosophy*, in *British Moralists: Being Selections from Writers Principally from the Eighteenth Century*, ed. L. A. Selby-Bigge (Oxford: Clarendon Press, 1897), 107. Quoted in Scarre, 54.

4. David Hume, *Enquiries Concerning the Human Understanding and Concerning the Principles of Morals*, ed. L. A. Selby-Bigge (Oxford: Clarendon Press, 1995), 231.

5. Hume, 212. Emphases added.

6. Jeremy Bentham, *Introduction to the Principles of Morals and Legislation* (New York: Hafner Publishing Co., 1961). Unless otherwise indicated, all quotations from Bentham are taken from this work, and their page numbers will be included parenthetically in the body of the text.

7. Jeremy Bentham, *The Rationale of Reward*, in *The Works of Jeremy Bentham*, ed. John Bowring (Edinburgh: Tait, 1838–1843), vol. 2, sec. 1, p. 253. (Reprinted by Russell Publishing, New York, 1962.)

8. Quoted by Scarre, 105.

9. John Stuart Mill, *Utilitarianism*, in *Utilitarianism, Liberty, and Representative Government* (New York: Dutton and Co., 1959), 8. Future references to this work will be included parenthetically in the body of the text.

10. For an interesting and readable defense of the doctrine of areté as understood as "quality," see Robert Pirsig, *Zen and the Art of Motorcycle Maintenance* (New York: Bantam Books, 1975).

11. John Stuart Mill, *Principles of Political Economy*, in *Collected Works: John Stuart Mill*, vol. 3, ed. J. M. Robson (Toronto: University of Toronto Press/Routledge and Kegan Paul, 1965), 947.

12. J. B. Schneewind, "John Stuart Mill, " in *The Encyclopedia of Philosophy*, ed. Paul Edwards (London and New York: Macmillan Publishing Co. & Free Press, 1972), vol. 5, 315.

13. Samuel Scheffler, *Human Morality* (New York: Oxford University Press, 1992), 12; quoted in Scarre, 23.

14. Peter Singer, "Famine, Affluence, and Morality" (1972), in *Ethics and Public Policy: An Introduction to Ethics*, eds. Tom L. Beauchamp and Terry P. Pinkard (Engelwood Cliffs, N.J.: Prentice-Hall, 1983), 196.

15. Hugo Meynell, *Freud, Marx and Morals* (Totowa, N.J.: Barnes & Noble, 1981), 164. Future quotations from this book will be cited parenthetically in the body of the text.

5
Evolutionary Ethics

The theory of evolution of Charles Darwin (1809–1882) hit the British social and cultural world like, as one commentator put it, a plow smashing through an anthill. It provoked confusion and panic, and chaotic scurrying around, as the inhabitants tried to salvage damaged and scattered eggs and rearrange them in a semblance of order. Traditional morality—and with it, moral theory—took a hard hit, or so it seemed at the time. Two basic reactive strategies were developed. The first was an offensive strategy—an attempt to refute Darwin's theory, or at least to demonstrate its irrelevance to ethical issues; the second was a revisionist strategy—to reframe ethics itself, so that ethics could be compatible with the theory of evolution or even become an "evolutionary ethics." Both of these strategies began immediately upon surveying the plow's damage, and the two strands have carried on into our century. In this chapter, we will first examine Darwin's theory itself, looking for the reasons that it was perceived as a threat to moral order and to ethical theory; then we will look at recent attempts to construct an evolutionary ethics that would incorporate biological theory into ethical theory.

Charles Darwin

Darwin was born in Shrewsbury, Shropshire, in 1809. His father was a physician, and he sent sixteen-year-old Charles to Edinburgh University to continue in the family tradition. However, the squeamish lad was horrified by the idea of performing surgery, so his disappointed father sent his son to Christ's College at Cambridge to study for the ministry. But Charles was no more

Charles Darwin (1809–1882)

interested in divinity school than he was in medical school; he was more interested in his hobby of natural studies. When he was twenty-two years old, a stroke of good fortune brought him an invitation to join the crew of the HMS *Beagle* on its surveying expedition into the Atlantic and Pacific oceans as the unpaid conversationalist companion of the twenty-six-year-old captain. To his father's chagrin, Darwin accepted and soon had upstaged the official naturalist hired by Her Majesty's government. For all practical purposes Darwin became the *Beagle's* acting naturalist on its five-year journey. He collected some 900 pages of notes based on his observations, and in the three-year period after his return to England in 1837 Darwin worked out his theory of evolution.

The organization of his data was guided by two theoretical models of recent vintage. First, while sailing on the *Beagle*, Darwin read Sir Charles Lyell's *Principles of Geology* (1830–33), which argued that the same natural forces that were at work in the nineteenth century had been at work in the remote past. The slow but inevitable process of these forces (heat, cold, wind, water, ice, and lava) meant that the earth was much older than the 5,834 years ascribed to it by Bishop Ussher, who, counting the generations mentioned in the Bible, concluded that the earth had been created in seven days in the year 4004 before Christ. (A fastidious disciple of Ussher located the exact moment of creation as 9 A.M., October 23 of that year.)

Bishop Ussher's Family Tree

Second, Darwin read Thomas Malthus's *Essay on Population* (1798), which argued that all species multiply at a rate beyond the environment's capacity to support them, leading to the notorious principle of the "struggle for survival."

Fortunately, Darwin had inherited enough wealth to allow him to work at his leisure, and he slowly compiled his notes in preparation for the eventual publication of his bombshell. Then in 1848 he was shocked to receive correspondence from an unknown admirer living in Borneo, Alfred Russel Wallace. It included an essay that summarized in a most concise manner the complete theory of evolution on which Darwin was laboring. Fearing that he would be upstaged if Wallace published his views

See what you've done now?

before Darwin had completed his study, Darwin hurriedly pared down his massive work and published his truncated revision a year later as *The Origin of Species by Means of Natural Selection* (1859). It immediately provoked both enthusiasm and hostility in the scientific community as well as among the lay public.

By the end of his life, Darwin had become very rich as a result of royalties from his books and his astute investments. He died in 1882 and was buried with honors in Westminster Abbey.

Theory of Evolution

Let me begin with an anecdote. Several years ago I reluctantly agreed to be a substitute instructor at San Quentin Prison in California for an anthropologist friend of mine who had fallen ill. Not wishing to let him down, I spent several hours boning up on the theory of evolution, the topic for the class I would be teaching. Once in the classroom, I soon realized that I had overprepared. Although a handful of students had read everything about Darwin available to them in the prison library, most of them had never heard of him and had no inkling of the meaning of the word "evolution." But I had never seen such eagerness to learn (so much so that I volunteered shortly after to teach philosophy at San Quentin). To achieve the goal, I devised on the spot a game I called "Invent-a-Bird." I cut paper into small cards and drew on each of seven cards a different bird head (e.g., one with a long, pointed bill; another, a strong nut-cracking beak; a third, a wide,

flat "duckish" bill; a fourth, a sharp, hooked beak for tearing flesh; a fifth, a cavernous fish-holding bill, etc.). Then, on another seven cards, I drew different legs and feet (e.g., webbed feet; feet with sharp talons; short, strong legs; long, thin legs, etc.). Then I made seven cards with similarly discrepant bodies, another seven with a variety of wings, and another with various tails. Finally, I made a pile of environmental cards: marshes, a snow scene, desert, ocean, prairie, and forest. Then I shuffled each pile and stacked them in a row along the front of my desk. Next I had each student—these former murderers, arsonists, rapists, and thieves—march one by one past the desk, picking up one card from each bird-part pile. Each student would then go to the blackboard and draw the bird he had randomly invented. Most drawings produced monsters: pathetic creatures with great, long, dainty legs on huge feet with gigantic hawklike beaks; or birds with huge bodies and teeny feet and head; a duck with talons; a hummingbird with webbed feet. The students laughed uproariously at each natural disaster produced. At last, after scores of failures, a bird was drawn that seemed to work: long, thin legs on webbed feet, with a large, round body, small tail, graceful long neck, and long, sharp bill—surely a proto-ibis or flamingo. But there was one more pile from which to choose— the environmental pile. There

This ain't gonna work.

was absolute silence as the husky, heavily tattooed inmate picked the card . . . a desert! This bird was doomed. I tried to restate our game in terms of Darwin's theory of "natural selection," "survival of the fittest," Mendelian genetic theory, and what little I could explain of DNA (deoxyribonucleic acid)—less than I hoped, as it turned out.

Mother Nature Selects

Upon his recuperation, my friend pointed out to me that my evolutionary game was somewhat misleading because there is no one-to-one relationship between DNA and body parts. A single gene may affect not just a single trait, but a whole trait complex, as the protein produced by DNA may be the basis of various otherwise unrelated bodily features. My only defense was that even Darwin could not have known this, because these discoveries were made after his death. Despite my inconvenient mistake, I felt that my class had been a pedagogical success, allowing me to introduce in a plausible way the various themes of Darwinian evolution to uninformed but intellectually eager students of a skeptical mind-set: the combination of randomness and natural laws that produced new forms, the ideas of **adaptation** and **speciation**. (During the class, my own enthusiasm had caused me to press the alarm buzzer in my pocket accidentally against the desk, provoking a charge into the classroom by heavily armed guards with weapons drawn, much to my embarrassment and to the pleasure of my already wired students.)

Teaching Darwin

"Natural Selection": Continuity and Variation

What, then, is Darwin's theory? It is deceptively easy to state. The theory can be divided into two parts: (1) All life is related. All living species have descended from earlier species as a consequence of branching out from those ancestral forms. (2) The fundamental mechanism of these developments is "natural selection."[1] Now the theory gets complicated. The first aspect of natural selection is *continuity*. Life-forms duplicate themselves; they reproduce. This process of reproduction generates many more duplicates than can in fact survive in the host environment; therefore, there is a constant "struggle for survival,"[2] either among members of the same species or among species themselves. Another aspect of natural selection, besides this process of continuity, is that of *variation*, which is ironically the result of breakdowns in the process of continuity. These breakdowns result in imperfect copies of the originals. These "flaws" are the product either of novel combinations of **genes** that were individually already present in the combined gene pools of the parental generation or of genetic **mutations** (chemical breakdowns in the gene), and they manifest themselves as new body traits. Most of these new characteristics will be damaging, resulting in the death of the offspring that carries them, but some of these new traits will, relative to the environment in which the individual organism finds itself, be advantageous, allowing it a more successful reproductive

> You see? I'm a perfect fit. The competition doesn't stand a chance.

rate (which is called "adaptation"). This advantage can lead to "speciation"—the development of new species that are more successful than were the parental species. A new species gives the appearance of having been intentionally designed for its environment, but in fact it is the accidental product of the process just described. (I should acknowledge that Darwin himself could not have stated his theory exactly as I have expressed it, because in his day nothing was known about genes.)

Religious Objections

Now, the first half of this two-part theory (namely, that species have descended from ancestral species) is, strictly speaking, *the* theory of evolution. It was first suggested in ancient Greece by the philosopher Empedocles and, by Darwin's time, had been accepted by many scientists and philosophers. Darwin's true originality appears in the second half of the theory, namely, the assertion that the *cause* of speciation (the emergence of new species) is natural selection in the context of the struggle for survival. But both halves of the theory encountered opposition from various religious camps, and the second half was also opposed by some scientists. Concerning the general theory of evolution, many religious-minded people objected to its obliteration of the distinction between humans and animals, and they claimed that, because humans have an immortal soul, there must have been a special creation of the soul by God that made humans independent of evolution.

I take offense at the aspersion that we are related.

SALOON

Literal-minded readers of the Bible went even further and denied that evolution was true of any level of nature. They believed that when, in Genesis 1:24, God says, "Let the earth bring forth the living creature after his kind, cattle and creeping thing, and beast of the earth after his kind: and it was so," this ruled out evolution of any sort. Some of these literal readers of the Bible explained the already voluminous fossil record as the result of Noah's flood, and a few, more dramatically, saw it as the work of the devil.

Other more liberal theologians believed that the fossil record could not be so easily dismissed, and they felt that the general theory of evolution was compatible with the idea of an all-seeing, all-powerful God who had simply used evolution to achieve

The Fossil Record as the Work of the Devil

his overall goal. But even this compromise was spoiled by the publication in 1859 of Darwin's *Origin of Species*, for his book had the effect of removing teleology (literally, the study of purposes, intentions, and goals) from nature. There were no "natural purposes" of the type described by Aristotle, and no references to divine purpose were needed to explain the process of evolution.

"Darwin's Dangerous Idea"

Many of Darwin's contemporaries were horrified precisely by the fact that Darwin replaced teleology with a purely mechanical form of causality—what Daniel Dennett has called "Darwin's Dangerous Idea" in his recent book of the same title.[3] In the eighteenth century, the favorite proof of God's existence had been what was called the "teleological argument" or the "argument from design," which compared the intricacies of natural entities such as eyeballs with the intricacies of designed artifacts like watches, and concluded that just as the subtlety of the watch entails an intelligent and purposeful master designer—namely, a watchmaker—so does the subtlety and perfection of the eyeball entail a master designer, an eyeball maker—namely, God.

Master Eyeball Designer

Yet Darwin's theory purported to show that even a phenomenon as complicated as the eyeball could be the product of natural selection—that is, of the laws of physics and chemistry, along with the laws of probability and randomness applied to the components of organic matter within the context of "the struggle for survival."

(Again, remember that Darwin could not actually present a complete account of natural selection because that turns out to involve the science of genetics and even an explanation of deoxyribonucleic acid [DNA]. Though Gregor Mendel published the first successful account of genetics in 1866, his book was ignored until the turn of the century, and DNA was not discovered until 1953 by Francis Crick and James Watson. Also, the completed theory of natural selection needs statistics, another science unavailable to Darwin.)

Isn't anybody listening?!

Father Gregor Mendel, the Founder of the Science of Genetics

Despite the technical complications of the theory, certain clear examples illustrate different ways in which natural selection works to favor one strain of **phenotype** (the physical creature that is the result of the interaction between genetic heredity and environmental conditions) over another. A well-known case involves a species of moth, *Biston betularia*, that inhabits the English Midlands. There are white and black varieties of this moth. Before the nineteenth century the white variety was overwhelmingly predominant, and the black form was scarce. It was too easily spotted by birds, the moth's natural enemy, against the white bark and lichen that covered the trees of the Midlands. In the 1800s the heavy industrialization of the region produced smoke and soot that killed the pale lichen and stained the bark, and both trees and buildings were left covered by a black layer of grime. As a consequence, the black moths began to find themselves safer from predators than their white relatives. The frequencies of the genes determining color in these moths rapidly changed, and now the black moths predominate. The white moths suddenly found themselves being "selected out" (or "selected in" . . . as bird dinners). There are no "intentions"—no teleology—involved in this process. It is purely mechanical.

Darwinism and the Human Being

But enough about moths. What implications does Darwin's theory of evolution have for us human beings? Oddly enough, the answer to this question is not clear. Darwin himself was certainly not anxious to answer it in *The Origin of Species*, where, speaking of the application of his theory to humans, he said only, "Much light will be thrown on the origins of man and his history."[4] Though his early notes show his interest in human evolution, he did not find the courage to publish *The Descent of Man* until 1871, twelve years after *Origin*. There he concluded that the facts compelled us to believe "that man is descended from some lower form, notwithstanding that connecting-links have not hitherto been discovered," and he asserted that the human being "is but one of several exceptional forms of Primates."[5]

Exceptional Primates

So then, humans are not all that much different from certain other animals. What are the moral implications of this aspect of "Darwin's Dangerous Idea"? Darwin is seen as one of the great revolutionaries of intellectual history, and by some as having dealt one of the three great blows to human self-importance. (The first: Galileo's proof that we are not at the center of the universe; the second: Darwin's discovery that we are mere animals; the third: Freud's demonstration that we are *sick* animals.)

The First Blow

Did Darwin himself draw revolutionary conclusions about human nature and morality from his theory of evolution, as would many of his self-proclaimed disciples? Apparently not. According to Darwin, human beings in a civilized state need not worry that their culture is the mere product of mechanical forces of natural selection. "For the moral qualities are advanced, either directly or indirectly, much more through the effects of habit, the reasoning powers, instruction, religion, etc., than through natural selection, though to this latter agency may be safely attributed the social instincts which afforded the basis for the development of the moral sense" (327–8). Furthermore, Darwin distinguishes between natural selection and **sexual selection,** which involves the conscious choice of the "selector," and he claims that in the cases of humans, sexual selection plays a larger role than does natural

Unnatural Selection

selection.[6] In fact, civilization takes over so much of the role that evolution plays in nature and in precivilized society that it preserves "a considerable number of individuals, weak in mind and body, who would have been promptly eliminated in the savage state" (45).

Mother Nature Cleaning Up

Darwinism and Morality

According to Darwin, humanity, based on its moral development, has risen "to the very summit of the organic scale" (328). Moral development is not a heroic, voluntary choice, of course. The foundations of morality are built into our biology as the result of natural selection.

Our predecessors experienced both selfishness and sympathy for others, and these opposing values synthesized into a desire to

help others, along with the hope that others would reciprocate. This combination of selfishness and sympathy would be open to natural selection, "for those communities, which included the greatest number of the most sympathetic members, would flourish best and rear the greatest number of offspring" (92).

According to Darwin, this would lead members of such communities to state with Immanuel Kant, "I will not in my own person violate the dignity of human-ity" (95). As you have seen, Kant (1724–1804) argued that rea-son imposes upon all rational crea-tures a moral duty (the cate-gorical imperative)

After you, my love.

No, no; after you. I insist!

Polite People Reproduce More Efficiently

to respect the dignity of all other rational creatures. In the nineteenth century, the main philosophical competition with Kant's moral ratio-nalism was utilitarianism, which, as you have also seen, was based on the writings of Jeremy Bentham (1748–1832) and John Stuart Mill (1808–1873). The utilitarians argue that morality is not grounded in reason but in feeling and passion, namely, on the desire for happiness. From this they deduce their primary principle of moral philosophy—that each act should be motivated by a desire for "the greatest amount of happiness for the greatest number of people." Darwin astutely disagrees with Bentham's claim that all actions are in fact motivated by a desire for happiness. Some are motivated by "instinct, or long habit, without any consciousness of pleasure" (104). But he agrees that the "greatest happiness principle" has justifiably become civilization's goal. So, in Darwin's mind, not only have natural selection and the general processes of civilization led to the categorical impera-tive and the principle of utility, but they also "naturally lead to the golden rule" (109–10), yet another stone in the foundation of morality.

If Darwin believes that the agency of natural selection has advanced the human race inexorably to embody a form of civilized morality that synthesizes Kantianism, utilitarianism, and Christian morality, then it must be said that the moral picture that Darwin believes follows from his theory of evolution is not a very radical one

Kant | Bentham | Mill | Jesus

Moral Evolution

after all, and it should not be one that evokes horror in his audience. As a commentator on this aspect of Darwin's theory has recently written:

Any nineteenth-century theory that entailed the truth of Kantian moral rationalism, the Benthamite and Millian doctrine of happiness, the Christian commandment of love, and the Aristotelian theory of virtue did not constitute a threat to the moral fiber of Britain.[7]

Yet Darwin's theory did evoke horror and rage. Some of his opponents believed that morality could be justified only if there was an immortal soul and a Final Judgment at the hands of an all-wise, wrathful God.

The Final Judgment: God (as Christ) in Consultation with Saint Matthew (as Angel) and Saint John (as Eagle) [Tympanum, Saint Pierre, Moissac, France]

Without belief in the eventual triumph of Good over Evil in eternity or, in some cases, without the fear of eternal punishment for moral transgression, people would become too dispirited to be willing to make the sacrifices required by morality or so emboldened as to pursue selfish and immoral acts. Clearly Darwin was not so pessimistic about the human race. A theological grounding was no more needed for morality than it was needed for the natural sciences.

How Darwin Undermines Traditional Ethical Theories, Despite Himself

You have seen that Darwin himself did not believe that his theory undermines traditional moral theories but that it supports them. Nevertheless, most of today's practitioners of evolutionary ethics disagree with him on this question. They do so for several reasons, one of which is that many traditional moral theories are based on a supposed difference in kind between human beings and other kinds of living beings. According to the traditional theories, this difference is supposed to bestow a certain kind of moral superiority on humans, an idea that contemporary Darwinism must reject. These traditional views are usually derived either from theology, or from empirical evidence, or from some combination of the two. The theological centerpiece is the claim that human beings were created "in God's image" (we might call this the noble cookie-cutter theory) and that

The Cookie Cutter Theory of Creation

therefore this link between nature and the supernatural gives the human being a special dignity. On this account, the goal of ethics is to honor this dignity.

Those moral theories that are not based on theology but on what are taken to be observable features of human life often see the great dividing line between humans and animals as being demarcated by the presence of reason—or rationality—in the human and its absence elsewhere. Some theories make the division between the human and nonhuman worlds depend on the human's capacity for language and the apparent absence of true languages in the rest of the animal world. Others draw the line at the human ability to make and use tools. Others have claimed that only human beings can have moral codes and that moral codes can only apply to the kind of beings that can have moral codes.

Contemporary evolutionary ethicists insist that Darwin's theory of evolution rejects any absolute division between human beings and the animal world. Of course, Darwin nowhere tries to prove that there exists in the rest of the animal world the level of rationality that exists in the human world; nor does he try to prove that in the animal world there are to be found true languages (systems of communication with grammars, vocabularies, and syntaxes [rules of meaning] that produce sustainable shared memory of the past, anticipation of the future, and innovative rationality and artistic creativity). Darwin's main point in this arena is that concepts like those of rationality, language, tool use, creativity, and morality are not absolutes; rather they are relative in the sense that there can be more or less of each of them. How could it be otherwise if human beings are descended from animal ancestors?

For Darwin, the gradation between our nearest primate relatives and ourselves is so smooth that hardly a ripple is caused. Rather than looking at our animal cousins and ancestors to discover the worst about them and then projecting that "bruteness" onto ourselves (as some later writers have done[8]), Darwin does the reverse. He looks first at us humans and then at simians, finding in them the same things that (or sometimes even better things than) he finds in us. He summarizes his analysis in *The Descent of Man*:

> It has, I think, now been shown that man and the higher animals, especially the Primates, have some few instincts in common. All have the same senses, intuitions and sensations—similar passions, affections and emotions, even the more complex ones, such as jealousy, suspicion, emulation, gratitude and magnanimity; they practice deceit and are revengeful; they are sometimes susceptible to ridicule, and even have a sense of humor; they feel wonder and curiosity; they possess the same faculties of imitation, attention, deliberation, choice, memory, imagination, the association of ideas and reason, though in very different degrees. The individuals of the same species graduate in intellect from absolute imbecility to high excellence. They are also liable to insanity, though far less often than in the case of man. (67)

Darwin admits that animals are not self-conscious, and they do not possess "the habitual use of articulate language . . . peculiar to man" (72). Nor do they have a belief in God; but neither are they plagued with the superstitions that terrify such a great part of humankind. They *do* have a sense of beauty and moral capacities. In fact, after describing various acts of heroism on the part of monkeys and baboons, Darwin concludes that he would prefer to think of himself as descended from a brave, heroic little monkey than from a superstitious human savage who treats his wives like slaves, delights in torturing his enemies, and offers up bloody sacrifices to imaginary gods.

According to evolutionary ethics, if we are not so very different from our animal ancestors, nor from our mammalian "cousins," then any moral theory that bases its arguments on the difference between humans and other forms of life is wrongheaded and, probably, cruel—cruel because it will condone what evolutionary ethicists think of as immoral behavior toward nonhuman animals. This objection will be directed primarily toward Kantian rationalism, but also against contractualism (which you will study in Chapter 7) and theological-based moralities. Recall that Kantian rationalism is based on the supposed autonomy of the human individual and on the uniqueness of human dignity. Contractualism sees a moral community as comprising only individuals who are capable of establishing contractual obligations with each other. Theological-based moralities, according to many evolutionary ethicists, are systems of self-flattery, invented by humans to glorify themselves.

If Darwin's theory of evolution does indeed undermine certain ethical theories, does it replace them with a moral theory of its own? I think the answer must be a resounding "No!" Darwin claimed that his writings were those of a scientific naturalist, not a moral philosopher. Nevertheless, he seemed to have thought that his theory of evolution could at least explain what he took to be the moral impulses of human beings. Writing in *The Descent of Man* about natural selection, Darwin said, "[T]o this . . . agency may be safely attributed the social instincts which afforded the basis for the development of the moral sense" (327–8).

In fact, as you have seen, Darwin thought his theory of evolution was compatible with almost every mainstream theory of ethics. The assumption seems to be that Darwin did not believe that a specifically *evolutionary* ethics was required by his biological discoveries. Then why do certain contemporary moral theorists believe, to the contrary, that a special moral theory is indeed in order? First, some believe that Darwin's fear of giving offense caused him to understate the implications of his insights. (Among those whom he did not want to offend was his pious wife, who often felt anxious about the outrage her husband's theory seemed to provoke.) That is, Darwin may have intentionally understated the radicalness of his theory insofar as it applied to the case of the human being.

A second reason for the suspicions against Darwin's own account of morality by contemporary evolutionary ethicists is that Darwin sometimes flirted rather seriously with now-discredited **Lamarckian** ideas and *especially* when dealing with human evolution and moral questions. Jean-Baptiste Lamarck (1744–1829) was a French naturalist preceding Darwin who developed a theory of evolution based on the idea of biological transmission of acquired characteristics. For example, he explained the giraffe's long neck in terms of generations of stretching by the ancestors of present-day giraffes. Individual giraffes, forced to reach ever higher into the trees for leaves to eat, passed on to their offspring the amount of neck elongation they had acquired in their lifetime of stretching.

Jean-Baptiste at Work

In most respects, Darwin's theory of natural selection is anti-Lamarckian. But in *The Descent of Man,* when speaking of moral qualities, Darwin said, "It is not improbable that after long practice virtuous tendencies may be inherited" (320) and, "we may expect that virtuous habits will grow stronger, becoming perhaps fixed by inheritance" (108). Also, "Habits, moreover, followed during many generations probably tend to be inherited" (114). These retrograde ideas are not ones that contemporary evolutionary ethicists are able to use (or, in some cases, even acknowledge).

A third reason for the rejection (or at least the ignoring) of the ideas of Darwin-the-moralist by contemporary Darwinians is that many theorists have felt that Darwin's account of natural selection's "choice" of social instincts such as altruism (the willingness to sacrifice one's own benefit for the benefit of others) does not square with the rest of his theory. For example, according to the late James Rachels, an articulate defender of evolutionary ethics:

> Darwin believed that the existence of social instincts could be explained as the result of natural selection. The key, as always, is to understand how individuals who possess this characteristic are better situated in the struggle for survival. This is not easy to understand; in fact, where altruism is concerned, just the opposite seems to be true; the tendency to behave altruistically seems to work against reproductive success. . . . How does altruism become a widespread characteristic within a group in the first place? Considering that individual altruists such as our heroic baboon seem to be at a disadvantage, why shouldn't the tendency to altruism be eliminated the moment it first appears?[9]

In summation, these three problems seem to have dissuaded most evolutionary ethicists from embracing Darwin's own account of the moral implications of the theory of evolution. (We will return shortly to the problem of altruism, because a recent theoretical contribution tends after all to support Darwin's views on this topic in dramatically new ways.)

There have been a number of contemporary attempts to develop viable forms of evolutionary ethics—that is, a moral theory that would not only be compatible with the key ideas of the theory of evolution but that would actually be driven by that theory. I have selected only one of them to represent evolutionary ethics, that of James Rachels (1941–2003). Rachels is well known to professional philosophers as a writer of textbooks and an editor of anthologies on moral philosophy. He was University Professor of Philosophy at the University of Alabama at Birmingham. I have selected his theory to represent evolutionary ethics both because of its scope (Rachels clearly had a good grasp of moral philosophy, Darwinian theory, and the philosophical implication of Darwinism) and because of its accessibility (Rachels's very readable *Created from Animals: The Moral Implications of Darwinism* is available in a manageable-sized paperback edition from the University of Oxford Press). Rachels called his theory "moral individualism."

James Rachels's Moral Individualism

According to moral individualism, the obligations that we have toward other individual living things do not depend on the general categories in which those living things find themselves placed (e.g., human or nonhuman); rather they depend on specific characteristics possessed by those *individuals*—hence the term, moral individualism. "If A is to be treated differently from B, the justification must be in terms of A's individual characteristics and B's individual characteristics" (173–4). So, according to moral individualism, instead of asking whether chimpanzees in general should be used in scientific experiments, we should ask whether this particular individual (who happens to be a chimp) has characteristics that would make it the object of moral consideration. Rachels writes, "If we think it is wrong to treat a human in a certain way, because the human has certain characteristics, *and a particular non-human also has those characteristics,* then consistency requires that we also object to treating the non-human in this way" (175). This is what Rachels calls the "principle of equality." Notice that Rachels's principle presupposes (correctly, probably) that we already have certain moral attitudes toward human beings. The issue for him is simply one of logic (". . . consistency requires that . . ."). Rachels, like Darwin, stresses the similarities between chimps and humans, rather than the differences. He holds that chimps are curious, intelligent, sensate creatures that experience feelings such as curiosity, boredom, pain and pleasure, fear and joy. If we take these qualities into consideration when deciding how we ought to treat humans, then we should also do so when dealing with chimpanzees. In deciding, for example, whether chimps should be used in medical experiments that may cause them death—or great pain, or fear, or even boredom—is it morally relevant to insist that chimps are not "masters of a syntactically complicated language" (188)? In other words, is it morally relevant to play the language card?

Playing the Language Card

Or, is it morally relevant to insist that chimps are unable to reciprocate our moral treatment of them? That is, is it morally relevant to play the contract card? Rachels doubts it.

Well, then, is it morally relevant that "humans . . . are more sensitive to harm than other creatures?" Rachels admits that this characteristic of most humans might well be morally relevant under certain conditions.

> Suppose we must choose between causing X units of pain for a human or non-human. Because of the human's superior cognitive abilities, the after-effects for him will include Y additional units of suffering; thus the human's total misfortune will be X + Y, while the non-human's total will only be X. Thus, the human has more at stake, and the principle of equality would recommend favouring him. (193)

But, insists Rachels, the principle of equality requires that in cases where the nonhuman's pain is more intense (say, it also equals X + Y), the justification for affording preference to the human disappears.

You have seen that Rachels does not deny that the peculiar characteristics that most human individuals have give them a moral priority over nonhuman animals. That is, Rachels admits that sometimes there is a significant sense in which it is correct to say that (some) human lives are more *valuable* than (some) nonhuman lives. The value of life, he says, is "the value that it has *for the person who is the subject of that life*" (198). (I think Rachels should have said "individual" rather than "person," because the latter term biases the theory more toward humans than Rachels means to do.) Rachels qualifies the idea of something having value for someone by saying that "X has value for P" means in this case "P would be worse off without X." This does not mean that person P must consciously realize that he or she would be worse off without X. Babies, for example, would be worse off without their eyes, even though babies do not realize that fact.

The sense in which Rachels's moral individualism often gives priority to humans over nonhumans is this: When Rachels says that the value of life is the value that it has for the individual that is the subject of that life, this formulation automatically gives more weight to what he calls "biographical lives" than to "biological lives." Amoebae have biological lives, and certain conditions are valuable for amoebae in Rachels's sense of the term "value." For example, a liquid environment has value for amoebae because they would be better off with it than without it. But can an amoeba really be the "subject" of its life?

What You Would Want to Say to an Amoeba

As far as we know, the facts about an amoeba's life are all biological in nature. But the facts about a biographical life are not exclusively biological facts. They are facts about our "history, character, actions, interests, and relationships. . . . our projects, our activities, our loves and friendships" (199). Biographical lives are, claims Rachels, more important than biological lives, because we value biological life only because it is a means to biographical life.

Now, Rachels's distinction between biological and biographical lives may appear to have reopened the gap between humans and non-humans that Darwin had tried to close, because it is not at all obvious that animals have biographical lives. But Rachels does not accept this conclusion:

> Do non-humans animals also have biographical lives? Clearly, many do not. Having a life requires some fairly sophisticated mental capacities. Bugs and shrimp do not have those capacities. They are too simple. But consider a more complex animal such as the rhesus monkey. The rhesus is a favourite research animal for experimental psychologists because, being so close to us from an evolutionary point of view, they share many of our psychological characteristics. They are intelligent and live in organized social groups; they communicate with one another; they care about each other, and . . . they behave altruistically towards one another. Monkey mothers and infants are bonded much as humans are. Moreover, they are not alike: the lives and personalities are surprisingly diverse. Their lives are not as intellectually and emotionally complex as those of humans, but clearly they do have lives. (208)

The conclusion to be drawn from the lives of rhesus monkeys is fairly obvious. Application of the principle of equality demands that most of the scientific experimentation with rhesus monkeys be suspended, for roughly the same reasons that similar scientific experimentation with humans should not be allowed.

But even in the case of animals that probably cannot be said to have biographical lives, if we find similarities between human suffering and animal suffering, then the principle of equality says that we should not make animals suffer just for the benefit, convenience, or pleasure of humans. Rachels characterizes some of the cruel treatment normally dished out to a variety of animals (civit cats, cattle [especially veal calves], and chickens) that are used by humans either as parts of consumer products or as food. He asserts that even the continuation of the production of meat products as food cannot withstand moral scrutiny. He concludes that not only must almost all animal experimentation be halted, but that vegetarianism is the only morally defendable posture to adopt.

Some people believe that we must work to eliminate suffering among animals but that the humane slaughter of animals for meat is not morally objectionable. Here is Rachels's response:

It would be impossible to treat the animals humanely and still produce meat in sufficient quantities to make it a normal part of our diets.

Cruel methods are used in the meat-production industry not because the producers are cruel people, but because such methods are economical; they enable the producers to market a product that people can afford. So to work for better treatment of the animals would be to work for a situation in which most of us would have to adopt a vegetarian diet, because if we were successful we could no longer afford meat. (212)

Implications of Moral Individualism for Our Attitudes toward Humans

I mentioned earlier that Rachels's theory presupposes that we already do have certain moral feelings about other humans. (After all, one consequence of the principle of equality is that we must be prepared to extend to certain nonhumans the same consideration that we now reserve only for humans.) But you should notice that in stressing individuals over whole species, Rachels's theory involves not just extending to animals some of the attitudes that we currently reserve for humans but also changing some of our current moral attitudes toward humans. For example, if supporting the possibility of a rich biographical life is the main reason for preserving a biological life, then the strictures against **euthanasia** (mercy killing) need to be reconsidered, according to Rachels. In the case of a patient in an irreversible coma, "[B]eing alive, sadly, does such a person no good at all" (199). Similarly, the moral and legal prohibitions against suicide must be rethought. Kant thought that suicide was a personal assault on one's own dignity, hence on human dignity itself. Rachels thinks otherwise. In cases in which one realizes that the prolongation of biological life can only produce a life of pain, misery, and degradation, one might well turn to suicide to protect one's personal dignity. He concludes that "when we consider the specific characteristics of human beings, we find nothing that can form the basis of an absolute prohibition against self-destruction. Kant's appeal to 'degrading human nature' seems, therefore, to be no more than puffery—when the emotional rhetoric is stripped away, nothing is left" (203).

Kant Exposed

Rachels and Darwin

What exactly is the connection between Rachels's moral individualism and Darwin's theory of evolution? Rachels, who is acutely aware of Hume's Guillotine and the naturalistic fallacy, has been careful not to try to derive a moral principle (an "ought") from Darwin's descriptions of the process of natural selection (an "is"). Rachels admits that Darwinian theory of evolution does not logically entail moral individualism (in the way that Darwinian theory of evolution *does* logically entail the assertion that the world is more than six thousand years old); but he argues that there is nevertheless more than a mere compatibility between the two theories. Let's look into this.

It may seem that the very name of Rachels's theory is anti-Darwinian. After all, a critic might say, Darwin speaks of species, not of individuals. (Darwin's book was not titled "The Origin of Individuals.") However, I believe Rachels is right to defend himself against that charge. One of the great ironies of Darwin's *Origin of Species* is his proof that there are no species. Well, I exaggerate, but that is roughly the effect of his work. Darwin declares that the term "species" is "arbitrary" (157), like the definitions that "decide whether a certain number of houses should be called a village, town or city" (156).

The only "natural order" around which species could be defined is genealogical. Yet Darwin warns that one "might with justice argue that fertility and sterility are not safe criterions of specific distinctions" (152). As philosopher Daniel Dennett points out, dogs, coyotes, and wolves do interbreed, though they are categorized as different species, and Chihuahuas and Saint Bernards can't mate except with extraordinary intervention. In addition, Dennett shows that declaration of speciation can only be made retrospectively. We can only designate something to be a new species with hindsight.

This discovery produces the oxymoronic idea of what Darwin calls "nominal essences" (95)—essences in name only—and threatens to put us strangely on the watershed side of **nominalism** (the theory of meaning, whose most radical expression is "We have only names"[10]) rather than **realism** (the theory that names can accurately denote real things). It also, it seems to me, justifies Rachels's decision to base his main moral category on individuals and still claim to be working within Darwin's scheme of things.

The Is/Ought Problem

From the fact (and Darwin does call it a fact) that there is a smooth transition between nonhuman animals and humans, Rachels deduces that no viable moral principle can be based on a supposed gulf between humans and animals. Is Rachels trying to deduce an "ought" from an "is"? (From the fact that animals *are* so-and-so, it follows that we *ought to do* such-and-such). I don't believe so. Rachels is in fact reversing the procedure. He knows that no "is" implies an "ought," but he also seems to see that, nevertheless, every "ought" does imply an "is."[11] That is, every moral principle presupposes certain factual states of the world. Consider some of the Ten Commandments. "Honor thy father and mother" presupposes that there are fathers and mothers. (Among some species that do not multiply sexually, there are no fathers or mothers.) "Thou shalt not covet thy neighbor's wife" presupposes the institution of marriage. (There have been cultures with no such institution.) "Thou shalt have no other God before me" seems to presuppose that there is more than one God (and may be evidence that the Jews in the times of Moses were **polytheists**). Now, what Rachels has done is to notice that a number of moral philosophers have presupposed as a factual state of the world that there is an unbridgeable gap between humans and nonhuman animals. Rachels believes (with Darwin) that there is no such factual state and therefore rejects those traditional theories based on that false idea. Their "ought" implies a false "is."

The Evolution of Altruism: Sober and Wilson's *Unto Others*

Altruism can be defined as the ability to forgo an advantage to oneself in order to promote the advantage of another. Is such a thing as altruism to be found in the natural world? The recent book on the question of altruism, *Unto Others*,[12] written by Elliott Sober, a philosopher of science, and David Sloan Wilson, a biologist, opens with a stunning if troubling example—that of the trematode parasite, *Dicrocoelium dendriticum*. This parasite passes the adult stage of its life cycle in the liver of sheep or cows. Its eggs are dispersed in the feces of these animals. The eggs are eaten by snails, and these eggs hatch inside the snails. The newly hatched worms spend their next stage in the snails' stomachs, until they eventually pass through the snails' digestive system wrapped in a mucus covering that is eaten by ants. Typically, about fifty of these mucus-covered parasites enter an individual ant. Once inside the ant, the parasites drill through the stomach wall of the ant. One of the fifty makes its way to the ant's brain, and in this stage it is called a "brain worm." The rest of the parasites form thick-walled cysts in the ant's body. The brain worm affects the ant's behavior; the ant now spends a great amount of time on the tips of blades of grass, where it is likely to be eaten by sheep or cattle.

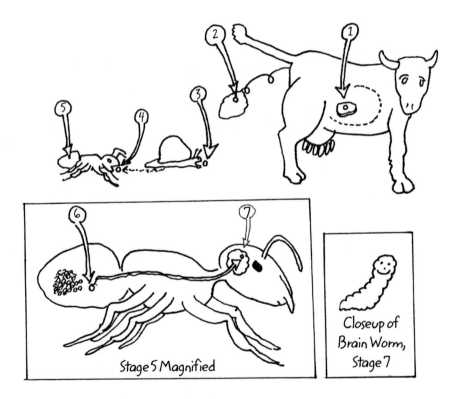

Stage 5 Magnified

Closeup of Brain Worm, Stage 7

The Seven Stages of Altruism

The brain worm (the one member of the group of fifty parasites that managed to get to the ant's brain) loses its life, but as the result of its sacrifice, the other forty-nine parasites manage to finish out their lives successfully in the stomach of their mammalian host.

This is a strange story, and it is also strange to call the brain worm an altruist. But if you look back at the definition of altruism used by biologists ("ability to forgo an advantage to oneself for the advantage of others"), you see that the brain worm qualifies. Notice that for biologists—unlike for moral philosophers—altruism has nothing to do with intentions or feelings. (We don't know if brain worms have feelings or intentions.) Shortly, we'll come back to the problem of altruism in humans, where feelings and intentions seem to matter. But first we have to try to understand how even "biological altruism" is possible. How can there be altruistic brain worms?

As you have seen, at least in his published works, Darwin himself saw no contradiction between his theory of evolution and the main moral principles of Western civilization, whether those principles were Kantian, utilitarian, Aristotelian, or Christian. Indeed, Darwin implied that these moral codes evolved out of the process of natural selection. Yet, all of those traditions—with the possible exception of the Aristotelian, which you will study in Chapter 6—presuppose the reality of altruism; and, as you have just seen, James Rachels has shown that the idea of altruism appears to be incompatible with Darwinism because it is difficult to see how species composed of individuals that are constitutionally disposed to altruism would be able to compete with species whose individuals were all motivated only by self-interest. Darwin himself was well aware of the problem of the natural selection of altruism, as we see from this passage from *The Descent of Man*:

> It is extremely doubtful whether the offspring of the more sympathetic and benevolent parents, or of those who were the most faithful to their comrades, would be reared in greater number than the children of selfish and treacherous parents of the same tribe. He who was

ready to sacrifice his life, as many a savage has been, rather than betray his comrades, would often leave no offspring to inherit his noble nature. (114)

Darwin nevertheless tried to extinguish this doubt and defend the view that nature indeed "selects" altruism over egoism. His awareness of the fact that altruism is problematic for evolutionary theory is noteworthy, but Darwin solved the problem to his own satisfaction by holding not only that individuals would be the beneficiaries of natural selection, but that groups also could be selected, and groups that had individual altruists would be more likely to survive than groups composed of egoists. (For instance, in Darwin's example just quoted, natural selection could favor *families* with altruistic members over families with only egoistic members.) However, in the recent history of biological science, the idea of "group selection" has been anathema (that is, a very big no-no). In fact, I believe that one motivation behind the search for a peculiarly *evolutionary* ethics has been the combination of the recognition of the presupposition of altruism behind almost all of the standard ethical theories and the recognition of the apparent elimination of the possibility of altruism from biology. Therefore, it seems to me that any current discussion of evolutionary ethics—indeed, any discussion of ethics at large—demands an attempt to sort out this question to the extent possible.

Group Selection

Darwin's idea, then, was that groups, and not merely individuals, could be the targets of natural selection. The idea of group selection was part of the mainstream Darwinian discourse until the 1960s, when a number of attacks were mounted against it. In *Unto Others*, Sober and Wilson give a short history of this series of attacks and their consequences. According to Sober and Wilson, the most thorough and devastating critique is G. C. Williams's 1966 book *Adaptation and Natural Selection*.[13] The arguments Williams puts forth claiming that natural selection works only at the individual level are thought to be so compelling, say Sober and Wilson, "For the next decade, group selection theory was widely regarded as not just false but as off-limits" (5). By 1982, Richard Dawkins could write what he took to be the obituary of group selection theory, comparing those biologists who tried to hang onto the theory to amateurs who try to square the circle or build a perpetual motion machine.[14]

Several attempts were made to explain the apparent existence of altruism without having recourse to group selection theory. The most impressive was W. D. Hamilton's theory of kin selection.[15] Hamilton stuck to the idea that natural selection worked only at the individual level and demonstrated that individuals sometimes helped other individuals who carried the same genes that the agent carries (that is, the agent sometimes behaved in self-sacrificial ways to aid its siblings). In doing so, according to Hamilton, the agent was actually guaranteeing the future transmission of its own genes; so, in one sense, its apparent self-sacrifice was not really altruistic but selfish. Hamilton was able to produce evidence that the closer the similarity between the genetic makeup of the helper and the helpee, the more likely that the agent would go to extremes in its willingness to engage in self-sacrificial aid. Brothers and sisters could expect major support from each other; first cousins (having only about an eighth of the genetic makeup of the agent) could expect a more diluted effort, and so on down the line.

Kin Selection Theory of Altruism

An extension of Hamilton's idea became popular in the form of Richard Dawkins's "selfish-gene" theory.[16] According to it, the "individual" at whose level natural selection works is really the gene itself.

Bodies (organisms with, in the case of human beings, a head, legs, arms, and a trunk) are simply hosts or carriers of genes, and they are discarded by these genes when their usefulness is over (i.e., these bodies die after they have given the gene the opportunity to multiply). As Sober and Wilson put it, "In Dawkins's fanciful language, individuals become lumbering robots controlled by genes whose only interest is to replicate themselves" (87).

Sober and Wilson respect the theories of Hamilton and Dawkins, claiming that these theorists have made major contributions to biology, but they nevertheless assert that the attempt to eliminate group selection theory has failed, and that group selection theory is now back in biology full force. They admit, however, that some biologists haven't kept up-to-date: "Many evolutionary biologists continue to play the 'group selection is dead' song from the 1960s with the same fondness they have for the Beatles" (51). This means that, according to Sober and Wilson, Darwin had it right all along. They write, "The only process to explain the evolution of altruism was the one that Darwin identified long ago" (77).

Well-Endowed Lumbering Robot

Sober and Wilson define a group as "a set of individuals that influence each other's fitness with respect to a certain trait but not the fitness of those outside the group" (92). It follows from this that groups are not necessarily geographically contiguous. Sober and Wilson give the example of a study group in a library. The individuals helping each other to research a particular assignment may be scattered all over the library, or even throughout several libraries, while the individuals gathered elbow-to-elbow at a specific library table may have nothing to do with each other. In fact, the type of group that may be available for "selection" might include members of different species.

Particular genes and cells are organized into the functional relation that we call individuals, and the individuals produced by these organizations are candidates for selection or elimination by natural selection. In the same way, groups of individuals can become organized into functional relationships producing groups that can also become candidates for selection or elimination. This is one of the main points that Sober and Wilson hope to have established in their book.

Cultural Norms

Another feature of Darwin's solution to the problem of altruism was the inclusion of cultural norms within his theory of evolution, insofar as that theory applies to humans and perhaps to other higher mammals. In other words, Darwin believed that cultural institutions themselves could be favored by natural selection. Many biologists regret this move on Darwin's part. Indeed, writers on evolution often see cultural norms (the laws, mores, customs, and moral rules of different cultures) as independent of biological evolution. Some of these theorists argue that culture picks up where evolution leaves off; other writers even see culture as *thwarting* the process of natural selection. That is, they have claimed that human biological evolution is at an end because cultural norms have superseded it, preventing natural selection and survival of the fittest from being causal factors in normal human communities under normal conditions. (For example, liberal democracies have a "safety net" that catches those who might otherwise fall below the minimum standards of well-being established by those communities. Individuals who might be eliminated from the gene pool in real fights for survival are thus protected.) This is *not* the tack taken by Sober and Wilson in their argument. Rather, they, like Darwin himself, see cultural norms as causal factors in producing the groups that might be candidates for "selection" or elimination. For example, they imagine two cultures called the "squibs" and the "squabs." A main social rule of the squibs is "Be altruistic to fellow squibs, punish those who don't, and punish those who fail to punish." The squabs have the rule "Solve your own problems; any way you can." According to Sober and Wilson,

> The altruistic squibs will outperform the quarrelsome squabs in all situations that involve between-group processes, such as direct conflict, foraging for a common resource, founding new groups, and so on. The problem of cheaters and freeloaders within groups, which is so often used to argue against the evolution of altruism, is not a problem for the squibs because cheaters and freeloaders are severely punished. (151)

Therefore, conclude Sober and Wilson, groups can evolve into adaptive units.

This formulation is indeed roughly what Darwin himself said, and it seems me that Sober and Wilson have even adopted some of Darwin's Lamarckism on this topic, though they do not say so. If social norms become a causal element in the makeup of the adaptive unit that "group selection" favors; and if social norms—or the behaviors that they generate—are acquired by individuals during their lifetime; and if these norms are inherited by future generations, then there is a serious sense in which "acquired characteristics can be inherited."[17] I think a lot of neo-Darwinians will not be pleased by this suggestion of Sober and Wilson's. (Still, after all, the main Lamarckian principle, "acquired characteristics can be inherited," may be more a part of orthodox Darwinism than many biologists are willing to admit. Mutations [sudden arbitrary changes or breakdowns in genetic structures] happen in the lifetimes of the individual whose genes suffered the mutation, and these mutations sometimes are passed on to the offspring of the individual, which, in radical cases, can be the first member of a new species. So we see, even according to orthodox Darwinism, sometimes "acquired characteristics can be inherited.")

Lamarck's Son

Psychological Altruism and Evolution

Recall that from a biological perspective, an individual organism behaves altruistically "if it reduces its own fitness and augments the fitness of others" (Sober and Wilson, 199). Notice that this thesis makes no reference to motivations, intentions, or mental states of any kind. At the end of their section on biological, or evolutionary, altruism—a bit less than two-thirds of the way through their book—Sober and Wilson make the following statement:

> It is important to stress that *everything* we have established so far has been without reference to the thoughts and feelings that guide human behavior. . . . If the brainworm has evolved to sacrifice its life so that its group will end up in the liver of a cow, who cares how (or if) it thinks or feels as it burrows into the brain of the ant? Similarly, if humans have evolved to coalesce into functionally organized groups, who cares how they think or feel? The fact is that they do it, just as brainworms burrow into the ant's brain and fruit flies develop wings. (193)

Interview with a Brain Worm

Yet when we speak of human morality, we almost always refer to the "thoughts and feelings that guide behavior." So, even if we grant that Sober and Wilson have made a strong case for biological altruism as a product of group selection, what is the connection between biological altruism and human morality? It does appear that sometimes humans sacrifice their own interests in the name of the interests of others. But if we found out that such occasions were merely instinctual responses or reflexes—the way, say, that a brain worm sacrifices its life, or the way that blinking is a reflex—then we might well think that such "altruistic" behavior had no moral significance. You saw in Chapter 2 that psychological egoism is the view according to which all acts are motivated by self-interest. The converse term, "psychological altruism," is the view that not all acts are motivated by the desire to benefit others but that at least some acts are so motivated. And, according to psychological altruism, such motives are conscious and intentional, unlike the motives of our tiny martyr, the brain worm.

Sober and Wilson defend psychological altruism. They hold that it is likely—though not certain—that it was "chosen" by natural selection. They argue that in the case of humans, beliefs and desires are causal factors in the process that generates the kinds of behavior that have survival benefits. In the realm of psychology they draw a distinction between "ultimate desires" and "instrumental desires." The desire to avoid pain is *psychologically* ultimate. That is, in terms of psychological motives it is ultimate in the sense that it is not for anything else. But if the desire to avoid pain is psychologically ultimate, it is at the same time *evolutionarily* instrumental. In evolutionary theory the desire to avoid pain has the function of ensuring the survival of the individual, because many acts that cause pain are also dangerous to the organism.

In this context, the question that Sober and Wilson want to ask is this:

> Do people ever have altruistic desires that are psychologically ultimate? Or do people want others to do well only because they think that this will provide a benefit to self? *Psychological egoism* is the theory that all our ultimate desires are self-directed; the motivational theory called *psychological altruism* maintains that we sometimes care about others for their own sakes. (201)

To defend their attempt to "establish the plausibility of psychological altruism as part of the human mind" (205), Sober and Wilson select as a case study the question of parental care of infants, because there is a fairly obvious propensity for human parents to care for their offspring, and this propensity definitely has evolutionary value. If human parents did not care for their offspring, those offspring would die, and the parents' genes would not be passed along to future generations. Sober and Wilson ask, "What sort of beliefs and desires might furnish the proximate mechanism for human parental care?" (206). There are basically three possibilities: (a) altruistic motivation (the psychologically ultimate desire on the part of parents that their children flourish); (b) egoistic motivation (the parental wish that their children flourish is a desire that is merely instrumental to the selfish desire for the well-being of the parents themselves); (c) some combination of altruistic and egoistic desire. (Sober and Wilson call this combination "motivational pluralism" [308].) Sober and Wilson experiment extensively with each of these possibilities. Their analysis leads to a conclusion that "natural selection is unlikely to have given us purely egoistic motives" (12) and that motivational pluralism is the most likely system to have been "chosen" by natural selection.

Any attempt to reduce all motivation to one category, such as the pleasure/pain syndrome (hedonism), would shortchange the benefits that derive from other forms of motivation available to us. Sober and Wilson ask, "Why should creatures with [their many] cognitive capacities have all their desires answerable to the ultimate tribunal of pleasure and pain?" (324).

Good News and Bad News

The main thrust of *Unto Others*, then, is the demonstration that the probability of natural selection favoring motivational pluralism is much greater than that of any other possibility. Sober and Wilson have made a strong case for the thesis that the altruism favored by natural selection applies beyond the circle of family members—self-sacrifices can be made even for individuals who do not carry one's genes. This is a great moral improvement over kinship selection theory. But, according to their theory, these altruistic motives toward nonfamily members can apply only within one's communal organization. In the words of Sober and Wilson,

However, if selection promotes an altruistic concern for the welfare of one's near and dear, it also may promote indifference or malevolence toward outsiders. Within-group selection is a competitive process, but so too is between-group selection; it promotes both within-group niceness and between-group nastiness. . . . [P]eople tend to empathize more with those whom they perceive as similar to themselves. . . . If empathy elicits altruistic motives with respect to those whom we take to be similar, its absence means that we are less inclined to be altruistically motivated toward those whom we take to be different. It is important not to lose sight of the symmetric logic of selection arguments. (326–7)

That is, based on Sober and Wilson's thesis, it is difficult to explain how nature could have selected altruism that extends to members of other groups with which one's group competes. Most moral theorists will surely hope that this pessimistic conclusion is false.

This rather significant development in Sober and Wilson's argument is disturbing, but at least it is an invitation for more thinking in the field of evolutionary ethics in order to bridge the gap between "us" and "them."

Us Against Them: The Big-Endians vs. the Little-Endians
(from *Gulliver's Travels*, I:4)

If Sober and Wilson are correct in saying that human thoughts and beliefs are "proximate mechanisms" that can lead to behavior with survival value, there is hope that our naturally selected altruism could be extended to individuals (and animals?) external to our own "we" group.

It appears that Sober and Wilson's arguments and conclusions escape any challenge from Hume's Guillotine, if only because Sober and Wilson have not recommended any values at all. If their argument is successful (and I for one am impressed), then they have shown not only that there is no need for evolutionary ethics to base itself on egoism, but that it would be an error to do so. Furthermore, they have shown that Darwinian biology, which by itself does not generate an ethical system, has a theory of human motivation that is at least compatible in principle with any of the traditional moral codes that presuppose the validity of psychological altruism. It may appear that this discovery is tantamount to admitting that no specifically evolutionary ethics is required, a conclusion that would seem to render the need for this chapter that you are reading null and void. However, I think that what Sober and Wilson have done is clear the way for an evolutionary ethics on the model of James Rachels's moral individualism. Such an evolutionary ethics demands that ethics heed Darwin's plea that the factual presuppositions behind ethical theories be consistent with human nature as it actually is ("ought implies is") and that ethical theories not isolate the human being in some fictitious space of nobility independent of its animal forebears and cousins.

Perceived Strengths and Weaknesses
Strengths

- Evolutionary ethics provides updated theories, inspired by and consistent with the current state of science.

- The philosophy offers the opportunity to transcend speciesism (chauvinism about the superiority of the species to which one happens to belong).

- We are forced to reconsider so-called moral views that may simply be cultural prejudices and conveniences (views about eating habits, the treatment of nonhuman animals, euthanasia, suicide).

- As put forth by James Rachels, the philosophy strongly supports and rationalizes a common moral intuition against cruelty to nonhuman animals.

Weaknesses

- If it stands too firmly on its biological foundation, evolutionary ethics is in danger of caving into the black hole of the is/ought problem; if it wanders too far away from its biological foundation, it is in danger of losing its claim to be an *evolutionary* ethics.

- It requires acceptance of a scientific biological theory resisted by many in the United States as a threat to traditional religious and moral values.

- The problem of altruism does not seem to have been solved in a broad enough manner.

Questions for Consideration

1. What features of Darwin's theory of evolution show the influence of Charles Lyell and Thomas Malthus, respectively?

2. Explain the Darwinian ideas of continuity, overproduction, struggle for survival, variation, adaptation, and speciation, and the relationships among these ideas.

3. Take the position of a particular religious tradition and write a short essay attacking Darwinism from the perspective you have chosen. (Characterize the religious point of view from which you will launch your attack.)

4. Take the position of a particular religious tradition (either the one in question 3 or a different one) and write a short essay from the perspective you have chosen showing that Darwinism and religion are compatible. (Again, clarify the religious point of view from which you will form your defense.)

5. Distinguish between "natural selection" and "sexual selection."

6. Some contemporaries of Darwin believed that his theory undermined the possibility of morality; yet Darwin denied that this is the case. Explain both positions.

7. Explain why some Darwinians in today's world believe that despite Darwin's denial, his theory does indeed undermine traditional morality and the moral philosophies that support traditional morality.

8. Discuss the debate about the uniqueness of human beings as distinguished from the rest of the animal world. Where does Darwin stand in this debate?

9. Explain James Rachels's principle of equality, and discuss its application to both human and nonhuman subjects.

10. Show how Rachels's distinction between biological and biographical lives sometimes gives moral priority to humans over nonhumans.

11. How does Rachels avoid the is/ought problem, if you think he does?

12. Explain the distinction between biological altruism and psychological altruism.

13. Why, according to Sober and Wilson, would human groups that exhibit some altruism be more likely to be adaptive (i.e., be "selected") than those that do not?

14. Explain why, according to Sober and Wilson, allowing that natural selection can favor groups, and not solely individuals (or even individual genes), can solve the problem of altruism in biology.

15. For Sober and Wilson's theory of altruism, discuss the significance of their claim that nature selects in-group altruism but does not select intergroup altruism (i.e., altruism by members of the in-group exhibited toward members of an out-group).

16. What, according to the author, is the "bad news" in the theory of altruism put forth by Sober and Wilson? Do you see any way out of this bad news within the framework of the arguments set forth in *Unto Others*?

Study Guide: Outline of Chapter Five

I. Influences on the development of Darwin's theory of evolution.

   A. Intellectual influences: Lyell and Malthus.

   B. Experiential influences: the voyage of the HMS *Beagle*.

II. Darwin's theory of evolution according to *The Origin of Species* (1859).

   A. Descent: the historical connection between all life forms.

   B. "Natural selection."

      1. Continuity (duplicative reproduction).

      2. Overproduction (more are reproduced than the environment can sustain).

3. The "struggle for survival" (some make it; some don't).

4. Variation (breakdowns in the process of duplication, e.g., mutations).

5. Adaptation (new organic configurations that find the environment less hostile).

6. Speciation (new communities of organisms that exhibit the same adaptive characteristics).

III. Religious objections to Darwin's theory of evolution.

   A. Biblical evidence against descent from lower species?

   B. No room for an immortal, eternal soul?

   C. No need for God the Creator?

   D. Theory as a diabolical temptation against faith?

   E. The elimination of teleology from nature?

   F. Darwinism vs. the "argument from design"?

   G. Undermines reasons for morality?

IV. Darwinism and the human being.

   A. Publication of *The Descent of Man* (1871).

   B. Like other life-forms, the human being is "descended from some lower form."

   C. The processes of both "natural selection" and "sexual selection" are at work in the human world.

V. Darwinism and morality.

   A. Darwin denied that the obliteration of the distinction between humans and animals threatens morality and moral theory.

      1. Humans have evolved to the "very summit of the organic scale."

      2. The foundations of morality are built into our biology.

      3. Darwin's respect for Kantianism, utilitarianism, and Christian ethics.

   B. How Darwin undermines traditional morality despite himself.

      1. The "distinction in kind" between animals and humans ("human dignity") required by many traditional moral codes and theories is rejected by Darwinism.

2. Darwin's fear of giving offense may have caused him to disguise the radicalness of his theory.

3. Darwin's occasional use of Lamarckian ideas to support traditional moral theories is rejected by most Darwinians.

4. Some believe that Darwin's theory lacks a strong enough account of altruism to satisfy traditional theories.

VI. Contemporary theories of evolutionary ethics.

    A. James Rachels's moral individualism.

        1. The obligations we owe to individuals (human or nonhuman) do not depend on their *species*, but on their individual characteristics.

        2. The "principle of equality": if both a human individual and a nonhuman individual have the same morally relevant features (e.g., ability to suffer pain or enjoy contentment), treat the nonhuman individual in the same way you treat the human individual.

        3. Rachels's theory of the value of a life.

            a. The value of a life is the value that life has for the subject of that life.

            b. The subject does not have to be conscious of that value.

            c. The distinction between biological and biographical lives, where biographical lives have more value.

        4. Moral implications of Rachels's evolutionary ethics.

            a. Experiments with animals must be greatly curtailed.

            b. Vegetarianism is morally required.

            c. Views on euthanasia and suicide must be reconsidered.

        5. Does moral individualism escape the is/ought problem?

    B. Sober and Wilson's theory of biological altruism in *Unto Others*.

        1. The biological definition of altruism: An individual organism is biologically altruistic if it "reduces its own fitness and augments the fitness of others."

        2. Many other biologists feel that biological altruism is impossible: The "fittest" organisms must be egoistic.

        3. They reject the role that Darwin gives to

            a. Group selection.

    b. Social norms.

    c. Lamarckism.

4. The attack on the theory of group selection: Nature selects selfish individuals (or even "selfish" genes).

5. Sober and Wilson's defense of Darwin's original view: Nature does "select" groups.

    a. Group characteristics can have survival value for its members.

    b. Altruism as such has survival value.

    c. Social groups exhibiting some altruism, and having social norms that support altruism, can evolve into "adaptive units."

6. Why nature is more likely to "select" not only biological altruism, but also psychological altruism, over psychological egoism: Child rearing is more successful.

7. The limitation of Sober and Wilson's theory: It appears that altruism could only have been selected when it is exhibited toward members of an in-group, not toward a competing outgroup.

For Further Reading

Cronin, Helena. *The Ant and the Peacock: Altruism and Sexual Selection from Darwin to Today.* Cambridge: Cambridge University Press, 1991.

Darwin, Charles. *The Origin of Species.* 1859. New York: Random House, 1993.

Darwin, Charles. *The Descent of Man.* 1871. Norwalk, Conn.: The Heritage Press, 1972.

Dawkins, Richard. *The Selfish Gene.* New York: Oxford University Press, 1976.

Dennett, Daniel C. *Freedom Evolves.* New York: Viking Penguin, 2003.

De Waal, Frans B. M. *Good Natured: The Origins of Right and Wrong in Humans and Other Animals.* Cambridge, Mass.: Harvard University Press, 1996.

Flew, Antony. *Evolutionary Ethics.* London: Macmillan, 1967.

Gould, Stephen Jay. *Ever Since Darwin.* New York: W. W. Norton, 1977.

Rachels, James. *Created from Animals: The Moral Implications of Darwinism.* Oxford and New York: Oxford University Press, 1990.

Regan, Tom. *The Case for Animal Rights.* Berkeley: University of California Press, 1983.

Regan, Tom, and Peter Singer, eds. *Animal Rights and Human Obligations.* Englewood Cliffs, N.J.: Prentice-Hall, 1976.

Singer, Peter. *Animal Liberation.* New York: Hearst Corporation, 1991.

Sober, Elliott, and David Sloan Wilson. *Unto Others: The Evolution and Psychology of Unselfish Behavior.* Cambridge, Mass., and London: Harvard University Press, 2000.

Stent, Gunther S., ed. *Morality as a Biological Phenomenon.* Berkeley: University of California Press, 1978.

Wright, Robert. *The Moral Animal: The New Science of Evolutionary Psychology.* New York: Pantheon, 1994.

Notes

1. In this chapter, I often put the phrase "natural selection" between quotation marks because the phrase is actually quite misleading, as Darwin came to realize after it was too late to change it. The phrase seems to imply an *agency* at work doing the selection (like a human being or a god), and a *teleology* (goals or purposes for the item selected). Ironically, it is precisely agency and teleology which Darwin's theory eliminates as unnecessary causal forces.

2. The phrase "struggle for survival," which Darwin borrowed from the philosopher Herbert Spencer (1820—1903), also proves to be misleading. Most of the organisms in the "struggle" do not know what the struggle is for, nor do they know that they are struggling; and many do *not* struggle—they just don't manage to pass along their genes.

3. Daniel Dennett, *Darwin's Dangerous Idea* (New York: Simon & Schuster, 1995). Page references to this work will be included in the body of the text in parentheses.

4. Charles Darwin, *The Origin of Species* (New York: Random House, 1993), 647.

5. Charles Darwin, *The Descent of Man* (Norwalk, Conn.: The Heritage Press, 1972), 128, 137. Future page references to this work will be included in the body of the text in parentheses.

6. The anthropologist Ashley Montagu believes that Darwin overestimated the role of sexual selection throughout the total history of human societies. In the preface to *The Descent of Man* (see note 5), he writes that "it has become increasingly evident that in most non-literate societies there is very little opportunity for the operation of sexual selection, for the simple reason that most individuals are not free to choose their mates" (x).

7. Leila S. May, "Monkeys, Microcephalous Idiots, and the Barbarous Races of Mankind: Darwin's Dangerous Victorianism," *The Victorian Newsletter,* no. 102 (Fall 2002): 20–6.

8. For example, Robert Ardrey, *The Territorial Imperative* (New York: Atheneum, 1966) and Desmond Morris, *The Naked Ape* (New York: McGraw-Hill, 1967).

9. James Rachels, *Created from Animals: The Moral Implications of Darwinism* (Oxford and New York: Oxford University Press, 1990), 152–3. Future references to this work will be cited parenthetically in the body of the text. Shortly you will see how Rachels tries to solve this problem.

10. ". . . *nomina nuda tenemus,*" the last line of Umberto Eco's novel, *The Name of the Rose,* trans. William Weaver (New York: Harcourt Brace Jovanovich, 1980), 502.

11. As far as I know, Arthur Danto was the first philosopher to point out that every "is" implies an "ought," in his *Mysticism and Morality: Oriental Thought and Moral Philosophy* (New York: Harper & Row, 1973).

12. Elliott Sober and David Sloan Wilson, *Unto Others: The Evolution and Psychology of Unselfish Behavior* (Cambridge, Mass., and London: Harvard University Press, 2000). Future references to this work will be included parenthetically in the body of the text.

13. G. C. Williams, *Adaptation and Natural Selection: A Critique of Some Current Evolutionary Thought* (Princeton: Princeton University Press, 1966).

14. Richard Dawkins, *The Extended Phenonotype: The Long Reach of the Gene* (New York: Oxford University Press, 1982), 115.

15. W. D. Hamilton, "The Evolution of Altruistic Behavior." *American Naturalist 97* (1963): 354–6.

16. Richard Dawkins, *The Selfish Gene* (New York: Oxford University Press, 1976).

17. Of course, these norms are inherited socially and not physically, so this is not the kind of example Lamarck himself had in mind. Remember, according to him, the giraffe physically inherits the additional length of the neck that resulted from its parents' stretching efforts.

6

Virtue Ethics

Throughout the modern period—roughly, the period after Descartes's death in 1650—Western moral philosophy has been dominated by Kantian rationalism (a philosophy of duty, derived from reason) and utilitarianism (a philosophy of the beneficial consequences of actions). During the past twenty-five years, it is not only evolutionary ethics that has been placed on the main stage of moral philosophy and claimed to be a worthy competitor of Kantianism and utilitarianism; a philosophy known as "virtue ethics" has made similar claims for itself. Its key concepts are not those of duty and rule following, nor of consequentialism and utility, but of human character and, as the name implies, virtue.

Despite its rather recent appearance on the philosophical stage, we cannot accurately say that virtue ethics is a new moral philosophy, because it is derived from the work of Plato and Aristotle, who taught in Athens during the fifth and fourth centuries B.C.E. But the works of the ancient Greeks—including Plato and Aristotle—were virtually lost to Europe during the so-called Dark Ages of Western history (roughly, 400 to 800 C.E., the violent beginning of the thousand-year medieval period), and what little ethical theory existed was derived from Biblical inspiration.[1] Virtue ethics experienced a revival in the thirteenth century because of the recovery of the writings of Plato and Aristotle. This was the result of intellectual exchange between the Christians and the Muslim world, where the works of Aristotle not only had survived, but had deeply influenced Muslim moral thought, and had been minutely commented upon. The key personage behind this European revival was Thomas Aquinas (1225–1274), who developed an influential Christianized version of Aristotle's virtue ethics. St. Thomas's moral philosophy has survived in Catholic intellectual circles to this day, but it still must be said that until its recent reintroduction upon the scene, virtue ethics has played a minor role in the larger drama of modern philosophical ethics.

Virtue Ethics in the Classical World

Because most contemporary versions of virtue ethics derive from the work of Aristotle, we will begin with a brief exposition of his theory. But such an exposition requires a few words about Aristotle's teacher, Plato.

Plato

Plato (427–347 B.C.E.) had divided reality into two basic components: the Forms, and copies of Forms. According to him, Forms are eternal, unchanging, nonmaterial archetypes, of which everything in the material world are mere imitations. Plato believed that each

Plato

human soul has been in direct contact with the Forms prior to the soul's embodiment during birth, an event so traumatic and degrading that the soul forgets its contact with the Forms. (Plato's Christian follower, St. Augustine [354–430], also saw birth as a degrading event. He reminds us that we were all born "between urine and feces.")

Therefore each human's main task (or at least each human that can demonstrate the intellectual capacity for the task) is to philosophize in order to try to recollect the memory of the Forms.

For Plato, this philosophical task, though partly epistemological (that is, a job of acquiring knowledge), is essentially a moral task, because the primary Form, the Form of all Forms, as we might put it, is the Form of the Good. Therefore, all attempts to acquire knowledge—to philosophize—are attempts to achieve knowledge of the Good, even if we do not realize that this is what is happening. Furthermore, Plato's moral theory was essentially a very optimistic one, not because he thought that most people could achieve knowledge of the Good (he didn't), but because he thought that whoever knew the Good would become good—that is, one would acquire all of the virtues. All moral error—or, to use a religious category, all sin—is really ignorance. No one who truly understands the Good can willingly do evil. The main reason for this is, surprisingly, an egoistic one; namely, that if I do evil, I damage my own soul, and in my right mind, I would not do damage to myself.

Aristotle

Aristotle

Aristotle (384–322 B.C.E.) incorporated some of Plato's thinking into his own views, but in many respects, he was critical of his teacher's theories. First, he was critical of Plato's dualism—the division of reality into two tiers and, worse yet, the assertion that one tier of reality is less real than the other. (For Plato, the material world is just a poor copy of the intelligible world.) Aristotle replaced Plato's dualism with a form of **pluralism**—the view that reality is composed of a multitude of different beings. Also, Aristotle was dissatisfied with Plato's account of change and movement. The problem of change had been a main concern in the earlier pre-Socratic philosophy, in which there were two extremes. On the one hand, Parmenides (ca. 515–ca. 440 B.C.E.) claimed that everything is eternally the same, and that change and motion are illusions; on the other hand, Heraclitus (flourished ca. 470 B.C.E.) claimed that the only thing real was change itself and that permanence and stability are illusions.

For Aristotle, Plato's solution is too close to Parmenides, because Plato's "most real" reality—the realm of the Forms—is eternally unchanging; change is only the result of poor imitation. Aristotle's compromise in some ways sides more with Heraclitus, because

Heraclitean
Hustle

for Aristotle, change is an essential part of reality. But change is not arbitrary. Each "substance" (Aristotle's term for a real being) is in a constant struggle for self-realization, that is, to fulfill its potentiality, to become what it really is. An acorn, for instance, is a potential oak tree, and all of an acorn's acts are directed toward that self-realization. The acorn is striving to achieve its essence, or its "form," said Aristotle, borrowing the term from Plato, but bringing it down to earth. For Aristotle, there are unchanging, eternal "forms," but they are in this world.

After having read the chapter in this book on Darwin and evolutionary ethics, you probably realize that Aristotle's picture of nature is exactly the type that Darwin would come to challenge 2,400 years later, because Aristotle holds that species do not evolve: Oak trees are eternally oak trees, eagles are eternally eagles, and roaches are forever roaches.

Furthermore, Aristotle's theory is a heavily teleological one. All motion is a kind of purposeful, goal-seeking, activity. There are in nature "natural" goals; in fact, nature is simply a system of natural purposes and attempts to realize those purposes—every substance in the world has an innate goal to achieve self-fulfillment. For many people, after Darwin, it is not possible to take seriously an Aristotelian picture of nature. Therefore, if modern virtue ethicists want to base their theories on Aristotle (as most of them seem to do), they must try to rewrite Aristotle's ethics in ways that will avoid his errors. Shortly, we will take a look at that effort, but first, we must lay out the outlines of Aristotle's moral theory.[2]

Well, then, human beings exist in reality, and therefore Aristotle, whose philosophy is a genuine metaphysics in that it tries to present an overall explanation of the totality of reality, needs to give an account of human beings and their status in the world. In fact, several of his books participate in this task. There is a book on politics, a book on aesthetics (particularly on drama and poetics), and a couple of books on ethics. The ethics book that is considered the most important now goes by the name of *Nicomachean Ethics*, named either after Aristotle's son, Nicomachus, or after a student by that name who may have transcribed Aristotle's book. It is to that work that we now turn.

Nicomachean Ethics

Aristotle's *Nicomachean Ethics* reflects his teleological metaphysics. The notion of a goal or purpose is the overriding one in his moral theory.

Luckily for modern-day defenders of Aristotle's ethical theory, even Darwin admits that human beings—unlike acorns—are motivated by goals and purposes. In fact, usually we

Teleology: Actions Are Like Arrows— They Are Aimed at Some Target.

distinguish between human behavior and the behavior of other objects in nature using teleological language about humans (except where there is a breakdown in the teleological system, such as a person's accidental tripping over a shoe) and nonteleological language about most other objects. (For example, we explain human behavior by talking about intentions and goals, but we explain acorn behavior by talking about their chemical nature in the context of the composition of dirt, and the role of wind, water, and sunshine in a causal, mechanical system).[3]

Aristotle opens the *Nicomachean Ethics* with this claim: "Every sort of expert knowledge and every inquiry, and similarly every action and undertaking, seems to seek some good. Because of that, people are right to affirm that the good is 'that which all things seek'."[4] It seems that to Aristotle this assertion is self-evident, yet many readers might disagree with it because it appears to be a version of Plato's controversial claim that nobody could willingly choose evil. But perhaps we could agree with Aristotle that when people choose to engage in a certain act, they do so because they take it to be better than its alternative in the circumstances under which the decision is made. Of course, one could be mistaken in one's choice. Acorns actually have the advantage here because their striving toward self-realization is instinctive and not conscious.

Oh goody! I've fallen from the tree. Now I can become a butterfly!

But humans make conscious choices, and therefore they sometimes make bad ones. Now, if there is no ultimate goal for us humans to seek, then our acts constitute an infinitely arbitrary series—a series of haphazard and unrelated choices—in which case our lives are unstructured and meaningless. Or the totality of our acts is an infinitely circular series (we get up in order to eat breakfast, we eat breakfast in order to go to work, we go to work in order to get money, we get money in order to be able to buy food in order to be able to eat breakfast, etc., etc., etc.)—in which case life again would be pretty meaningless. But if there is some ultimate good toward which the purposes of all acts are directed, we should try to come to know that ultimate good so that we can adjust all our acts toward it in order to avoid that saddest of all tragedies—the wasted life.

In fact, believes Aristotle, there is a rough verbal agreement both among philosophers and the general public that the end toward which

all human acts are directed is happiness (*eudaimonia*). It seems universally agreed among Aristotle scholars that the Greek word *eudaimonia* has no exact translation into English. It is usually rendered as "happiness," but sometimes as "well-being," or "good living," or "thriving." The main reason that none of these translations is completely satisfactory is that the quality that Aristotle seeks to characterize is a quality that attaches to a whole life, and not just parts of it (yesterday I was happy, but not today; I was happy to see her, but then she spilled spaghetti sauce on my comic book collection), nor features of it (my marriage, my job, my comic book collecting).

Aristotle says, "[A] single swallow does not make spring, nor does a single day; in the same way, neither does a single day, or a short time, make a man blessed and happy" (102/1098^{a}18–21). Aristotle goes so far at one point to suggest that only after a person's death can a judgment be made about whether that person's life was *eudaimon*. Despite the discrepancy between the Greek and the

English, I will usually stick with the traditional translation of *eudaimonia* as "happiness," but will choose other translations from this list when they seem contextually superior, or occasionally use the Greek word itself to remind us of the slight conceptual incongruity here. Happiness is recognized by everybody as the human good, according to Aristotle, because we seek happiness for its own sake, not for the sake of something else. The question *Why do you like to travel (or collect comic books, or read gourmet cooking books, or help others, etc.)* makes sense; but there is something odd about the question *Why do you want to be happy?* Yet, there is much disagreement about what happiness is. Unless we philosophize about it, and come to know exactly its nature and how to achieve it, our claim to know that happiness is the human good will be quite empty.

To determine the nature of happiness, Aristotle turns to his teleological metaphysics and asks the question What is the function of the human being? When you know the function of an artifact like a knife, you can determine its "good." (A good knife is one that is held comfortably and cuts with precision.) Or, to use another example of Aristotle's, if we know the function of a bodily organ, we can determine that organ's "good." (A good eye is one that, without the support of artificial devices, can detect similarities, differences, and changes in external reality at a distance or close up.)

For many post-Darwinians, Aristotle's question What is the function of the human being? is highly suspect. (In fact, for some hard-core Darwinians, even the question about human organs is suspect. Can we talk about the *function* of the eye or the heart without making teleological assumptions about purposes in nature?[5]) At any rate, it is clear that Aristotle is completely comfortable with his question. People today with certain religious convictions might also be satisfied with the question, which they might pose as Why did God put us here? Furthermore, it does seem that it might be possible to ask what the function of a human being is in the same spirit that we talk about the function of the heart or eye without making egregious teleological assumptions. (The function of the heart is whatever it actually *does* do—pump blood, as it turns out—not what it was "meant" to do.)

Aristotle frames his answer in three different but related formulas:

> [T]he function of a human being is activity of the soul in accordance with reason, or not apart from reason. (102/1098ᵃ8–9)
>
> [A] human being's function we posit as being a kind of life, and this life as being activity of soul and actions accompanied by reason, and it belongs to a good man to perform these well and finely, and each thing is completed well when it possesses its proper excellence. (102/1098ᵃ13–17)

> [T]he human good turns out to be activity of the soul in accor-
> dance with excellence (and if there are more excellences than
> one, in accordance with the best and most complete).
> (102/1098ª16–18)

Take note of the appearance of the term "excellence" in the second and third definition. This is a translation of the Greek word *areté*,
and it is often translated as "virtue"—hence the term "virtue ethics."
Areté is that quality of any act, endeavor, or object that makes it a
successful act, endeavor, or object. Before we can understand Aristotle's definition of happiness, we must look into *areté* and see what
kinds of excellences and virtues there are, and how we can achieve
them.

But even before this, as an aside, I must mention that Aristotle
believed that certain material conditions must hold before happiness
can be achieved. This list of material conditions reveals Aristotle's
elitism: We need good friends, riches, and political power. We need a
good birth, good children, and good looks ("for the person who is extremely ugly, or of low birth, or on his own without children is someone
we would be not inclined to call happy"
[104/1099ᵇ4–6]). Neither is happiness available to people who are
very short.

In addition, we must be free
from the need of performing man-
ual labor. ("No man can practice
virtue who is living the life of a
mechanic or laborer."⁶) Furthermore, the bulk of Aristotle's work
testifies to his belief that true hap-

piness eludes anyone who is not a male. Obviously, modern virtue
ethicists reject this list, which is not hard to do, because Aristotle's moral theory is left virtually intact when his elitist bias
is deleted. The only substantial contribution that it adds is the
recognition that achieving *eudaimonia* is not totally up to the indi-

vidual agent; "moral luck"[7] also plays a role in the achievement of happiness.

Moral Bad Luck

Moral Virtue

For Aristotle, there are two kinds of virtue: intellectual and moral. Intellectual virtues are acquired through a combination of inheritance and education, and moral virtues through imitation, practice, and habit. The habits that we develop result in "states of character"— that is, in dispositions to act in certain ways—and these states of character are virtuous for Aristotle if they result in acts that are in accordance with a "golden mean of moderation." For Aristotle, a "mean" is a position taken between two extremes; he calls one extreme "deficiency" and an opposite extreme "excess." Both extremes are vices, and the mean is a virtue. For example, when it comes to facing danger, one can act with excess, that is, show too much bravado (foolhardiness). Or one can act deficiently, showing too much fear (cowardliness). Or one can act with moderation, and hence virtuously, by showing the right amount of fear (courage). (General George Custer was certainly no coward, but was he courageous or foolhardy?)

Aristotle lists the following examples to illustrate his idea. (Some of the awkward language you will find here has to do again with Greek words that have no direct counterpart in English. For example, *mikropsychia* ("smallness of soul") and *megalopsychia* ("greatness of soul") are not concepts we recognize, but they are very important to Aristotle.)

ACTION	DEFICIENCY	EXCESS	MEAN
Search for pleasure	insensateness	self-indulgence	moderation
Giving of money	avariciousness	wastefulness	generosity
Spending of money	stinginess	vulgarity	munificence
Accepting honors	smallness of soul	conceit	greatness of soul
Feeling anger	spiritlessness	irascibility	mild-temperedness
Expressing humor	boorishness	buffoonery	wittiness
Casual relationships	contentious	obsequiousness	friendliness
Expressing shame	shamelessness	no name for this state (but the person is ashamed of everything)	sense of shame
Describing one's achievements	humility	boastfulness	pride
Expressions of feelings about those who are overly honored	spite	envy	righteous indignation
Pursuing aspirations	lack of ambition	overambition	no proper name for this state

We can diagram Aristotle's account of the location of the moral virtues or excellences as follows:

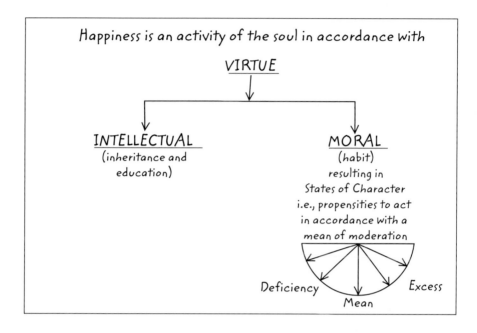

Happiness is an activity of the soul in accordance with
VIRTUE

INTELLECTUAL
(inheritance and education)

MORAL
(habit)
resulting in
States of Character
i.e., propensities to act
in accordance with a
mean of moderation

Deficiency   Excess
Mean

The misleading feature of this diagram is that it might make the search for the golden mean appear to be simply a mathematical issue (the mean is exactly halfway between deficiency and excess, so all you really need is a ruler). But Aristotle insists that the choices we must make if we are to learn moral virtue cannot be made scientifically but must be approached through trial and error, and they are always contextualized. For example, concerning the giving away of money, where generosity is the virtue, when Aristotle says that the generous man gives away just the right amount, that amount is always relative to what he can afford. Moreover, the virtuous person here does not give money to just anybody, but to the right person, and in a timely manner, and for a good reason. Giving generously to a drunken spendthrift is not a virtuous act, hence is not true generosity.

When I say that trial and error are involved in Aristotle's theory of moral choice, I do not mean to leave the impression that the process of making these judgments is purely hit-or-miss. As we will see, one must reason well at each stage, and one must have a grasp of the circumstances in which one is making these decisions. The whole process of experimentation here is an exercise of reason, not a gambler hoping for luck.

Aristotle summarizes for us his theory of moral virtue:

> Excellence, then, is a disposition issuing in decisions, depending on intermediacy [i.e., means] of the kind relative to us, this being determined by rational prescription and in the way in which the wise person would determine it. And it is intermediacy between two bad states, one involving excess, the other involving deficiency; and also because one set of bad states is deficient, the other excessive in relation to what is required both in affections and in actions, whereas excellence both finds and chooses the intermediate. (117/1106^{b}36–1107^{a}6)

Two comments on this passage: First, notice that Aristotle's idea of virtue or excellence as a "disposition" is not merely a behavioristic account (i.e., not an account that depends only on observable physical behavior and excludes mental or emotional states) because Aristotle says that both the right "affections" (that is, emotions) and actions are required. You've got to have the right attitudes, feelings, and thoughts when you make your decision and take your path. Second, notice that the choice of the mean is finally explained as the one that is as the "wise person would determine it." (Other translations have "as the man of practical wisdom would determine it.") Some critics feel that this move is circular. We want to know which actions are virtuous, and we are told that they are the actions that virtuous people make. But how are we going to recognize virtuous people (the "wise person," or the "man of practical wisdom") if we don't know what virtue is? Certainly, modern virtue ethics philosophers will have to address this issue.

Before turning to the question of intellectual virtue, let us inspect

Circular System

one more example of moral virtue—one that tells us something interesting about the difference between Aristotle's world and our own, hence, yet another issue that modern virtue ethicists must address. Speaking of actions performed in the pursuit of honors or avoidance of disgrace, you saw that Aristotle says that the excess is "conceit" (or "vanity"), the deficiency is *mikropsychia* (being "small-souled"), and the mean is *megalopsychia* (having "greatness of soul"). As was mentioned, these Greek words have no exact English equivalents, but let's look at some of Aristotle's examples of *megalopsychia*.

It is, then, honours and dishonours that the great-souled person most has to do with; and in the case of great honours, accorded him by people of excellence, he will be moderately pleased, on the grounds that he is getting what belongs to him, or actually less than that—for there could be no honour worthy of complete excellence. All the same, he will accept it in so far as they have nothing greater to mete out to him. As for honour from just anyone, and given for small things, he will wholly despise it, because that is not what he is worthy of. . . . This is why great-souled people seem to be arrogant. . . . [T]he great-souled person is justified in looking down on people (since his judgements are true). . . . [H]e is the sort to speak his mind, since he tends to look down on people. . . . He is not the sort to feel admiration either; for nothing impresses him. . . . [S]low movement seems to be characteristic of the great-souled person, and a deep voice, and steady speech; for the person who takes few things seriously is not the sort to hurry, nor is someone who is impressed by nothing the sort to be tense— and these are the causes of a high-pitched voice and hasty movement. (149–151/1124ª1–1125ª15)

Aristotle's small-souledness now looks very much like our idea of humility, and his great-souledness seems very much like pride. Perhaps because of two thousand years of Jewish and Christian moral traditions in the West, Aristotle's great-souled man will seem to many of us today to be quite obnoxious—his behavior seems totally staged, his actions contrived, and his arrogant condescension is intolerable. He is the kind of person we might name not

(squeak)
Oh, how very exciting.
(squeak)

by calling him a great-souled person, but by calling him . . . well, perhaps by calling him a jerk. Now, this is no small issue, because Aristotle calls greatness of soul "a sort of adornment, as it were, of the excellences; for it augments them, and does not occur without them" (149/1124ª5). It seems to be for Aristotle the virtue crowning all other virtues.

Intellectual Virtue

By combining the three definitions of "the function of the human being" given by Aristotle earlier, we get the idea that happiness, the human end, is "an activity of soul and actions accompanied by reason . . . in accordance with areté (virtue or excellence)." At this point in our analysis, we are supposed to understand something about the actions to which Aristotle refers (namely, the means between two extremes) and hence about moral virtues (characteristics of those mediating actions), but we still need to know what he refers to as the "activity of the soul." In order to get at that, we must look at the intellectual virtues, of which there are two kinds: practical wisdom and philosophical wisdom.

Practical Wisdom

Practical wisdom is still very closely related to the virtues, because it is the ability to deliberate well about one's decisions and actions. According to Aristotle,

> It is thought characteristic of a wise person to be able to deliberate well about things that are good and advantageous to himself, not in specific contexts, e.g. what sorts of things conduce to health, or to physical strength, but what sorts of things conduce to the good life in general. (180–1/1140ª25–1140ª29)

So the man of wisdom is capable of deliberating well about decisions that lead to the good life, to eudaimonia, and this ability is, on most interpretations of Aristotle, an intellectual virtue.[8]

Because of Aristotle's addition of this distinction between the two kinds of intellectual virtues, I will now add to the diagram provided earlier.

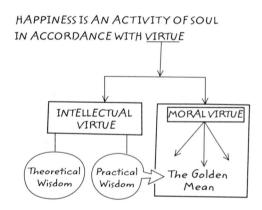

Philosophical (or Theoretical) Wisdom

I have yet to say anything about the other of the two important intellectual virtues, philosophical—or theoretical—wisdom, that "best and most complete virtue." If the virtue of calculative reason was practical wisdom, the virtue of pure reason is philosophical wisdom. You saw that practical reason deliberates over the strategies for achieving the good life. We only deliberate over things that are in our power. As Aristotle says, "[N]o one deliberates about things that cannot be otherwise" (177/1139ᵃ14). We do not deliberate over the past, nor about eternal truths, because we cannot change them. There is no *practical* component in them. But, as opposed to practical reason, *pure reason* contemplates precisely those features of reality about which we can do nothing.

Despite being what some might consider to be "useless knowledge," the philosophical wisdom that is the product of contemplation is awarded a very high standard by Aristotle:

**Contemplating That about Which
We Can Do Nothing**

> But if happiness is an activity in accordance with excellence, it is reasonable that it should be activity in accordance with the highest kind; and this will be the excellence of what is best. Whether, then, this is intelligence or something else, this element that is thought naturally to rule and guide, and to possess awareness of fine things and divine ones—whether being, itself too, something divine, or the divinest of things in us, it is an activity of this, in accordance with its own proper excellence, that will be complete happiness. That it is *reflective activity* has been said. . . . [T]his is the highest kind of activity, since intelligence too is highest of the things in us, and the objects of intelligence are the highest knowables. . . . Again, reflective activity would seem to be the only kind loved because of itself; for nothing accrues from it besides the act of reflecting, whereas from practical projects we get something . . . besides the doing of them. (250–1/1177ᵃ13–1177ᵃ24; 1177 ᵇ1–1177 ᵇ4)

If the human being is "the rational animal"—if reason is the human essence, as Aristotle believes ("Man is the rational animal")—then philosophical contemplation (or reflection, in this translation) proves to be the highest goal of human life, the "function" of human existence, and the happiest human being is THE PHILOSOPHER (the philosopher, it is very important to note, who does not simply sit around thinking, but who engages actively in everyday life with "practical wisdom"). Of course, we may be a little suspicious to find a philosopher writing a book in which he tries to figure out what the best form of life is and discovering it to be . . . his own! Would someone with the same ideas as Aristotle but working in a different profession have arrived at a different conclusion? But it is comforting, at least to me, to learn that the human being is *Homo philosophicus*.

Virtue Ethics in Our World

We will now leap ahead about two thousand and five hundred years to observe the revival of virtue ethics in the twentieth and twenty-first centuries. In doing so we are also sailing over one of the most adept virtue ethics theorists of all time, St. Thomas Aquinas, who thrived during the thirteenth century. If someone is introduced to you as General Thomas, you know you are being presented to a military person who (probably) has been highly regarded in his or her field; similarly, if some (now dead) person is introduced to you as *Saint Thomas*, you know you are being presented to a highly regarded person of the Church. But it was not so from the beginning. Though Thomas is now one of the luminaries of Catholic philosophy, a few years after Thomas's death in 1274, the University of Paris outlawed the teaching of Aristotle and banned Thomas's own massive works. It is sometimes said, only semi-facetiously, that Aquinas's main historical achievement had been to "baptize" Aristotle; but this was no mean trick, not only because there is much in the Christian world that is antagonistic to the Greek world, but also because in the thirteenth century, conservative elements in the Church associated Aristotelian philosophy with the intellectual tradition of the Muslims. The Muslims of Spain had access to the thought of Aristotle long before it

The Baptism of Aristotle
(kicking and screaming)

was fully known in the Catholic world, and outstanding Spanish Arab and Jewish scholars had absorbed it into their own systems. Indeed,

St. Thomas acquired much of his knowledge of Aristotle from the Spanish philosopher Averroës (known in his own language as Al-lul Walid Muhammad ibn Hafid ibn Rushd), who lived between 1126 and 1198. If the transition between the Christian world and the Greek world looks easy to us today, this is partially due to St. Thomas's efforts. We will touch upon his ideas again and mention some of the difficulties that he faced in developing a successful Christian Aristotelian virtue ethics.

In our time, a great number of Catholic philosophers continue to be adherents to Aquinas's version of virtue ethics, but there are also a number of moral philosophers who do not write specifically as religious philosophers (some of them are, and some are not) who have become dissatisfied with the traditional ethical camps, dominated by hedonism, utilitarianism, and Kantianism. They have reconsidered virtue ethics and deem it a viable competitor on the still-combative scene of moral philosophy. Most—but not all—of these contemporary virtue ethicists still see Aristotle as their main champion, though, like St. Thomas before them, they find that in rebaptizing Aristotle into a different world from fourth-century Athens, they have to make a few adjustments and compromises and experience a few embarrassments. (How could it be otherwise?) Before looking back to the various features of Aristotle's philosophy that contemporary virtue ethicists accept or reject, I will try to characterize the contemporary movement as I see it.

Contemporary Virtue Ethics

Each ethical system seems to have a key moral concept from which all its other concepts are derived. The foundational concept of hedonists and consequentialists alike (such as utilitarians) is that of the "good," and secondary moral concepts such as right and wrong, virtue, duty, and obligation—insofar as they exist at all in these systems—are derived from this concept. Deontologists such as Kantians ground their theories in the idea of "duty" and derive the other moral concepts from it. This structure is tantamount to a kind of

reductionism in that all features of the system are explicable in terms of one basic concept. Now, virtue ethics is reductionist in this same way;[9] however, it seems to waver in its choice of a fundamental category between the idea of virtue itself (as the name of the movement would imply) and the idea of the virtuous person. Then the secondary concepts (right and wrong, duty, obligation), if they apply at all, are derived from one or the other of these two foundational concepts. In some ways, the concepts of virtue and virtuous person fuse, because a virtue is not an action, or a duty, or an event, or even just a disposition, but a quality or a characteristic that some individuals possess. The result is that virtue ethics is usually described as "agent-centered" rather than "act-centered," as concerned with "Being rather than Doing."[10]

Furthermore, it is seen as rejecting the idea that morality can be codified (i.e., set forth in a list of binding rules, like a legal code), because its idea of a moral agent is always contextualized in actual historical situations, hence, in a sense, relativized (as you saw with Aristotle's claim

Doing and Being

that morality can never be an exact science because it is always experimental and creative). As virtue theorist John McDowell says, "Occasion by occasion, one knows what to do, if one does, not by applying universal principles but by being a certain kind of person:

one who sees situations in a certain kind of way."[11] In many ways, this approach represents a radical departure from, for example, Kant, or Mill (but not from Aristotle). Besides rejecting as artificial the kind of program of codification and absoluteness that we found in Kant, virtue ethics also mounts an attack on the consequentialism of the utilitarians. Elizabeth Anscombe, one of the pioneers of modern virtue ethics, writing in the mid-twentieth century, argued that because it is impossible to know (all) the consequences of any act, consequentialism is empty because it cannot advocate any act at all except the most simple and uncontroversial ones. She says that a consequentialist

> has no footing on which to say "This would be permissible, this not"; because by his own hypothesis, it is the consequences that are to decide, and he has no business to pretend that he can lay it down what possible twists a man could give doing this or that. . . . [H]e has no right to say he will, in an actual case, bring about such-and-such unless he does so-and-so.[12]

Unforeseen Consequences of Kicking Puppies

Virtue ethics also rejects the demands for moral sainthood apparently put forth by Kantianism, utilitarianism, and religious-based ethics. In an influential article from 1982, Susan Wolf argues that moral demands, though very important, are not the only demands made upon us. Other goals, relationships, activities, and interests besides moral ones (such as hiking, reading, gardening, art, music, relaxation, sex, and religion—not necessarily in that order; make up your own hierarchy!) are or can be important components of one's life. It is not clear to Wolf that one can say on an *a priori* basis that moral interests *always* trump these interests. Wolf writes that "our non-moral reasons for the goals we set ourselves are not excuses, but may rather be positive, good, reasons which do not exist *despite* any reasons that might threaten to outweigh them. In other words, a person may be *perfectly wonderful* without being *perfectly moral*."[13]

Aristotle Today

As was mentioned, most contemporary virtue ethicists tout their relationship to Aristotle.[14] For example, Rosalind Hursthouse, a philosopher at Auckland University in New Zealand, and one of the most forceful and articulate members of the virtue school, calls herself a "neo-Aristotelian" in her recent book, *Virtue Ethics* (8). However, this does not prevent her from rejecting out of hand Aristotle's elitism or from saying forthrightly that Aristotle is "just plain wrong" on certain topics, such as slaves and women. (Aristotle thought that slavery was justified because slaves had different kinds of souls from other folks, and that women did not have complete souls.) Nor does she feel that we must stick with Aristotle's specific list of the virtues or with what Aristotle took to be the ultimate virtue.

Aristotle, still thinking about humans the way he thought about artifacts and about physical capacities like eyesight, asked what is man's highest function and concluded that it was philosophy. Most contemporary virtue ethicists, even though they are philosophers, refuse to go there with Aristotle, both because they reject his anti-

Darwinian teleology of "ultimate functions" and because they feel slightly embarrassed about this self-serving conclusion that Aristotle served up to himself. (Also, because of their rejection of teleological metaphysics, and because of their **naturalism,** they reject St. Thomas's claim that our ultimate end is preparation of the soul for the life hereafter.) Hursthouse says that one need not follow Aristotle "in specifying the life of contemplation as the only one that truly constitutes eudaimonia (if he does)."[15] Well, he *does*, and therefore Hursthouse's disagreement with Aristotle constitutes a rather large-scale revision of the *Nicomachean Ethics*. Still, I suppose it had to happen. And it is related to what Hursthouse calls "avoiding the Platonic fantasy."

> This is the fantasy that it is only through the study of philosophy that one can become virtuous (or really virtuous), and, as soon as it is stated explicitly, it is revealed to be a fantasy that must be most strenuously resisted. Of *course* people can be virtuous, really virtuous, without having spent clockable hours thinking about *eudaimonia*. (137)

Despite these significant revisions of Aritotelianism, Hursthouse and most others of her group want to hold fast to Aristotle's views about the nature of virtue. You saw that, for Aristotle, a virtue is not only a character trait, but an *excellence* of character. Each virtue, as Hursthouse says, "involves getting things right" (12), and the individual who always or usually gets things right is what Aristotle called the person of "practical wisdom." (Well, all right, Aristotle actually said "man" of practical wisdom, and he *meant* "man," but I think we have already disposed of that embarrassment.) So Hursthouse and others remain committed to Aristotle's complicated idea of *phronesis*, or practical wisdom, a theme to which we will return after a bit more discussion of the nature of virtue.

The Nature of Virtue

A virtue is not simply a tendency or disposition to behave in a certain way; a virtue is a state of one's character. If you display the virtues of honesty, justice, and kindness, then you *are* honest, just, and kind—but not in an empty sort of way. The virtues link your character with the world. When you act kindly, it is because you have a *reason* to act kindly, that is, because you have taken into consideration the feelings of others as part of the motivation behind your actions. Because you have (good) reasons for your actions when they are expressions of virtues, the virtues are *rational.* But they also involve emotions. The virtue theorists are convinced that one of Kant's major errors was to characterize the emotions as always irrational and hence as a target of moral effort, never as a motive of moral effort. In contrast, Aristotle had said that virtuous actions are performed with the *right* feelings and emotions behind them. Sometimes we *should* feel love, sometimes we *should* feel righteous indignation, or even anger, as we act in the world. (Of course, Aristotle also thought we should feel disdain for short, ugly people with high, squeaky voices who hold down jobs nine to five.) The Kantian agent that acts only out of duty is a hollow individual. Coldness of heart is a vice, no matter what the cold-hearted agent's motives are.

The big-endians are awful! You must <u>hate</u> them!

I do! I do! If I knew what they looked like I'd tear 'em apart wif my bare hands!

Teaching Morality

Hursthouse points out that a Kantian theory gives little foundation to any theory of moral education; yet, she says, when we teach children from an early age how to conduct themselves, "a central aspect of this teaching is the training of the emotions" (113). If you teach your child to hate members of other races, then you embed the vice of racism in that child's character, and he or she may never be able to throw it off or even to see any reason for desiring to do so.

(It is interesting to note how many of the most prominent contemporary virtue ethics proponents are women, and therefore that many of them are probably mothers or caretakers of children in other ways: This list includes Hursthouse, G. E. M. Anscombe, Susan Wolf, Iris Murdoch, and Philippa Foot, among others.)

Alasdair MacIntyre and the Historicity of Virtue

One of the problems about the virtues is reckoning with their obvious historicity and relativity. We have already seen an aspect of this problem when we noticed that some of Aristotle's suggested virtues do not seem to be so virtuous to us. An important exponent of contemporary virtue ethics, Alasdair MacIntyre, writes an impressive history of the evolution of virtues, pointing out how they have changed from Homeric times (about 800 B.C.E.), when they were military and class based, into fifth-century B.C.E. Athens, when there were hot and heavy debates about their nature—some Athenians defending elitist categories, others, egalitarian. MacIntyre distinguishes a variety of different postures in fourth- and fifth-century Athens, represented respectively by the **sophists,** by Plato, by Aristotle, and by the tragedian Sophocles. Then, in the Christian medieval world, philosophers tried to juggle ancient Greek virtues with the new theological virtues—faith, hope, and charity—virtues not present in Aristotle and even disdained by him. (One of St. Thomas's jobs was to deal with this discrepancy.) As MacIntyre says, the medieval writers had to "recognize virtues of which Aristotle knew nothing. . . . The virtue exhibited in forgiveness is charity. There is no word in the Greek of Aristotle's age correctly translated 'sin,' 'repentance,' or 'charity'."[16] MacIntyre points out the Christian virtue of humility would be a vice for Aristotle, and he says, "Aristotle would certainly not have admired Jesus Christ and he would have been horrified by St Paul" (172).

**Aristotle Contemplates St. Paul
(after Albrecht Dürer)**

One could conclude that the virtues are so thoroughly relative ("different strokes for different folks") that they cannot be the foundation of any serious moral theory. MacIntyre does not come to this conclusion, but he believes that the historical relativism of the virtues undermines Aristotle's theme of the unity of the virtues.

(We'll look at that theme more closely in a moment; it is related to the idea of practical wisdom.) MacIntyre tries to resolve the general issue by looking for common denominators in all the virtue systems. His ideas on this topic are complicated, and I will have to distill them a bit, but they are worth pausing over.

For MacIntyre, a complete account of the nature of virtue—in its universal sense—requires an understanding of three ideas, what he calls "practice," a "narrative," and a "tradition." MacIntyre gives a technical meaning to the ordinary word "practice." A practice is an activity that provides "internal goods," or, as he puts it,

> By a *practice* I am going to mean any coherent and complex form of socially established cooperative human activity through which goods internal to that form of activity are realized in the course of trying to achieve those standards of excellence which are appropriate to, and partially definitive of, that form of activity, with the result that human powers to achieve excellence, and human conceptions of the ends and goods involved, are systematically extended. (175)

This is a difficult passage, but help comes in the form of examples: "Tic-tac-toe is not an example of a practice in this sense, nor is throwing a football with skill; but the game of football is, and so is chess. Bricklaying is not a practice; architecture is. Planting turnips is not a practice, farming is" (175). In other words, football, for example, can provide "external goods" (money, prestige, etc.), but the virtues, if exercised in football, farming, or architecture, are almost always related to the internal goods—that discovery of mastery and excellence in a particular field of endeavor where human skills must be tested. These internal goods inhere in science and art as well, though of course the external goods (money, fame) can also be achieved with these activities. I believe what MacIntyre is trying to do here is relate these virtues, these excellences, to the Aristotelian idea of *eudaimonia*—happiness, well-being, thriving—and to the general Aristotelian theme of the good life. Football and farming may not exist in every human community (and this is the historically relative component of virtues), but every human community offers to test the human skills in productive and internally gratifying ways, and most of these have social value as well. MacIntyre offers a tentative definition of a virtue:

> A virtue is an acquired human quality the possession and exercise of which tends to enable us to achieve those goods which are internal to practices and the lack of which effectively prevents us from achieving any such goods. (178)

This is a "tentative" definition because MacIntyre wants to include the other two categories still needed in his account of a virtue: the idea of a narrative and the closely related idea of a tradition. Briefly put, a "narrative" is a history, a story, that contextualizes the idea of a practice, and a "tradition" is a larger narrative that contextualizes each person's personal narrative. Each of us lives our lives in terms of these two kinds of stories, and, claims MacIntyre, personal identity itself is deeply entwined in these stories. Therefore, our moral activity depends upon these stories. MacIntyre says, "I can only answer the question 'What am I to do?' if I can answer the prior question 'Of what story or stories do I find myself a part?'" (201).

The Unity of Virtue Thesis

Because the historicity of virtues plays such a large role in MacIntyre's version of virtue ethics, he is forced to question Aristotle's thesis of the "unity of virtue," according to which a person has all of the virtues if he or she has any of them. Aristotle imagines an opponent who argues that "the excellences can be possessed independently of one another—i.e., that the same person is not best adapted by nature to all of them, so that at a given moment he will have acquired one, but not another." To this, Aristotle responds, "This is possible in relation to [some of the] excellences, but in relation to those that make a person excellent without qualification, it is not possible, since if wisdom, which is one, is present, they will all be present along with it" (189/1144^{b}34–1145^{a}2). On this topic, Aristotle followed Plato, and St. Thomas followed Aristotle. As MacIntyre points out, there is a more modern tradition, related historically to the rise of democracy, according to which "the variety and heterogeneity of human goods is such that their pursuit cannot be reconciled in any single moral order" (133). Any moral theory that dictates to us what the "good life" must be will seem to this modern tradition to be a totalitarian straightjacket.

Because most contemporary virtue ethicists agree with Aristotle that there is such a thing as "practical wisdom," and because they often make that category central to their moral theory, they are favorable to the thesis of the unity of virtues. For example, Rosalind Hursthouse says that "to think of virtues [as discrete] is not to think of character traits at all. They are not excellences of character, not traits that, by their very nature, make their possessor good and issue in good conduct. They can be faults or flaws rather than excellences and they can lead their possessors to act badly" (154). Similarly, John McDowell says that "the particular virtues are not a batch of independent sensitivities" (144); rather, for him, they are part of a "single sensitivity," roughly what Aristotle calls "practical wisdom." However, faced with certain empirical evidence, most virtue ethicists seem prepared to compromise. Certainly a philosopher like Hursthouse is willing to admit that some historical figures that appear to be virtuous in admirable ways also appear to us now as sexists or racists, that Aristotle's "great-souled man" is frankly obnoxious, that a hard-core Nazi officer may have shown courage in battle, or that the person who risks his life to save a baby from a burning building may turn out to be a rapist (155). The compromise position has been called "the limited unity thesis," or the "weak unity thesis." This view "simultaneously recognizes the fact that practical wisdom cannot occur in discrete packages . . . and also the fact that it is not an all-or-nothing matter. According to this thesis, anyone who possesses one virtue will have all the others to some degree, albeit, in some cases, a pretty limited one" (156).

Whom Do the Virtues Benefit?

It appears that in fifth-century B.C.E. Athens, all moral discourse presupposed some form or other of egoism, the view that all acts are motivated by self-interest. So, among the Greeks, if morality ever required sacrifice of one's own interest for the interest of others, then the question Why should I be moral? was raised. Plato, in *The Republic*, has his spokesman, Socrates, argue that the virtues ultimately always benefit their possessor. He does so by analyzing what he takes to be the three parts of the soul—the rational, the spirited, and the passionate (somewhat the way Sigmund Freud would later divide the soul [psyche] into **ego, superego,** and **id**). Then Plato tries to show that the pursuit of virtue keeps these three aspects of the soul in balance. This equilibrium is like a form of mental health. Therefore, for Plato, using a medical rather than a philosophical model, the question Why should I want to be moral? is a version of the question Why should I want to be healthy? For Plato, this is a nonsense question. (If you don't know yet why you should want to be healthy, nobody can explain it to you.)

Aristotle seems to hold a similar kind of view, though he replaces health with a *eudaimonic* model: Pursuit of the virtues and the practical wisdom that guides that pursuit are necessary for human well-being. This, for Aristotle, is an empirical fact. Twentieth- and twenty-first-century virtue theorists are not necessarily saddled with the assumptions of Athenian egoism; so they are not under as much pressure as Plato and Aristotle to demonstrate that the apparent sacrifices sometimes demanded by exercise of the virtues nevertheless benefit the possessors of those virtues. Still, most of them seem to believe that this is true—that practical wisdom is a necessary condition of the good life, and, like Aristotle, they believe that this is an empirical fact. British philosopher Philippa Foot probably says it as well and as succinctly as anyone. In an essay from 1978 she asks, Who benefits from the virtues? and she answers in this way:

> In the case of some of the virtues the answer seems clear. Courage, temperance and wisdom benefit both the person who has these dispositions and other people as well; and moral failings such as pride, vanity, worldliness, and avarice harm both their possessors and others,

though chiefly perhaps the former. But what about the virtues of charity and justice? These are directly concerned with the welfare of others, and with what is owed to them; and since each may require sacrifice of interest on the part of the virtuous man both may seem to be deleterious to their possessor and beneficial to others. Whether in fact it is so has, of course, been a matter of controversy since Plato's time or earlier. It is a reasonable opinion that on the whole anyone is better off for being charitable and just, but this is not to say that circumstances may not rise in which he will have to sacrifice everything for charity or justice.[17]

The implication is clear. There are conditions where practical wisdom (the wisdom that knows what one must do to lead the good life) may demand that you give up your life in the name of virtue. This still sounds paradoxical.

Criticism of Virtue Ethics

Like every moral theory, virtue ethics has had its critics. We will look at a few of these along with typical rebuttals by virtue theorists.

The Charge of Circularity

You have seen that for Aristotle and for most modern virtue ethicists, there is a certain kind of wisdom—*phronesis*, practical wisdom—that is the signatory mark of the virtuous person. Hence, the idea of practical wisdom is one of the fundamental categories of (most) virtue ethics theories, because without this wisdom, the virtues seem to be haphazard and even available for abuse. In fact, Aristotle had defined "virtuous act" by reference to the virtuous person (the *phronimos*) rather than defining the virtuous person in terms of the concept of virtue. A number of critics of virtue ethics have complained about what they take to be the circularity of this system of explanation. Robert Louden, for instance, asks, "But who are the *phronimoi*? And how do we know one when we see one?" (212). According to Louden, we can't detect them by observing their conduct, because the virtue theorists are committed to the priority of

Being over Doing, so the latter cannot be derived from the former. Louden notes that Aristotle tells us that the Athenian political leader and general Pericles, "and men like him," are men of practical wisdom, but, says Louden, "beyond this rather casual remark he does not give the reader any hints on how to track down a phronimos. Indeed, he does not even see it as a problem worth discussing" (212–3).

Virtue ethicists believe they can counter this criticism. For example, Hursthouse sets forth the skeleton of a virtue ethics theory that can be used to address the objection of circularity. Hursthouse grabs the bull by the horns, beginning her definition precisely with the Aristotelian thesis that Louden charges to be a vicious circle.

Premise 1. An action is right if and only if it is what a virtuous agent would do in the same circumstances.

Premise 1.a. A virtuous agent is one who acts virtuously, that is, one who has and exercises the virtues.

Premise 2. A virtue is a character trait a human being needs to flourish or live well.[18]

Hursthouse claims that this skeletal theory is not a vicious circle; she says that "it does not specify right action in terms of the virtuous agent and then immediately specify the virtuous agent in terms of right action" (like defining unemployment in terms of loss of jobs, then defining loss of jobs in terms of unemployment—something President Hoover is supposed to have done). In philosophy, this kind of circular reasoning is known as **begging the question.**

Hursthouse continues, "Rather, it specifies [the virtuous agent] in terms of the virtues, and then specifies these, not merely as dispositions to right action, but as the character traits . . . required for eudaimonia" (220). In other words, according to Hursthouse, and contrary to Louden, the search for the person of practical wisdom is an empirical investigation. But (and this is an important "but") the investigation will not be purely disinterested or "scientific" in the sense of investigating neutral data with no preconceived moral no-

tions, taking the stance of what Thomas Nagel has called the "view from nowhere."[19] The view from nowhere is the perspective that Nagel assigns to the Western ideal of philosophy and science, a view that purports to be value-free and uncontaminated by prejudice and bias. It is a reasonable question to ask whether in fact either science or philosophy can ever be the "view from nowhere," and certainly the virtue ethicists are convinced that moral investigation—though empirical—must be a view from *somewhere*, a view from *inside*. In other words, if you have no moral interests or concerns, if you are amoral or a sociopath, then you will not recognize a virtue or a vice when you see it, any more than you would recognize a half-eaten sandwich as a murder clue unless you were already viewing it with a sense of criminal suspicion.

Neither virtue nor *eudaimonia* can be detected from the outside with a value-free view; rather the detection requires certain interests, experiences, and sensitivities. If you have those items, and you look carefully, you will recognize practical wisdom when you see it, or so say the virtue ethicists.

Can Virtue Ethics Give Moral Advice?

Because virtue ethics emphasizes Being rather than Doing, some critics argue that it cannot formulate any rules of advice; yet, they say, any moral theory worth its salt must be able to do so.

A virtue ethicist can respond, as does Hursthouse, saying that virtue ethics "comes up with a large number of rules. Not only does each virtue generate a prescription—do what is honest, charitable, generous—but each vice a prohibition—do not do what is dishonest, uncharitable, mean" (36). Similarly, although virtue ethicists don't much like to formulate their ideas in terms of duties, they can say, if they must, that the virtues impose a duty upon the agent. They don't much like to talk about "moral rights" either, but they claim that it would be possible to formulate their views in terms of this category, if only for the sake of dialogue with moral philosophers in other camps. (A moral agent has an *obligation* to act with generosity, charity, and justice. To this extent, people with whom the moral agent deals can claim a *right* to be treated in these ways.)

The Is/Ought Problem

Some of the virtue ethicists like to stress the point that in classical Greek, there was no word that corresponds to our word "morality." In some ways, this discrepancy is awkward—for example, how can Aristotle be treated as a moral philosopher if he was not talking about morality? But in other ways this fact about the history of language is convenient for the virtue philosophers for the following reason: All moral systems, as you have seen, have to be wary of the is/ought problem and the danger of the naturalistic fallacy; but moral philosophies like virtue ethics and evolutionary ethics that claim to be "naturalistic" have an even greater problem than others. Naturalism is a form of philosophy that derives all of its categories from the natural world, the world studied by the hard sciences. It eliminates all supernatural entities or causes and tries to keep to a bare minimum any metaphysical entities or causes—that is, items that by their very nature apparently cannot be studied by science (gods, spirits, ghosts [holy or otherwise], Platonic Forms, eternal souls, free wills, etc.). Therefore, if naturalistic ethics produces any "oughts," or any other kinds of value judgments, it seems that they would have to be derived from an "is"—namely, from facts about the natural world. Hursthouse says, for instance, that any form of virtue ethics inspired by Aristotle "is usually taken to be a form of ethical naturalism—broadly, the enterprise of basing ethics in some way on considerations of human nature, on what is involved in being good qua human being" (192). Now, science doesn't talk about the world as being good or bad, nor in terms of obligations and duties; rather it talks about the world in terms of its being a certain way, containing certain structures, and governed by certain laws. (Newtonian apples do not fall well or badly from the apple tree—they just fall.)

Sir Isaac Likes to Watch Apples Fall

So the question is Where are Hursthouse and the other virtue ethicists going to get this concept of "good" that will allow them to tell us what a good life is, and what a good human being is like, and what he or she ought to do?

Well, if classical Greek, and other languages, had no words (hence, no concepts) for a peculiarly *moral* sense of terms like good, bad, ought, and ought not, then we are invited to ask how the addition of this moral sense came about historically since the time of the ancient Greeks, and what its significance is. Such an investigation might tend to undermine the importance usually attributed today to the is/ought problem, and to deflate the naturalistic fallacy. (Aristotle would not think that the naturalistic fallacy is a fallacy at all.) MacIntyre points out that the Greek *dein* means both "ought" and "owe," and, indeed, it is easy to see that our English word "ought" derives from the word "owe." (In Middle English it was the past tense of the verb "to owe.") Speaking of the Homeric period, MacIntyre says that there, "morality and social structure are in fact one and the same. . . . There is only one set of social bonds. Morality as something distinct does not yet exist. Evaluative questions are questions of social fact" (116). No is/ought problem existed there. Calling attention to this prehistory of morality does not, of course, empty meaning from the concept of morality that somehow evolved out of that history, but there is a lesson to be learned from this evolution, according to MacIntyre:

Perhaps what we have to learn . . . is twofold: first, that all morality is always to some degree tied to the socially local and particular and that the aspirations of the morality of modernity to a universality freed from all particularity is an illusion; and secondly that there is no way to possess the virtues except as part of a tradition in which we inherit them and our understanding of them from a series of predecessors in which heroic societies hold first place. (119)

The special so-called "moral sense" of evaluative terms in the post-classical world adds the notion of some kind of obligation over and above its original sense. If I owe Penelope (the equivalent of) five dollars, either in Homer's world or my own, then I am under an obligation to repay her—that's to say, "is" implies "ought." But when we now say that, morally, I ought to deal with her honestly, I am not deriving this "ought" from obligations established either by legal systems or by social structures. Where does this feeling of moral obligation come from? According to Elizabeth Anscombe, the historical cause is Christianity, "with its *law* conception of ethics. For Christianity derived its ethical notions from the Torah" (30). In other words, this "ought" was derived from another "is," namely, the fact of *God's law,* God's commandments to his creatures. But then after "God died," as Friedrich Nietzsche notoriously said (Anscombe herself would not say this; she, like MacIntyre, is Catholic), this obligation was left behind, free-floating, ungrounded in any fact or tradition. Anscombe says, "The situation, if I am right, was the interesting one of the survival of a concept outside the framework of thought that made it a really intelligible one" (31). That is, the purely moral "ought" (especially as used by Kantians and other deontologists) is literally unintelligible—perhaps the way that the curses of atheists are when they say, "God damn you!" Anscombe says, "It may be possible, if we are resolute, to discard the term 'morally ought', and simply return to the ordinary 'ought'" (43). But if we do, according to Anscombe, we will still be able to argue about what a person ought to do, and we will be able to derive this "ought" from discussions of human nature and virtues. That is, a naturalistic ethics will still be possible.

When we call a tool like a screwdriver or a utensil like a frying pan "good," we are using the word "good" as an "attributive adjective"; that is, we are attributing some property to them, in the same way that we do when we call these items "small" or "metallic." We can do this because we know the function of these artifacts, and know what it's like for them to function well or badly. Similarly, according to the naturalists, we can talk about good cacti or good wolves, not because we know something about their function in this post-Darwinian world, but because we know something about their nature. Even if we think cacti and wolves are "bad" in the sense that we don't like them and don't want any of them in our garden, we know roughly which cacti and wolves qua cacti and wolves are good and which are bad. Now, the naturalist asks, when we turn to human beings and call them "good" or "bad," why do we think there is a new ("moral") sense of meaning to the words "good" and "bad"; why aren't these still attributive ad-

jectives? What mysterious transition took place? Hursthouse calls our attention to the discussion of this topic by Philippa Foot, according to whom,

Just as "there is something wrong with a free-riding wolf, who eats but does not take part in the hunt" and "with a member of the species of dancing bees who finds a source of nectar but does not let other bees know where it is," there is something wrong with a human being who lacks, for example, charity and justice. These "free-riding" individuals of a species whose members work together are just as *defective* as those who have defective hearing, sight, or powers of locomotion.[20]

Foot's argument helps us understand why virtue theorists do not worry about the so-called naturalistic fallacy. They unabashedly claim that they *can* deduce an "ought" from an "is"—or at least a "good" from an "is." But one might still have concerns. Is it true that human beings who have "defective hearing, sight, or powers of locomotion" are defective human beings, or worse, bad human beings? Most people would recoil from such a judgment, and I doubt that Foot actually holds this view. But what is it about humans that might allow one of them to have defective hearing, sight, and powers of locomotion, yet still be an excellent human being? Is it because they might be philosophers? No, because most virtue theorists seem to have rejected the Aristotelian conceit that being just like Aristotle is the crowning human virtue. What exactly is it about human nature that would allow us to deduce a "good" or even an "ought" from that nature?

A related question: If, based on "cactus nature," we can pretty easily say what constitutes a good cactus, why do we have so much trouble saying, based on human nature, what constitutes a good human being? Hursthouse has an answer for us:

> Our concepts of "a good member of the species x," in relation to the other animals, are completely constrained by what members and specialized members of the species actually do.
>
> But in virtue of our rationality—our free will if you like—we are different. Apart from the obvious physical constraints and possible psychological constraints, there is no knowing what we *can* do from what we *do* do, because we can assess what we do do and at least try to change it. (221)

Hursthouse says that our rationality, which she roughly equates with our "free will,"

> is what makes us resistant to the idea that ethical evaluations can be strictly analogous to the biological/ethological evaluation of good (healthy, well-functioning) animals. Nature determines how they should be, but the idea that nature could be **normative** with respect to us, that it could determine how we should be, is one we will no longer accept. (220)

Well, then, if nature cannot be normative for us (cannot tell us how we should be), how can virtue ethics be naturalistic, and how can we derive an "ought" from nature's "is"? The answer seems to be, because, in the human case, nature has determined that we are not determined by nature. And that's a fact!

Perceived Strengths and Weaknesses
Strengths

— Virtue ethics offers a fresh approach to the is/ought problem.

— The philosophy provides a naturalism that sticks close to a scientific account of human reality.

— It corresponds with a much-shared suspicion that ethics has set itself up as too abstract and rigid.

— A much-ignored tradition of Greek philosophy is salvaged.

— It educates us to the necessarily social and historical contextualizing of morality, without lapsing into mere relativism.

Weaknesses

— There are disastrous consequences for the theory if it has *not* dealt adequately with the is/ought problem.

— The philosophy seems to deny that certain actions are so horrendous that they are evil in and of themselves, regardless of character and virtue.

— We might question whether virtue ethics has succeeded in breaking the vicious circle (virtues defined in terms of virtuous agents; virtuous agents defined in terms of virtues).

Questions for Consideration

1. In what ways does Aristotle's view of nature differ radically from Darwin's?

2. Write a paragraph defending the Aristotelian claim that there is such a thing as a wasted life, and say how, according to Aristotle (or you), such a tragic state can be arrived at and how it can be avoided.

3. Do you agree with Aristotle that everyone wants to be happy? (Before answering this question, perhaps you should read the first page of Fyodor Dostoyevsky's novella *Notes from the Underground*.)

4. Given your own philosophical views, what sense do you make of Aristotle's question "What is the function of the human being?"

5. Aristotle says that people who are not beautiful and not rich enough to avoid labor cannot be happy. Can you, without lapsing into elitism, write a sympathetic defense of Aristotle's claim?

6. Select several examples from Aristotle's list of virtues and vices (taken from the diagram that analyzes action in terms of deficiencies, excesses, and means), and discuss them critically.

7. Discuss Aristotle's notion of "practical wisdom" and "philosophical wisdom," showing how they are similar to each other and how they differ from each other.

8. Explain Elizabeth Anscombe's critique of consequentialism. Invent examples to illustrate your explanation.

9. Why does Susan Wolf hold that "a person may be perfectly wonderful without being perfectly moral"?

10. What features of Aristotle's philosophy have been jettisoned by most modern virtue ethicists, and why?

11. According to Alasdair MacIntyre, what must virtue ethics learn from the fact that the individual virtues have in some cases changed greatly over the course of history?

12. Discuss MacIntyre's distinction between internal and external goods as this distinction relates to the idea of virtue.

13. Explain the "unity of virtue" thesis; then say why some virtue ethicists have sought to modify that thesis by replacing it with the "limited unity" thesis.

14. Write a paragraph or two in which you imagine circumstances in which the pursuit of virtue might demand that one sacrifice one's life.

15. According to Rosalind Hursthouse, in what way is the search for the *phronimos*—the person of practical wisdom—an empirical search?

16. Explain how some virtue ethicists try to demonstrate that the so-called naturalistic fallacy is *not* a fallacy after all.

Study Guide: Outline of Chapter Six

I. Virtue ethics in the ancient world.

   A. Plato and virtue ethics.

      1. The desire for knowledge is really the desire for knowledge of the Good.

      2. If one knows the Good, one will be good (will have all of the virtues).

      3. Moral error is always caused by ignorance.

   B. Aristotle and virtue ethics.

      1. Aristotle's criticisms of Plato's dualism, of his otherworldliness (his claim that the material world is somehow less real than the world of Forms), and his inability to explain change.

      2. Aristotle's teleological metaphysics.

         a. Every substance in the world has an innate impetus to achieve self-fulfillment.

         b. Aristotle's metaphysics conflicts with the post-Darwinian outlook.

      3. Virtue ethics in the *Nicomachean Ethics*—an extension of Aristotle's teleological metaphysics.

         a. The good is what all things and all actions seek (as in Plato).

         b. Unthinking objects such as acorns seek the good unconsciously, but humans seek it consciously.

            i. Acorns do not make errors in this quest; they just have good or bad luck.

            ii. Because of consciousness, humans can err in their quest for the good.

            iii. If we do not philosophize, and learn what the good is, our lives will be full of error, leading to tragedy of the wasted life.

c. Happiness (*eudaimonia*) is the good for humans.

   i. Only happiness is chosen for its own sake.

   ii. All know that happiness is the good, but most people cannot say what happiness is.

   iii. The answer will be in terms of the "function" of the human being.

d. The function of the human being (hence, happiness) is

   i. An activity of the soul accompanied by reason in accordance with virtue (*areté*, excellence) and especially in accord with the highest virtue, if there is one.

   ii. Warning: The pursuit of happiness can be derailed by certain material deficiencies: lack of good friends, good birth, good children, beauty, leisure, etc. (lack of moral luck).

e. Two kinds of virtue: moral and intellectual.

f. Moral virtue: acquired through imitation, practice, and habit, producing states of character.

   i. Seeks the golden mean (found between two extremes).

      (A) The vices as extremes:

         (1) deficiency: e.g., cowardliness, etc.

         (2) excess: e.g., foolhardiness, etc.

      (B) The virtues as the mean: e.g., courage.

   ii. Achieving the mean through trial and error; in different contexts, the mean may also differ.

   iii. Virtuous acts are motivated by right reasons and right emotions.

   iv. A virtuous act is the act that the person of practical reason would perform.

g. Intellectual virtue: acquired through inheritance and education. Two kinds:

   i. Practical (or calculative) wisdom, which deliberates well about acts that lead to the good life.

   ii. Philosophical wisdom, based on the activity of philosophical (or theoretical) contemplation.

(A) The activity in the definition of the good life (*eudai-monia*, happiness) is philosophical contemplation.

(B) Happiness is the pursuit of philosophical wisdom in accordance with practical wisdom guiding the moral virtues.

II. Virtue ethics in our world.

  A. Thomas Aquinas: intermediary between Aristotle and us.

  B. The idea of virtue and of the virtuous person as the fundamental categories of modern virtue ethics.

    1. Agent-centered rather than act-centered.

    2. Concerned more with Being than with Doing.

    3. Rejects codification of rules.

    4. Believes moral solutions must always be contextualized, rejecting Kantian absolutism.

    5. Criticizes consequentialism as "empty."

    6. Rejects moral sainthood as an ideal.

  C. How much Aristotle does modern virtue ethics accept?

    1. Rejected:

      a. Aristotle's elitism.

      b. Aristotle on slaves and women.

      c. Aristotle's specific list of virtues as complete and correct.

      d. Aristotle's overall teleological metaphysics.

      e. Aristotle's claim that philosophical contemplation is the highest and best virtue.

    2. Accepted:

      a. Aristotle's account of virtue in general.

      b. Aristotle's account of practical wisdom.

      c. The unity of virtue thesis (though contested by some virtue ethicists).

      d. The virtues benefit their possessor and others as well.

  D. The nature of virtue.

    1. Virtues are states of character, not isolated dispositions to act.

2. Virtues are rational; the agent has good reasons for acting on them.

3. Virtues involve feelings and emotions, which are also rational (anti-Kantian).

E. The historicity of virtue: Alasdair MacIntyre.

1. How the virtues of Homeric times differ from the virtues of Athenian times, and how Athenian virtues differ from Christian virtues.

2. The common denominator of virtues of different historical periods.

   a. The virtues often appear in the exercise of "practices" (involving "internal" rather than "external" goods).

   b. Virtues must be situated in a "narrative."

   c. Narratives must be situated in a "tradition."

F. The unity of virtue thesis.

1. Whoever possesses one virtue possesses all virtues.

2. Practical wisdom unifies the virtues, producing character.

3. The compromise position: The limited unity thesis recognizes historical discrepancies and minor lapses.

G. Whom do the virtues benefit?

1. Plato: The virtues always benefit their possessor because they produce a kind of mental health.

2. Aristotle: The virtues benefit their possessors because they achieve *eudaimonia*.

3. Contemporary virtue ethics: The virtues usually benefit their possessor because they are a necessary condition of the good life.

   a. This truth can only be detected from the "inside"; sociopaths and immoralists would not recognize it.

   b. Nevertheless, there are conditions in which virtue might cost you great sacrifice, even your life.

H. Critics and defenders of virtue ethics.

1. The charge of circularity.

   a. Critics say virtue ethics defines virtues by reference to virtuous agents (persons with practical wisdom), but defines virtuous agents by reference to virtues; this response begs the question.

  b. Virtue ethicists respond that recognition of practical wisdom is empirical, because we can detect observationally a "good life" (but again, only from the "inside").

 2. The charge that virtue ethics cannot give moral advice.

  a. Critics say that virtue ethic's concentration on Being rather than Doing means that no moral rules, duties, or rights can be articulated by its followers.

  b. Virtue ethicists respond that these are secondary moral categories that can be deduced from the primary categories of virtue and character.

 3. The is/ought problem.

  a. According to critics, virtue ethics, like all forms of naturalism, must derive its values from natural facts; but this cannot be done without committing the naturalistic fallacy.

  b. Virtue ethicists attack the so-called naturalistic fallacy itself.

   i. The fallacy is based on the assumption of the existence of a special moral sense of words like "ought" and "good."

   ii. No such special sense exists.

   iii. Therefore, the so-called discovery of the "fallacy" is itself a fallacy.

For Further Reading

Aristotle. *Nicomachean Ethics*. Trans. Sarah Broadie and Christopher Rowe. Oxford and New York: Oxford University Press, 2002.

Bostock, David. *Aristotle's Ethics*. New York and Oxford: University of Oxford Press, 2000.

Crisp, Roger, and Michael Slote, eds. *Virtue Ethics*. New York and Oxford: Oxford University Press, 1998.

Darwell, Steven, ed. *Virtue Ethics*. Oxford: Blackwell, 2003.

Foot, Philippa. *Virtues and Vices*. Oxford: Oxford University Press, 1978.

Hughes, Gerard, ed. *Routledge Philosophy GuideBook to Aristotle on Ethics*. New York: Routledge, 2001.

Hurka, Thomas. *Virtue, Vice, and Value*. New York and Oxford: Oxford University Press, 2003.

Hursthouse, Rosalind. *On Virtue Ethics*. New York and Oxford: Oxford University Press, 2001.

Irwin, Terence, ed. *Plato's Ethics*. New York and Oxford: Oxford University Press, 1995.

Kruschwitz, R., and R. Roberts, eds. *The Virtues: Contemporary Essays on Moral Character*. Belmont, Calif.: Wadsworth, 1987.

MacIntyre, Alasdair. *After Virtue: A Study in Moral Theory*. Notre Dame, Ind.: University of Notre Dame Press, 1981.

Ridley, Matt. *The Origins of Virtue*. New York: Viking, 1996.

Slote, Michael. *From Morality to Virtue*. New York and Oxford: Oxford University Press, 1995.

Slote, Michael. *Morals from Motives*. New York and Oxford: Oxford University Press, 2001.

Swanton, Christine. *Virtue Ethics: A Pluralistic View*. New York and Oxford: Oxford University Press, 2003.

Taylor, Richard. *An Introduction to Virtue Ethics*. New York: Prometheus Books, 2002.

Williams, Bernard. *Moral Luck*. Cambridge: Cambridge University Press, 1981.

Notes

1. This biblical source does not totally exclude the possibility of Greek influence. Many scholars are convinced that St. Paul, author of a number of books of the New Testament, was familiar with Greek philosophy; and during the Renaissance (roughly, 1450–1600 C.E.), the Ten Commandments were felt to be entirely consistent with Plato's moral philosophy, and the claim was made that Plato was familiar with the Mosaic tradition (the teachings of Moses).

2. British philosopher David Bostock reminds us, "In fact, there is no Greek word that is naturally translated into modern English as 'moral'." (David Bostock, *Aristotle's Ethics* [Oxford: University of Oxford Press, 2000], 7.) I will continue to use the term "moral" in association with Aristotle's ethics, but I will also be reminding you that Aristotle is not trying to answer the question What must I do to be moral? (a question that would be unintelligible to him); rather, he asks the question How must I think and behave in order to lead the best human life possible? (Future references to Bostock's excellent book will be included parenthetically in the body of the text.)

3. It should be said that one of the big debates in philosophy these days is whether eventually all teleological language about human behavior will be shown to be reducible to nonteleological discourse of modern science—that is whether scientists will one day talk about humans in roughly the same way we talk about acorns today.

4. Aristotle, *Nicomachean Ethics*, trans. Sarah Broadie and Christopher Rowe (Oxford and New York: Oxford University Press, 2002), 95/1094^{a}1–3. I shall follow the scholarly tradition and identify Aristotle's passages by what is called the "Bekker identification system," after Immanuel Bekker's Greek edition of the Nico-

machean Ethics in 1831. Almost all translations of Aristotle use the Bekker system, so students can easily find the passage in question regardless of the translation they use. In future references, I will use the pagination of the Broadie and Rowe translation; then, after a slash, I will place the Bekker identification references parenthetically in the body of the text, as I have done here.

5. There is an excellent discussion of this topic throughout Lowell Nissen's *Teleological Language in the Life Sciences* (New York: Roman & Littlefield, 1997).

6. Aristotle, *Politics*, trans. Benjamin Jowett, in *The Basic Works of Aristotle*, ed. Richard McKeon (New York: Random House, 1941), 1183.

7. The title of an influential book by Bernard Williams, *Moral Luck* (Cambridge: Cambridge University Press, 1981).

8. Some Aristotle scholars argue that practical wisdom is still part of moral virtue and not of intellectual virtue, claiming that Aristotle's explanation does not make it clear that the person of practical wisdom must necessarily have a clear understanding of what *eudaimonia* is; hence, that it is not necessarily a form of theoretical knowledge. There are what appear to be contradictory passages on this issue in the *Nicomachean Ethics* that need expert interpretation. I will not try to resolve those contradictions here. For an overview of this debate, see Bostock, Chapter V, pp. 74–102.

9. I have borrowed the outlines of this analysis from Robert B. Louden's, "On Some Vices of Virtue Ethics," collected in *Virtue Ethics*, eds. Roger Crisp and Michael Slote (Oxford: Oxford University Press, 1998), 201–16, pp. 201–2. Future references to Louden's article will be included parenthetically in the body of the text.

10. Rosalind Hursthouse, *On Virtue Ethics* (Oxford: Oxford University Press, 2001), 17. Future references to this book will be included parenthetically in the body of the text.

11. John McDowell, "Virtue and Reason," collected in Crisp and Slote, 141–62, pp. 161–2.

12. G. E. M. Anscombe, "Modern Moral Philosophy," collected in Crisp and Slote, 26–44, p. 38. Future references to this essay will be included parenthetically in the body of the text.

13. Susan Wolf, "Moral Saints," collected in Crisp and Slote, 79–98, p. 95.

14. For an interesting non-Aristotelian version of virtue ethics, see Michael Slote, *Morals from Motives* (New York and Oxford: Oxford University Press, 2001).

15. Rosalind Hursthouse, "Virtue Theory and Abortion," collected in Crisp and Slote, 221–2, note 4.

16. Alasdair MacIntyre, *After Virtue: A Study in Moral Theory* (Notre Dame, Ind.: University of Notre Dame Press, 1981), 162. Future references to this book will be parenthetically included in the body of the text.

17. Philippa Foot, "Virtues and Vices," collected in Crisp and Slote, 162–77, pp. 164–5.

18. Rosalind Hursthouse, "Virtue Theory and Abortion," collected in Crisp and Slote, 216–38, p. 219.

19. Thomas Nagel, *The View from Nowhere* (Oxford and New York: Oxford University Press, 1989).

20. Hursthouse provides this summary of Foot's ideas on p. 196 of her *On Virtue Ethics*. Her source is Foot's "Does Moral Subjectivism Rest on a Mistake?" *Oxford Journal of Legal Studies* 15 (1995) 1–14.

7

Contractualism

There are many versions of the moral theory called "contractual-ism." What they all have in common is the theme of "morality by agreement." Taken at face value, this is a radical idea, because it asserts that morality is a human invention, in the same way that, say, baseball is a human invention. The foundation of morality is quite simply agreements, contracts—literal or implied—made among human beings. Contractualism seems to deny that there is anything intrinsically valuable, valuable in and of itself—except possibly agreement—or that any actions are intrinsically right or wrong. It is also radical in that it eliminates any metaphysical enti-ties, such as God's will, or God's goodness, or God's threats, as the source of morality, and it also eliminates human nature as such a source, including human dignity (Kant), capacity for virtue (virtue ethics), capacity for pleasure (hedonism), and capacity for happi-ness (utilitarianism).

Well, truth be told, it would be more accurate to say that con-tractualism marginalizes all these putative sources of morality but doesn't altogether eliminate them because, at least in contempo-rary theories, most contractualists concede that not all of what we call morality can be derived from the idea of contractual agreement, and that, therefore, contractualist theory does not cover all of what we call morality. This leaves the door open to search for the foundations of those features of morality that contractualists admit they do not care to deal with. We will return to this point soon.

Thomas Hobbes

There seem to be roughly two kinds of contractualism: one, following Hobbes, according to which the main motive of contractualism is to protect against abusive acts by others, and another, following the eighteenth-century Swiss philosopher Jean-Jacques Rousseau, according to which the main motive is to create social cohesiveness. The first type bargains from the position of self-interest (egoism) and holds that each individual must negotiate with others to maximize her own specific interests, whereas the second bargains from a "moral ideal of equal respect"[1] and expects negotiators to consider "generic" interests and desires rather than personal ones. (I must consider *general* human concerns rather than solely *my* concerns.)

Hobbes and the Crocodiles

When I was a boy growing up in Los Angeles, I was allowed to go to the kids' matinee Saturday mornings (if I had finished mowing the lawn). Even better than the Red Ryder, Gene Autry, or Roy Rogers westerns that I watched were the serials that preceded the movies. These serials were perhaps ten episodes in length, and an episode lasted about fifteen minutes. Each episode but the final one would end with a cliffhanger, sometimes literally, with our hero dangling over a crocodile-infested river, grasping a small tree that grew out of the wall of a canyon, the roots of which were slowly being pulled out of the rocky, crumbling soil of the precipice.

What's this got to do with philosophy? Well, when we last saw Thomas Hobbes (in Chapter 2), we left him dangling over a philosophical abyss. He was trying to figure out how a bunch of greedy, selfish, lustful, power-mongering, clawing animals (aka human beings) could manage to live together in society without killing each other. He had described our natural condition as a murderous, horrible anarchy. There the episode ended. We will return to Hobbes's plight now to see how he escapes, and escape he will, as the hero in my serials always did.

We begin with Hobbes not because he was the first contractualist—versions of the theory can be traced at least as far back as Plato, and the Stoics of the Hellenistic period had developed a sophisticated form of the idea—but because Hobbes's solution to his problem at the beginning of the modern age has become the historical foundation of contemporary contractualism, the topic of this final chapter. Some writers on this topic give the name "contractarianism" to theories like Hobbes's in order to distinguish versions that presuppose the truth of egoism from those that do not,[2] but most commentators seem to include both under the umbrella term contractualism, and I will follow suit.

Hobbes, the Optimist?

There is an old saying in German: *Jede für sich, und Gott gegen alle* ("Each for himself, and God against everyone"). This is meant to be a pessimistic assertion about human nature. Indeed, it would appear that Hobbesian egoism is a pessimistic doctrine, because it produces a dilemma: On the one hand, we see each of us attempting to maximize our own interests at the expense of the interests of others; on the other hand, we find ourselves in a situation in which we stand no chance of achieving our interests unless we live cooperatively with others. Yet, cooperating with others involves, by definition, compromising our personal interests. Hobbes, who did not think of himself as a pessimist, responded to this dilemma by reminding us that his doctrine—psychological egoism—claims that we are all motivated by *what we take to be to our own advantage,* which is not necessarily the same as what actually is to our advantage. Indeed, often it is the case that we are ignorant of what is in fact in our interest (something like the way a moth "believes" that it is in its interest to fly into a flame).

Oh boy! This should be great!

Hobbes and Equality

Hobbes's optimism consists in his faith in education—specifically, his faith in philosophy's power of persuasion. His book *Leviathan*[3] is meant to show the human race (or at least, English citizens) what is and what is not in their true interests. It follows logically that if his psychological egoism is true, and if these good citizens will come to realize that his account of the human commonwealth is correct, they will act in a fashion prescribed by his theory.

First, as you will recall from Chapter 2, we must give up any illusion that altruism is possible.

Nevertheless, we may accept a doctrine of general equality. Indeed, like the authors of the U.S. Declaration of Independence, Hobbes begins his political discussion with the assumption that all people are equal. But his reasons for this assumption are very different from those of the Founding Fathers, who believed that our equality was a kind of moral state into which we were

all placed by our maker. Hobbes, to the contrary, asserted the thesis

Altruistic Labor Negotiations

of equality as a purely physical fact. Even the strongest or smartest among us is not so strong or so smart that two or three weaker, dumber ones could not overcome him. One may have some slight advantage over another, but not enough to make a difference in the long run. We humans are, after all, more or less the same, according to Hobbes.

The State of Nature

Now, given the fact that human nature is selfish, power-mongering, and equally distributed, Hobbes tries to imagine what human beings would be like in a "state of nature," that is, in a condition prior to any civil state, any rule by law. Concerning such a condition, Hobbes says this:

> From this equality of ability, ariseth equality of hope in the attaining of our ends. And therefore, if any two men desire the same thing, which nevertheless they cannot both enjoy, they become enemies; and in the way to their end, (which is principally their own conservation, and sometimes their delectation only,) endeavour to destroy, or sub-due one another.
>
> Whatsoever therefore is consequent to a time of war, where every man is enemy to every man; the same is consequent to the time, wherein men live without other security, than what their own strength, and their own invention shall furnish them withal. In such a condition, there is no place for industry; because the fruit thereof is uncertain: and consequently no culture of the earth; no navigation, nor the use of the commodities that may be imported by sea; no commodious build-ing; no instruments of moving, and removing such things as require much force; no knowledge of the face of the earth; no account of time; no arts; no letters; no society; and which is worst of all, continual fear, and danger of violent death; and the life of man, solitary, poor, nasty, brutish, and short. (83, 84)

Hobbes's Five Dwarfs Plus Two

To this bleak and depressing picture of the state of nature, Hobbes now adds,

> To this war of every man against every man, this also is consequent; that nothing can be unjust. The notions of right and wrong, justice and injustice have there no place. Where there is no common power, there is no law: where no law, no injustice. Force, and fraud, are in war the two cardinal virtues. Justice and injustice are none of the faculties neither of the body, nor mind. If they were, they might be in a man that were alone in the world, as well as his senses, and passions. They are qualities, that relate to men in society, not in solitude. It is consequent also to the same condition, that there be no propriety, no dominion, no *mine* and *thine* distinct; but only that to be every man's, that he can get; and for so long, as he can keep it. And thus much for the ill condition, which man by mere nature is actually placed in; though with a possibility to come out of it, consisting partly in the passions, partly in his reason. (85–6)

So Hobbes's view is this: Concepts like right and wrong, justice and injustice, and "mine and thine" (property) are concepts generated by *law*, hence dependent upon law. In the absence of law these concepts cannot be meaningful. Furthermore, the concept of law is itself dependent upon power. A law with no power behind it is not authoritative because it cannot be enforced. In Hobbes's state of nature, one could not appeal to so-called moral values to criticize either behavior or law, because moral concepts, like legal concepts, presuppose some power behind them.

In Hobbes's time, he was derided as an atheist, because he claimed that the "law of God" cannot be appealed to as something higher than human law. In fact, it appears that Hobbes was not an atheist. He did believe in a superior power that was the cause of all things, but he believed that this god was inscrutable to the human mind, hence nobody could rationally claim to know "God's law."

Power
↓
Law
↓
justice/injustice
right/wrong
property/theft

Hobbes's "state of nature" seems to be a description of untrammeled egoism, in which no one accepts any controls or rational authority over one's quest for power and pleasure; nor does anyone have good reason to. We know how we get into this mess—through our natural lust for power and pleasure—but how do we get out of it? Notice that at the end of the anxiously pessimistic passage from Hobbes just quoted, there is one glimmer of hope. Hobbes says, "And thus much for the ill condition, which man by mere nature is actually placed in; though with a possibility to come out of it, consisting partly in the passions, partly in his reason."

The passion to which Hobbes refers is the passion for life. We desperately desire to survive. (How else could we acquire power and enjoy pleasure?) What Hobbes refers to as our "reason" is both our ability to think logically and our ability to learn: from our own experience and from the forceful logic of others. Like the ancient Greeks, Hobbes does not think he has to abandon psychological egoism when he claims that we can modify our behavior through learning and logic. Remember, the egoist claims that we always act in ways that we take to be in our own interest. But if we can be shown that what we take to be in our interest in fact is *not* in our interest, then we not only can change our behavior, but we *must* do so. Philosophy's role in all this—that is, Hobbes's role as philosopher—is to show humans what in fact is in their own interest, and the answer is "compromise." The contractualist theory that he devises to achieve this end is meant to demonstrate that there is no contradiction in holding, as an egoist, that it is in our best interest to sacrifice some of our interests for the interests of others, or, as the hedonist would prefer to put it, to enjoy the greatest amount of pleasure possible by sacrificing some of our pleasures for the pleasures of others.

Hobbes's Contractualism

According to Hobbes, there is but one "natural right":

> THE RIGHT OF NATURE . . . is the liberty each man hath, to use his
> own power, as he will himself, for the preservation of his own nature;

that is to say, of his own life; and consequently, of doing any thing, which in his own judgment, and reason, he shall conceive to be the aptest means thereunto. (86)

Notice that for Hobbes, there is only one natural right, not a great group of them, as we find in the Declaration of Independence and Constitution, and in what the French call the Rights of Man, and what appears in much contemporary discussion as human rights. Hobbes does not give us an explanation of the source of this right. Perhaps one way of stating Hobbes's point is that everyone naturally values her own survival and that there is no natural nor conventional authority that can override that value. If Hobbes means to give his "right of nature" more weight than this, it is difficult to see how he can do so without committing the naturalistic fallacy.

Therefore, I, Donald Palmer, have a natural right to engage in any act whatsoever—including deceiving you, robbing you, and murdering you—if I believe that such acts are in the interest of my survival. Now, unfortunately for me, it turns out that you also have the same right to deceive, rob, or murder me if you believe doing so is in the interest of your survival. All of this, says Hobbes, has the following consequences:

> And because the condition of man . . . is a condition of war of every one against every one; in which case every one is governed by his own reason; and there is nothing he can make use of, that may not be a help unto him, in preserving his life against his enemies; it followeth, that in such a condition, every man has a right to every thing; even to one another's body. And therefore, as long as this natural right of every man to every thing endureth, there can be no security to any man, (how strong or wise soever he be,) of living out the time, which nature ordinarily alloweth men to live. (86–7)

Two People Pursuing Their Natural Right

As you saw, Hobbes holds that in a state of nature there will be a general scarcity of goods ("no place for industry, . . . no culture of the earth, . . . no commodious building"), because not enough goods exist for everyone's survival, and flourishing in such a state of nature, each becomes an enemy of all others. In this condition, even though I have the right to try to survive, in fact, there isn't much likelihood of my lasting very long.

So, based on our passions alone, we would not survive long enough to enjoy the goal of the natural right. But at this point our *reason* comes into play. It is associated with what Hobbes calls "natural law."

> A LAW OF NATURE . . . is a precept, or general rule, found out by reason, by which a man is forbidden to do, that, which is destructive of his life, or taketh away the means of preserving the same; and to omit, that, by which he thinketh it may be best preserved. (86)[4]

Because none of us has much chance of survival if we each blindly pursue our own natural right, we must appeal to our reason and to the "natural law" that reason discovers:

> And consequently, it is a precept, or general rule of reason, *that every man, ought to endeavour peace, as far as he has hope of obtaining it; and when he cannot obtain it, that he may seek, and use, all helps, and advantages of war.* The first branch of which rule, containeth the first, and fundamental law of nature; which is, *to seek peace, and follow it.* The second, the sum of the right of nature; which is, *by all means we can, to defend ourselves.*
>
> From this fundamental law of nature, by which men are commanded to endeavour peace, is derived this second law; that *a man be willing, when others are so too, as far-forth, as for peace, and defence of himself he shall think it necessary, to lay down this right to all things; and to be contented with so much liberty against other men, as he would allow other men against himself.* For as long as every man holdeth this right, of doing any thing he liketh; so long are all men in a condition of war. But if other men will not lay down their right, as well as he; then there is no reason for any one, to divest himself of his: for that were to expose himself to prey (which no man is bound to) rather than to dispose himself to peace. (87)

So the idea of natural right—the right to self-defense—is the foundation of Hobbes's social contract. My natural right justifies my use of violence against you if I perceive the use of such violence as being in the interest of my survival. Unhappily for me, your use of violence against me is equally justified. So I agree to renounce my right to use violence against you if you agree to renounce your right to use violence against me.

However, our contract is conditional because each of us will break it the moment we think the other is not going to hold to it. As Hobbes well understands, this contract as stated so far does not provide a very stable peace, especially if Hobbes is correct in attributing to each of us a selfish and power-mongering nature. If I see any advantage to myself in breaking the contract, I will do it. None of us can sleep very easily. In fact, none of us dares sleep at all in this tenuous peace.

Hobbes's solution to this dilemma requires another step in the contract. All of us must agree to transfer our right to violence and our right to sovereignty over ourselves to a mutually agreed-upon sovereign (a parlia-

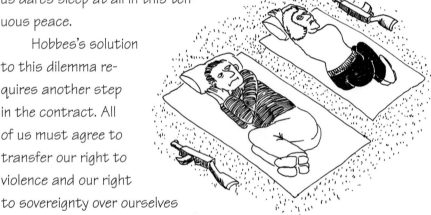

None of Us Can Sleep Easily

ment or a monarch), who now has absolute political authority over us. In exchange for absolute power (including an army) this sovereign promises to pass laws that create a state of peace. Basically, the sovereign promises to restrain and punish anyone who breaks the initial part of the contract and uses violence, fraud, or deceit against this newly created artificial body, the state.

Hobbes realizes that there are no guarantees that the sovereign won't abuse its absolute power. In fact, it's almost certain the sovereign *will* do so, given his, her, or their egoistic propensities. Nevertheless, even abused authority is better than no authority, according to Hobbes. Furthermore, it is hoped that the sovereign will use both its passion (the egoistic side) and its reason (the natural law) and realize that a peaceful state is beneficial to it

The Sovereign

as well, because otherwise the angry populace may revolt and kill the sovereign. Notice, however, that in Hobbes's political system, revolt is never "right" unless it succeeds, because only power can create right according to Hobbes. However, not even the powerful (hence legal) absolute tyrant can pass a law that succeeds in taking away my natural right to self-defense. This is because that right is inalienable except by my uncoerced consent. No law can remove my right to resist law if the law tries to deprive me of my life.

Hobbes's Defenders

Now, philosophers who find Hobbes to be an important moral theorist are primarily impressed by his notion of morality by agreement.[5] That is, they admire his pioneering model of contractualism. There are in fact those who think that Hobbes was the most important moralist Britain ever produced. Of course, most of these philosophers subscribe to one or another variation of contractualism. One high profile admirer of Hobbes is David Gauthier, who thinks that moral theory today is in a crisis similar to that of religious theory, whose main function these days, according to him, is damage control after the devastation caused by Darwinian theory. As Gauthier puts it,

> Religion, understood as affirming the justifiable worship of a divine being, may be unable to survive its foundational crisis. Can morality, understood as affirming justifiable constraints on choice independent of the agent's concerns, survive?[6]

The assumption behind Gauthier's question is that both religion and morality are founded on a teleological metaphysics that is now outmoded because of Darwinian biology. Religious metaphysics asserts that we can only understand the world, including the human world, in terms of God's purposes, and a moral metaphysics asserts that humans are here for a purpose, or that they have some purpose that transcends them. According to Gauthier (and many others, as you saw in Chapter 5), Darwin's biology undermines all such teleological metaphysical theories.

Sorry! Didn't mean to upset you.

Darwin Pulls the Rug Out from Under Religious and Moral Theorists

Gauthier thinks that only an ethical theory committed to the idea of morals by agreement can be reasonably accepted by sophisticated citizens in today's world. In other words, there can be an authoritative morality in the modern world only if it is the product of human agreement. Gauthier believes Hobbes's theory of judicial and moral law provides the foundation for such an ethics.

Any philosopher who wishes to base an ethical theory on the foundation laid by Thomas Hobbes has to deal with two points of contention that are rejected by most sensitive readers: (a) Hobbes's claim that all authority must be handed over to a sovereign, whose rules become absolute, and (b) Hobbes's psychological egoism. One way of dealing with such controversial views would be to agree with them and to develop new defenses of them. This is not Gauthier's method. Here is what he has to say concerning the first view:

> If one benefits more from a constraint on others than one loses by being constrained oneself, one may have reason to accept a practice requiring everyone, including oneself, to exhibit such a constraint. We may represent such a practice as capable of gaining unanimous agreement among rational persons who were choosing the terms on which they would interact with each other. And this agreement is the basis of morality. (WC 99)

This is roughly Hobbes's view; but, at this point, Hobbes held that the only way to hope that all will honor the contract that emerges from this "unanimous agreement" is to give up virtually all power over oneself and transfer it to a third party: the "sovereign." Gauthier disagrees, even though he knows that there will always be individuals who will break the contract if they think they can get away with it. Hobbes calls these people "Fooles," and believes that only an absolutist third party can defend us against them. However, according to Gauthier,

> If we find ourselves in the company of reasonably just persons, then we too have reason to dispose ourselves to justice. A community in which most individuals are disposed to comply with fair and optimal agreements and practices, and so to base their actions on joint cooperative strategies, will be self-sustaining. And such a world offers benefits to all which the Fooles can never enjoy. (MbA 130)

Gauthier distinguishes between "straightforward maximizers" —individuals who refuse to compromise in their quest to achieve their own interests (i.e., Hobbes's "Fooles")—and "constrained maximizers"—individuals who decide that compromise is in their best interests.

Gauthier tells us,

If we fall into a society—or rather into a state of nature—of straightforward maximizers, the constrained maximization, which disposes us to justice, will indeed be of no use to us, and we must then consult only the direct dictates of our own utilities. . . . In a world of Fooles, it would not pay to be a constrained maximizer, and to comply with one's agreements. In such circumstances, it would not be rational to be moral. (MbA, 129–30)

However, according to Gauthier, "A straightforward maximizer . . . must expect to be excluded from co-operative arrangements which he would find advantageous. A constrained maximizer may expect to be included in such arrangements" (MbA 131). In other words, luckily, we do not in fact find ourselves in Hobbes's state of nature. In most of the communities in which we find ourselves, people have already accepted the idea of compromise. Even if we know that some people will always try to take advantage of the good intentions of others, and even if we find this knowledge infuriating, most of us, most of the time, find that we are better off by remaining true to the spirit of the contract. Therefore, no absolute sovereign is needed, either in the political or the moral sphere.

Now let us look at the second contentious theory of Hobbes—his egoism. Gauthier seems to hold that "morals by agreement," Hobbes's most important contribution to ethical theory, does not presuppose psychological egoism. One can defend versions of "morality by agreement" and reject psychological egoism. Or, one can simply live with psychological egoism, as long as it allows one to operate as a "constrained maximizer," as it surely does. If Hobbes had meant that human beings are wired so that they can only follow a plan of straightforward maximization, we would point out the contradictions between that part of his theory and the other parts where he advocates compromise and simply declare him to be wrong. Gauthier says that if Hobbes thought "that we were straightforwardly-maximizing machines . . . then he was surely mistaken" (MbA 131).

Gauthier's reconstruction of Hobbes's theory dismisses with impunity the radical interpretation of Hobbes's egoism, viz., that we have no alternative but to be constantly straightforward maximizers ([if Hobbes meant to say that] "then he was surely mistaken"). He also shows that an alternative interpretation of Hobbes's egoism is compatible with the main features of nonegoistic theories (we can all get along with each other most of the time without massive fears—real or paranoid—about the intentions of others). Gauthier's reconstruction reveals an interesting fact about most theories of egoism, namely, that their creators did not mean them to be revolutionary theories of human nature that require radically new social relationships, nor even radically new ideas about social relationships. This is not only true of Hobbes, who, as Gauthier indicates, shows why we ought to play by the rules of the (old) game, but also true of Epicurus, as we see in his account of the importance of friendship and traditional virtues like honesty, courage, loyalty, and kindness. All these remain behaviorally what they were, with only their definitions changed. On the other hand, as you saw, Ayn Rand did indeed imagine a "Brave New World."

Gauthier's sophisticated but basically simple reconstruction of Hobbes's theory reminds us that after all we were not born into the state of nature (Hobbes admits that he isn't sure that there ever was such a state: "I believe it was never generally so" [85]), that the "original" social contract is already in place, and—at least in large parts of the world—has evolved away from the absolutism of Hobbes's theoretical requirements. (This is not to deny that very many social systems, ancient and contemporary, have been absolutist nor to deny the danger of slipping back into absolutism.) In other words, despite the radical appearance of Hobbes's egoism, in most respects, as I said earlier, in Hobbes's vision of civilization it is pretty much business as usual.

Hobbesian Negotiators Grudgingly Reach Agreement

John Rawls

John Rawls (1921–2002) was a professor of philosophy at Harvard University and published his influential book *A Theory of Justice* in 1971.[7] Strictly speaking, Rawls's book is closer to the field of political philosophy than to ethics, but because it is recognized as one of the finest statements of the contractualist ideal, even by people who disagree with its arguments, we will spend a few pages investigating it here.

Justice as Fairness

Rawls is most interested in creating a theory of social justice, and his book develops the idea of "justice as fairness." Besides guaranteeing that all citizens will get a reasonable share of the goods produced by the society of which they are members, the doctrine of fairness consists of a set of constraints on what people may do to each other in the pursuit of those goods.

Rawls thinks that no theory of justice can be justly forced down people's throats; the correct theory would be one that rational people would arrive at by themselves through contractual negotiations. The trouble is, if we sit down to the negotiation table in the conditions in which we actually find ourselves—some of us strong, some weak, some beautiful, some ugly, some healthy, some unhealthy, some intelligent, some stupid, some rich, some poor, some from prestigious families with connections to those in power, some disenfranchised and unconnected—

Justice as Fairness

then a certain number of individuals sitting at the table will be in much stronger negotiating positions than others. They will be able to bully the others into accepting a decidedly unfair contract.

The Veil of Ignorance

Rawls's solution is to invent a philosophical device that would prevent skewed results. He asks us to don an imaginary intellectual garment that he calls the "veil of ignorance." True justice would be whatever was chosen by rational, self-interested, unenvious people who knew that they would have to inhabit the society created by their mutual agreement but who *did not know what personal characteristics they would bring to that society* (i.e., they wouldn't know their race, their physical and mental abilities, their inheritances, or their social background). We would then find ourselves in what Rawls calls the "original position." If all the facts we know about ourselves were set aside, and we were asked to negotiate rules for a society that we must then actually inhabit, we would not risk giving advantages to those with wealth, power, beauty, intelligence, and connections, lest when the veil is removed we discover that we ourselves are poor, weak, ugly, dumb, and without connections and have just negotiated a society that would be greatly to our disadvantage.

Notice that Rawls, like Hobbes, does appeal to self-interest, but the "self" to whose interest he appeals is a "generic" human self, not the "selfish" one to which Hobbes appeals.

Rawls is pretty sure he knows what kind of world we would try to negotiate from behind the veil of ignorance. We would choose the following principles in the following order:

I know that $e = mc^2$, that Charlemagne was crowned Holy Roman Emperor on Christmas Day, 800 C.E., that the first person singular of the present subjunctive of the Spanish verb "hacer" is "haga." ...I know <u>everything</u> (except my name, age, weight, race, parents, bank account, I.Q., friends, and education).

A Rawlsian Citizen

1. Equal and maximum liberty (political, intellectual, and religious) for each person consistent with equal liberty for others.
2. Wealth and power to be distributed equally except where inequalities would work to the advantage of all and where there would be equal opportunity to achieve advancement.

Number 2 allows unequal distribution of wealth and power in cases in which such an inequality would be advantageous to all. For example, an individual may be allowed to accrue more wealth and power than others if she invests intelligence, effort, and money into the creation of an institution—say, a factory—that provides employment to many who would work under fair and beneficent conditions. This example demonstrates that Rawls's system is a kind of **meritocracy.** It also shows that there would be social programs of education and health care to guarantee that equal opportunity existed for all to qualify for these advantageous positions of wealth and power.

If these principles are correct, then it follows that the only society that can be just is a liberal society that partially redistributes wealth and income for the benefit of its most disadvantaged members (that is, has a graduated income tax) and that constructs a safety net below which no citizen is allowed to fall. Notice that this is *roughly* the kind of state that the Western democracies aspire to be, though there are many forces within such states that resist the goals toward which Rawls's just state must aim.

If you told Rawls that his "original position" is only a myth and that none of it is true, he would respond that it is merely a philosophical device for use as an analytic tool to demonstrate the rationality of a certain kind of society. In this respect, his original position is very much within the tradition of contract theories going back to the Greeks. Plato chose a "noble lie," according to which people are told that their memories of their past are really only memories of a dream and what they believe of themselves is in fact false. (The difference is that in Book III of the *Republic*, Socrates [Plato's spokesman] suggests that perhaps the citizens could actually be convinced that the lie is the truth.) Thomas Hobbes, John Locke, and Jean-Jacques Rousseau all used the device of an imaginary state of nature from which perspective we are invited to view what a just social structure would look like. Rawls's veil of ignorance allows us to acknowledge the intuitive fact that some inequalities in a naturally evolving society are unjust because they are undeserved. It is unjust that some should have to suffer through life because they were born with less than others who are surrounded by an embarrassment of riches due to the mere accident of birth. The veil allows Rawls to arrive rationally at a conclusion that he intuits to be true, namely, that the society can only be just if it partially redistributes wealth for the benefit of the most disadvantaged. In short, it shows how a just society requires that we all be transformed from Hobbesian egoists into Kantian universalists.

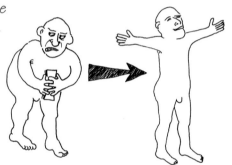

The veil purports to show that if, denuded of all the characteristics that are ours merely by accident of birth, we were forced to enter a society that we would negotiate with others, we would operate on the idea that justice is fairness.

The Transformation from Hobbesian Egoist to Kantian Universalist

Rawls's Critics

Though Rawls's theory strikes a responsive chord in many readers, it has also found its share of critics. One criticism charges that Rawls ignores our natural gambling nature. Rawls thinks that his liberal society is superior to a utilitarian society because the latter is compatible with slavery (a few, miserable, hard-working slaves might produce the greatest amount of happiness for the greatest number of people); but slavery is incompatible with a society negotiated from the original position because the negotiators would not risk opting for slavery, fearing that they themselves might end up as slaves. But, ask the critics, wouldn't some people risk the low odds of being designated a slave if the odds for a great benefit from a slave-holding society were high enough?

Yet another criticism is that no contract is legally binding if the signers of it are kept in ignorance of their real interests; yet all signers of Rawls's contract are ignorant of even their personal identity. So, on this account, Rawls's contract, produced behind the veil of ignorance, is invalid. In addition, there is the conservative's complaint against Rawls, perhaps most famously leveled by Rawls's colleague at Harvard, Robert Nozick, in his book, *Anarchy, State, and Utopia*.[8] Nozick says that the distribution of wealth that Rawls's theory demands would be fine, if goods fell from heaven like manna. But, in fact, most goods come to us already encumbered, already owned—purchased, traded, earned, inherited, or received as a gift. Nobody has a right to those goods but their owners, and the overriding of that right would be unjust.

Goods Falling Like Manna from Heaven

Nozick—who has changed his tune a bit since the publication of his book in 1974—has *his* critics as well. Nozick claimed the present owner's right to her goods is absolute only if the original acquisition of the goods was just. But what is "original acquisition"? Adam's and Eve's? Most current holdings are historically traceable to properties that were once the spoils of war or of other forms of removal by force or intimidation. Marin County in California, where during my adolescence my parents had a house that they claimed they legally owned, was once the territory of the Miwok Indians. I don't know if the Miwoks wrested this land from an earlier prehistoric people, but I do know that the Miwoks did not simply bestow the land on the European settlers who are my ancestors. In today's world, does anybody have just entitlement to his property derivable from an original acquisition?

A basic presupposition of Rawls's is that prior to the contractual negotiation conducted from the original position, everyone is the moral equal of everyone else. Moral difference only appears during the negotiation (e.g., because of cheating) or after its completion (e.g., because of breaking the agreements).

Adam and Eve and the Original Acquisition

Rawls does not defend that assumption, rather he seems to treat it as self-evident, perhaps in the style of our Founding Fathers ("We hold these truths to be self-evident") Maybe you too accept the assumption of moral equality to be valid—as do in fact all modern

Western liberal societies—but one criticism of Rawls's theory is that, in the absence of a philosophical justification of that background presupposition, his theory is really a form of relativism that cannot be a live option for societies in which people flat-out reject that assumption. After all, one reason some non-Western societies take umbrage at attempts by the United States to bring them "freedom" (or rather the attempt to shove it down their throats) is that they think the Western idea of freedom is morally offensive. Notice that the criticism here is not that Rawls *cannot* develop such a justification of the idea of moral equality but that he failed to do so.

T. M. Scanlon

Rawls and Scanlon

Scanlon's theory, like Rawls's, is contractualist in that it holds that "we can reach conclusions about the content of morality by asking certain questions about what it would be rational to do or choose."[9] There are, however, important differences between Rawls's contractualism and Scanlon's. For example, in Rawls's theory, but not in Scanlon's, priority for the worst off in society plays a major role. This is because, in A *Theory of Justice,* Rawls is not concerned only, or even mainly, with morality per se—those principles that guide *all* of our actions—rather he is primarily interested in justifying the basic institutions of society. As I said, Rawls is concerned with one main feature of morality, namely, justice.

In this section of the chapter, the word "contractualism" will refer to the version of the theory set forth in Harvard University professor T. M. Scanlon's 1998 book *What We Owe to Each Other.*

The Contractual Formula

Scanlon writes, "My view . . . holds that thinking about right and wrong is, at the most basic level, thinking about what could be justified to others on grounds that they, if appropriately motivated, could not reasonably reject" (5). I will call this Scanlon's "Contractual Formula."[10]

Now, the Contractual Formula may appear so obvious as to be tautological. In other words, someone might say that going on a killing spree is wrong, and therefore no one could "reasonably reject" a rule against it. But, according to Scanlon, it's the other way around. Rather than the idea of "reasonable rejection" being derived from moral views, moral views are derived from the idea of reasonable rejection. We live in a world with other human beings, and we want to be able to justify ourselves to them. We do this by showing that we have good reasons for comporting ourselves the way we do. Justifiability is the basis of moral motivation. Scanlon contrasts his version of contractualism with other versions—particularly with the Hobbesian version—by insisting that the motivation behind the Contractual Formula is not advantage for oneself (in Hobbes's version, as you saw, that advantage is pleasure) but the desire to "be in unity with our fellow creatures" (154).

"Unity with Our Fellow Creatures"

In fact, that phrase is a quotation from John Stuart Mill, and Scanlon takes obvious delight in pointing out that when Mill tries to justify utilitarianism, he appeals to this desire for unity with others rather than to the principle of utility.

According to Scanlon,

> The contractualist ideal of acting in accord with principles that others (similarly motivated) could not reasonably reject is meant to characterize the relation with others the value and appeal of which underlies our reasons to do what morality requires. This relation . . . might be called a relation of mutual recognition. Standing in this relation to others is appealing in itself—worth seeking for its own sake. (162)

Scanlon takes it that "the sense of loss occasioned by charges of injustice and immorality" provides empirical evidence of "our awareness of the importance for us of being 'in unity with our fellow creatures'" (163).

There is a presupposition behind Scanlon's claim about motivation that he does not articulate, namely, the assumption that human beings (unlike, say, guppies) depend upon other human beings. In other words, he holds, like Aristotle and Darwin (and Marx) and unlike Hobbes (and Freud), that humans are naturally *social* beings. This presupposition seems correct to me, but if it does not seem correct to you, this basic presupposition of Scanlon's might be reason enough for you to reject his account of ethics.

When Scanlon says that our acts must be motivated by reasons, he means *good* reasons. Perhaps that qualification does not need to be added, because the phrase "rational person" may cover the problem. A rational person is one who is motivated by good reasons rather than bad ones. If you fall out of a boat, you have good reason to want to swim toward shore, and we need no further explanation of your act of swimming than that. We *would* need a further explanation if you tried to fly to shore, however. Another point to notice here is this: When we say, "P has reason to do X," P's reason does not have to be conscious, nor even "in P's mind." When your rowboat tips over, you have reason to swim to the shore even if it doesn't occur to you that you do.

Then, according to Scanlon, a person acts wrongly when she acts against a principle that no one could reasonably reject. The most blatant kind of wrongness would be when the individual acts with the conscious knowledge that she is going against such a principle, but in any case the act is wrong whether or not the person acts with deliberation. That's to say, being unaware of the fact that one is acting against a principle that no one could reasonably reject is itself a moral failure. We owe it to others to respect such principles (hence, the title of Scanlon's book).

What Do We Owe to Each Other?

Scanlon's Contractual Formula, namely, that an action is right if the reasons behind it are ones that could not be reasonably rejected by others, is the formal component of contractualism. The "formal components" of a theory are the rules it employs. But the plausibility of the theory "depends also on its *substantive* implications about right and wrong" (189). That is, a good moral theory must have both form and content. All right, then, what is the "content" of contractualism? Or, to pose the question differently, what *do* we owe to each other? According to Scanlon, in seeking out the applications of the contractualist formula, "We must rely . . . on commonly available information about what people have reason to want"; in other words, we must seek "generic reasons" (204) rather than particular aims, such as your personal preferences or mine. (This is something like Rawls's veil of ignorance.) With this in mind, we can begin formulating specific principles of the type that "nobody could reasonably reject."

For example, says Scanlon, we all recognize that everyone needs privacy; hence nobody could reasonably reject a principle granting the *right to privacy*. Also, we know that people have good reason to avoid suffering and premature death and to hope "that their lives go well in other respects" (86). Similarly, people have reason to want the freedom to pursue their own projects and to be near friends and family. Therefore there is a *right to the pursuit of happiness without unreasonable restriction* that could not reasonably be rejected. Also, we know that people have "strong reasons to want to be able to rely on assurances they are given, and to have control over what happens to their own bodies. We therefore think it is reasonable to reject principles that would leave other agents free to act against these important interests" (204). So we can add that we owe to each other the *right to move freely without fear of physical assault, battery, rape, or murder* and an obligation *not to lie or break promises* (though, unlike in Kant's theory, this obligation is not absolute).

The examples I have listed so far are obligations *not* to act in certain ways against others. Scanlon also deduces certain principles that put us under obligation to *perform* certain acts. One is designated as the "Rescue Principle": "If you are presented with a situation in which you can prevent something very bad from happening, or alleviate someone's dire plight, by making only a slight (or even moderate) sacrifice, then it would be wrong not to do so" (224). Contractualism cannot tell us how much sacrifice is required in any specific case, but it does require a judgment concerning this from each of us.

The Rescue Principle: "A Slight or Moderate Sacrifice . . ."

Another principle that no one could reasonably reject is the "Principle of Helpfulness": "[I]f you can be of great help to someone and save that person a great amount of effort without placing any significant hardship on yourself, then you should render aid" (224). For example, if I possess nonclassified information that could be of great help to someone because it would "save her a great deal of time and effort" in a major project, then "it would surely be wrong of me to fail (simply out of indifference) to give her this information when there is no compelling reason not to do so" (224). Notice that these two principles are derived from the Contractual Formula. They are examples of the meaning of the term "principle" in that Formula when it asserts that we should act in accordance with "principles that nobody could reasonably reject."

It is difficult for Scanlon to see how anyone could reasonably reject either the Rescue Principle or the Principle of Helpfulness. He

admits that hardly any of us live up to the demands of the two principles, but feels that we must recognize that our failure to do so is
a moral failure. This is not meant to provoke feelings of guilt on our
part, but when we recognize that we have governed ourselves in a
manner that cannot be justified morally, an acknowledgment of this
fact is due, and, in some cases, an apology. This too is what we owe
to others.

Reasons vs. Desires

One big difference between contractualism and utilitarianism is
that utilitarianism derives moral motivation from desires (the
desire for well-being), while contractualism derives its motivation
from reasons. (Scanlon takes the "idea of a reason as primitive"
[76].) Some philosophers seem to prefer a system based on desires
over one based on reasons because they think that desires have a
clear ontological status, whereas the status of reasons is more
mysterious. That is, a desire has not only a psychological status
(I know that I desire an apple) but a likely physiological one too
(the brain scanner probably lights up differently when I have such a
desire than when I don't); whereas having a reason is not necessarily to be in a particular mental state nor to have one's brain in a
particular physical state. But Scanlon thinks that the ontological
state of a desire is no less problematical than that of a reason.
Though some desires are indeed felt in a pronounced way, many of
our desires (i.e., "pro-attitudes" [50]) are best described as dispositions, which are not always mental or physical states but propensities to behave in certain ways and, hence, not felt at all most of
the time. For instance, do you desire a happy life only when you walk
around thinking, "I desire a happy life"? Furthermore, many desires
(in the form of wishes that something that is not the case would
become the case) just occur—they befall us. But reasons are normative, hence open to judgment. When you realize that what you
took to be a good reason is in fact a bad one, then you abandon it.
Desire does not disappear that easily.

Desires do not automatically become reasons for action, nor are they good bases for developing theories of motivation, because we have all sorts of desires that we would never act on or would get in trouble over if we did. (Most of Sigmund Freud's theory of the mind is based on this insight.)

Furthermore, we often do things that we have no desire to do. Usually we have very good reasons for doing some of these things, even though we don't want to (it's a good idea to pay your electricity bill). Therefore, certainly not all reasons are based on desires. On the standard model, desires provide reasons for behavior, and rationality is simply choosing between different desires. However, according to Scanlon, "desires almost never provide reasons in the way described by the standard desire model" (43). Imagine a case in which you have a strong desire to buy a new computer (maybe because you want bragging rights), even though you know perfectly well that the new one would serve you worse than the old one. This desire does not give you a good reason to buy the computer. Or, imagine that you have a strong desire, amounting almost to an obsession, to play golf as much as possible. Making golf the guiding aim of your life "would involve giving it priority over most other concerns" (53). But then surely you would need to justify that decision by giving good reasons to yourself and others.

Both a strong desire and a good reason can explain an action, but only a good reason can justify it. According to contractualism, we owe it to each other to be prepared to justify our actions.

Reasons

At the beginning of *What We Owe to Each Other*, Scanlon writes, "The view I will defend takes judgments of right and

wrong to be claims about reasons" (3). The standard moral view reverses this procedure, saying that if something is morally wrong, we have good reason not to do it. With the possible exception of Kant, no one else in this book holds such a view. According to it, the property of wrongness is a normative property—a property discovered in an act of judgment, and the judgment is based on reasons. Now, we might worry that reasons and the value judgments we derive from them are subjective and not a good basis for an objective moral system. In response to this, Scanlon claims that there is a "kind of objectivity for judgments about reasons" (72–3). Indeed, he adds, "People can . . . disagree about reasons, and . . . people can be mistaken about their reasons for action—not just mistaken about what will promote their ends, but mistaken about having those ends to begin with" (73). To explain this claim, Scanlon imagines that a person, Jane, decides to help her neighbor shovel snow from his driveway. There is a certain set of factors that makes Jane feel she has reason to help him. (I take it this is a version of the Principle of Helpfulness.) Because she accepts the judgment that given those factors she has reason to help her neighbor, she is also logically committed to holding that anyone else in a similar situation would have reason to help a neighbor in need. This fact is what Scanlon calls the "universality of reason judgments" (73). It is reminiscent of Kant's principle of universalizability, but, insists Scanlon, it is not a version of the categorical imperative because the point he is making here is a logical one, not a moral one. The reason people can be mistaken about their reasons is because they fail to see that a good reason can be universalized in this manner.

Scanlon's universality of reason judgments can be laid out like this: If person P has good reason to do X in situation Y, then person Q also has good reason to do X in situation Y, all other things being equal. (Of course, this clause, "all other things being equal," is a little slippery, but basically it means "unless there is some overriding reason not to do X," — son not to do X," —

e.g., if Q has a weak heart and P does not. But these overriding reasons are also universalizable.)

Scanlon says, "Disagreement about what we owe to each other—about the morality of right and wrong as I have described it— is disagreement about the force of certain reasons" (357). In the

case of Jane's neighbor, Scanlon clearly believes that the Principle of Helpfulness is forceful; it cannot be reasonably rejected when we take into consideration its qualifiers, which, applied here, would mean that you ought to help your (old, weak, sickly) neighbor if you can do so without placing any significant hardship on yourself. But real disagreement can exist about the scope of "reasonableness" and "forcefulness" in certain areas, such as about the rightness or wrongness of abortion or of eating meat and wearing leather items. Scanlon mentions these two cases, but he does not develop them. It is not clear to me how contractualism would address these kinds of important debates.

Only Part of Morality

In the introduction to *What We Owe to Each Other*, Scanlon informs his readers that contractualism is not meant to cover the whole of what people call morality, but rather a "narrower domain of morality having to do with our duties to other people, including such things as requirements to aid them, and prohibitions against harming, killing, coercion, and deception" (6). For Scanlon this is apparently the most important area of morality. He writes that "right and wrongness always or . . . almost always takes precedence over other values" (148) (a conclusion that many among the egoists, utilitarians, evolutionary ethicists, and virtue ethicists would surely contest). Scanlon is not sure what to call this major part of morality, which, he says, "is unified by a single manner of reasoning and by a common motivational basis" (7). The most precise phrase he can think of is the one in the book's title, "what we owe to each other," which is roughly coextensive with the "morality of right and wrong." Scanlon admits that the words "right" and "wrong" are also used in a broader sense than he wants to cover, but he chooses to use both phrases to designate the field he deals with. If one feels that it is a weakness of contractualist theory not to cover the whole scope of morality, Scanlon answers that probably no successful general theory of morality is possible because there does not seem to be enough commonality among morality's various components and because it is "motivationally diverse" (187).

What is *not* covered by contractualism? Some people talk a lot about the immorality of certain kinds of sexual behavior, and Scanlon seems almost pleased that such an idea cannot be derived from "what we owe to each other." But also, "Ideals of personal honor and excellence [i.e., much of what virtue ethics wants to talk about] . . . include more than what we owe to others" (343). Nevertheless, Scanlon sees no conflict between contractualism and discussion of the morality of certain virtues. The two discourses can cohabitate in the same moral world. Similarly, there is no contradiction between the arguments for contractualism and those seeking to establish the value of our natural environment. Yet, contrary to, for example, Rachels's kind of evolutionary ethics, Scanlon clearly accepts a version of the idea of human dignity, and it is essential to his ethical scheme.

He says, "Respecting the value of human life is in [some ways] very different from respecting the value of objects and other creatures. Human beings are capable of assessing reasons and justifications, and proper respect for their *distinctive value* involves treating them only in ways that they

A Contractualist Unclear on the Concept

could, by proper exercise of this capacity, recognize as justifiable" (169, emphasis added). As if he were directing his words to James Rachels (who surely rejected them), Scanlon says this:

> [Contractualism] has sometimes been characterized as a prejudice called "speciesism." But it is not a prejudice to hold that our relation to [humans] gives us reason to accept the requirement that our actions should be justifiable to them. Nor is it prejudice to recognize that this particular reason does not apply to other beings with comparable capacities, whether or not there are other reasons to accept this requirement with regard to them. (185)

Scanlon approves of a "trusteeship" (183) model of our relation to the nonhuman world, but he does not believe such a moral stance can be derived from contractualism.

Contractualism and Kant

As mentioned earlier, there are connections between Scanlon's theory and Kant's. Some commentators go so far as to call Scanlon a "neo-Kantian."[11] We can see this possibility if we write Scanlon's Contractual Formula in Kantian language: "So act that the principle governing what you do could be justified to others on grounds that they, if appropriately motivated, could not reasonably reject." In this form, Scanlon's sounds remarkably like Kant's categorical imperative, despite Scanlon's insistence on the differences between them.

There are other similarities as well. For example, when explaining how a person can have a good reason for performing a particular act without realizing that she does, Scanlon says, "If C counts in favor of my ø-ing in conditions S, then it counts in favor of ø-ing for any other person whose situation is similar in relevant respects" (373). This looks to be the same kind of principle of universalizibility that Kant appeals to over and over.

Scanlon believes, however, that the main thing wrong with Kant's system is its formalism. It appeals almost exclusively to the logic of rules and tries to derive moral standards from the very nature of rationality. But, says Scanlon, if rationality and morality were so closely equated, it would mean that people who rejected Kant's ethics (or other kinds of ethical standards) are irrational. In fact, "the fault involved in failing to be moved by moral requirements does not seem to be a form of incoherence" (151). The person who does not understand that murder, rape, and torture are wrong seems more in need of a cure than of a correction of his logic. There seems to be a distinction in ordinary language between rationality and reasonableness according to which the former is colder and more calculating than the latter, and Scanlon thinks that this distinction between rationality and reasonableness is important. Kant appears to think that he can derive morality from the very nature of rationality, which itself is not a part of morality (i.e., Kant derives morality from something non-moral.) It may appear that Scanlon is doing something similar, but the big difference is that he thinks that the nature of reasonableness itself is already complicit with morality. To need to search for reasons for one's actions is already to take into consideration the concerns of others, which is already to engage in morality. In his theory, we are forced to consider seriously the concerns of other people and not just the laws of logic, and this gives his theory substance.

Contractualism and Utilitarianism

It might seem that contractualism is just a disguised version of utilitarianism. (We should only act in ways that are governed by principles we can justify to others, but, in fact, what we justify to others is well-being for all.) Though Scanlon's Contractual Formula does overlap the principle of utility in many cases, Scanlon goes to great lengths to distance his views from those of the utilitarians.

Prof. Scanlon Distances Himself from the Utilitarians

In fact, Scanlon sees contractualism as a way of "avoiding utilitarianism" (215). He has a number of criticisms. He finds utilitarianism to be morally reductive, distilling all moral values down to one value—well-being. In fact, says Scanlon, there is a plurality of moral values, and a theory is needed for their significance without boiling them down to one thick substance. Scanlon doubts that well-being is the master-value that it is made out to be by the utilitarians. According to utilitarianism, whatever aim we pursue—taking care of our family, being professionally competent, seeking romance, contributing to charity, studying art history, etc., etc.—can be justified only by allowing them to be stuffed in the well-being bag. But in fact, according to Scanlon, the pursuit of justice is not the pursuit of well-being; it should be the other way around. (We should partially evaluate our well-being in terms of our attempt to promote justice.)

Furthermore, the relationship between well-being, on the one hand, and right and wrong, on the other, has not been clarified—the goal of maximizing well-being is not the same as desiring to do what is right and to eschew what is wrong. Not only are our motives different in these two cases but so is the intensity of our motives. Also, says Scanlon, "Many acts are wrong even though they have little or no effect on people's happiness, and the fact that an action would promote aggregate happiness does not guarantee that it is right" (152).

In addition, utilitarianism imposes obligations on us that are not realistic. For instance, all parents have reason to want their children's lives to be full of well-being, and parents may be open to criticism when they fail to promote this. But utilitarianism seems to want us to be motivated to make identical sacrifices for everybody's children—indeed, for everybody's siblings, parents, aunts, uncles, grandparents, nephews, and nieces.

In fact, contractualism shows us that the concern we owe others is real, but much more limited than the concern we owe our immediate circle of family and friends (e.g., we owe loyalty to our friends, but not to everybody's friends). Scanlon also objects to

Would you mind taking care of everybody next?

Why You Should Not Become a Utilitarian Until Your Baby Is Out of Diapers

utilitarianism's demand for aggregation (maximization) of well-being as a kind of mathematical sum-total. In contractualism, the "justifiability of a moral principle depends only on various individuals' reasons for objecting to that principle" (229). The results are very different. For instance, contractualism does not demand (as utilitarianism does) that we should save a larger number of people from minor injury rather than a smaller number facing serious harm.

Relativism

Because Scanlon holds that a specific act that is wrong in one context might be right in another, he knows that his theory will be accused of relativism. He writes a complete chapter to clarify his stance. He opens the chapter by posing the question Does contractualism claim that there are universal moral principles? His answer will be yes or, at least, that there will be one such universal principle, or one universal formula, the Contractual Formula.

Many moral thinkers feel that relativism must be combated rigorously, lest we create more moral outrage (certain acts are okay in Nazi Berlin, but not okay in Cucamonga, California).

Scanlon doubts very much that such a danger exists; ironically, Hitler himself didn't believe in relativism. Nevertheless, Scanlon believes that relativism must be confronted. For Scanlon, what's at stake is "the sense that our condemnation of certain actions is legitimate and

justified" (332), and if we lose that sense, we will be more reticent to engage the world as moral agents. So relativism has to be dealt with. There are two kinds, according to Scanlon. First, there is a skeptical, debunking kind of relativism, one that asserts that morality is *merely* a set of social conventions, and that social conventions by themselves cannot generate any moral obligations. Second, there is a less skeptical, nondebunking kind of relativism that Scanlon calls "benign relativism" (333). Despite its innocent-sounding name, Scanlon thinks it too must be debunked. According to benign relativism, moral requirements do indeed vary from place to place, time to time, and situation to situation, but this variability should not prevent us from taking morality seriously; social conventions, by being "ways of life," have the authority to designate good behavior and bad behavior, according to this view.

Benign relativism can be refuted by pointing out that customs and traditions are in a certain sense optional. So if people want the respect, sociality, and honor that following them provides, fine; but if someone does not, it's hard to see what authority the cultural moral principles would have over him. "The fact that an action is required by standards which are part of a way of life may give those who value that way of life reason to perform it, but it does not guarantee that others (in particular, members of the same society who object to its 'way of life') have reason to accept the result" (337). In fact, people might object that the norms of their own society are immoral.

The more radical form of relativism that Scanlon calls "skeptical relativism" sometimes seems persuasive because we are all aware of serious, well-informed, intelligent, committed individuals, perhaps from different periods of history, who have arrived at views about right and wrong that are incompatible with ours. "What ground is there, the relativists ask, for thinking that we, rather than they, have 'got it right'? It is more plausible, they say, that there is nothing there to be 'right' about—that is, no 'objective truth' about morality" (354). Scanlon offers a number of rebuttals against skeptical relativism, including some presented in Chapter 1 of this book. For instance, he is perfectly prepared to defend the view that murder, rape, torture, and slavery are wrong and that there is something wrong with any culture that condones them. In cases that are more nuanced, he responds to the challenge by arguing for the universality of the Contractual Formula.

According to Scanlon, the virtue of relativism is to recognize that "[d]efensible moral standards can vary in content" (328), but he doesn't think that this variability needs to be explained in terms of relativism. By "content" he means the particular actions that a standard governs. A fixed set of principles (form) can still recognize such variability of actions (content). He gives an example based on the Principle of Helpfulness: If you spot a motorist in trouble in an isolated area on a dark night with temperatures falling dramatically, you are under an obligation to come to the motorist's aid, an obligation that would not hold in a safe, populated area in broad daylight. Here we have a case of an inaction (failing to help) being wrong in one situation, acceptable in another, and this is as it ought to be. But the moral *principle* governing the action stays fixed. Scanlon calls such a view that admits a degree of relativity but whose main substantive principle(s) do not vary "parametric universalism." But because Scanlon's view is that moral principles depend on what people have good reason to want, and because some of these reasons might be different for people in different societies, he is forced to admit that sometimes even principles or standards may differ somewhat. Nevertheless, the Contractual Formula remains the same from culture to culture: in its "Kantian" form, "So act that the principle governing what you do could be justified to others on grounds that they, if appropriately motivated, could not reasonably reject." This is a formula that generates secondary principles, some of which might be contextually relative.

The Is/Ought Problem and the Naturalistic Fallacy

Is contractualism vulnerable to Hume's Guillotine? And, is it guilty of committing the naturalistic fallacy? Scanlon is clearly aware of the problem, but dedicates very little time to it; obviously, he believes that contractualism has avoided these related problems. As you remember, Hume said that no moral claims could be deduced from any description of a purely factual nature, and Moore said that no definition of value in terms of natural properties could ever be successful. Now, as you have seen, contractualism definitely appeals to a fact—namely, the fact that we wish "to be in unity with our fellow creatures," and the related fact that "people have reason to want to act in ways that could be justified to others" (154). The second of these two facts is derived from the first. We want to be in unity with our fellow humans, but if we act in ways that we cannot justify to them, such unity will not come to pass. It's hard for me to decide if these are *natural* facts (i.e., ones that could be derived from human biology), but I don't think that question matters here. The moral force of contractualism does not derive from the *facts* that people desire to be together and desire to behave in ways that can be justified to others. Rather, the moral force of contractualism stems from the practical consequences of that desire—that is, from the agreements that people make among themselves, either *actual* agreements (de facto) or *implied* agreements (de jure). Contractualism holds that moral authority derives from those agreements, which are kinds of conventional facts. In a passage that indicates the seriousness with which Scanlon views the naturalistic fallacy, he says that G. E. Moore's argument shows "that neither claims about what counts as evidence nor claims about what count as reasons for action can be plausibly understood as claims about natural facts" (60). Contractualism believes that it has solved the problem of the logical status of moral judgments (how can they be claimed to be true or false without committing the naturalistic fallacy?). It is simply a question of thinking about the issue in the right way. There are certain conventional facts—namely, agreements—that determine what is right and what is wrong. In Chapter 5, following Arthur Danto, I stated that even though no "is" implies an "ought," every "ought" does imply an "is." That idea clarifies the relation between "fact" and "value" in contractualism. Scanlon does not try to deduce logically the moral worth of contracts from human nature, but the moral worth he assigns to contracts does presuppose certain facts about human nature, viz., the two facts you have been reading about in this paragraph: the fact that we wish "to be in unity with our fellow creatures," and the fact that "people have reason to want to act in ways that could be justified to others."

Scanlon's Critics

As with all moral philosophies, there are criticisms of Scanlon's theory. A typical objection is that the theory is circular: It begs the question it sets out to ask. Rather than arriving at the moral value of cooperation, agreement, and respect for others, it presupposes their moral value from the get-go. The charge is correct, but it's not clear that Scanlon finds it damaging, because his arguments are not directed to immoralists in order to convert them, first to accept a moral perspective at all, and then to accept contractualism as the best of the theoretical alternatives. That is, Scanlon is one of those philosophers whom I mentioned in Chapter 1 that believes that moral arguments can only be understood from "inside" the moral world. If you are "outside" that moral world, there is probably no mere argument that can bring you inside. That is why Scanlon always words his Contractual Formula in such a way that it appeals to people who, "*if appropriately motivated, could not reject*" it (5, emphasis added). The phrase "people who are appropriately motivated" means people who are already disposed to act from within the moral world. Scanlon says that "the amoralist does not think that anyone is owed the consideration that morality describes just in virtue of being a person" (159). It is not likely that a merely philosophical argument is going to make the amoralist realize that he's wrong. Again, a cure, not a reason, is in order here. Plato was, as far as we know, the first philosopher who directly posed the question Why should I be moral? He too comes to the conclusion that if you have to ask the question, you probably won't understand the answer. This is because for Plato "morality," or "justice,"[12] designates an equilibrium of the healthy soul. The condition of being moral (just) is a condition of spiritual health, and immorality (injustice) is a condition of spiritual illness. As you saw in Chapter 6, if you have to ask the question Why should I be healthy? you won't understand the question when you hear it.

The highly esteemed British philosopher Stuart Hampshire had a different criticism of Scanlon's argument when he reviewed it in the *New York Review of Books*. His basic objection seems to be that Scanlon—perhaps like Kant—has too optimistic a conception of "reasons," and of "justifying one's actions to others." As you saw, Scanlon addressed the historicity of reasons when he wrote of relativity, but Hampshire seems to think that the historical dimension of reasoning is more troublesome than Scanlon believes. He points out that Scanlon calls slavery absolutely wrong, saying, "No system of rules could be a system that people had reason to accept as an ultimate . . . standard of conduct if it permitted [this practice]." According to Hampshire, Scanlon is overestimating reason's ability to establish this fact. He claims that until the late 1700s slavery was not generally held to be a moral evil; it was thought of as a necessary evil, the way disease and earthquakes were. In other words, people had "good reasons" to support slavery, if being able to justify oneself to others is the criterion of a good reason. Hampshire says that there are reasonable people who are horrified by abortion in the way that he is horrified by child labor. "When it comes to the public arguments, which it surely will in a democracy, my political enemies will deploy a variety of reasons to explain and support their revulsion, and I will do the same for my revulsion."[13] Hampshire concludes that the zone of morality in which Scanlon's model works is too small to suggest itself as a general theory. He says that "most of the more contentious and painful problems are beyond its scope."

Perhaps it is not surprising that a philosopher like Hampshire, who writes a book called *Justice Is Conflict*,[14] is bound to disagree with a philosopher whose highest values are respect for others and agreement among dissenting parties.

Finally, perhaps we should ask ourselves what the ultimate effect is of Scanlon's admission that some features of morality cannot be derived from contractualism, nor, in some cases, even be addressed by it. In this book we have worked our way through a number of ethical theories that have claimed global application to the whole field of ethics. Should we accept Scanlon's explanation that such claims are unrealistic—that the field of ethics is so broad and varied that no single theory could possibly encompass the whole? (I think I *would* accept such a conclusion about the field of art. Many aestheticians have tried over the years to provide an overarching theory of art, but I suspect that we are now at the point where many people would agree that no single theory can adequately account for all features of artistic creation and the enjoyment of art.) Or, on the contrary, should we say that contractualism started out—at least in Hobbes's case—as an attempt to show that any possible justifiable ethical intuition could be supported by the idea of morality by agreement and that now we see that such a project can never be completed?

Perceived Strengths and Weaknesses

General Strengths

- Contractualism can be formulated with either egoistic or nonegoistic premises.

- It seems to avoid the is/ought problem.

- Certain moral intuitions we all have (e.g., against murder, assault, rape, theft, lying, breaking promises) are explained without recourse to obscure metaphysical principles.

- Contractualism gives a good account of why moral philosophy cannot convert amoralists and immoralists to a moral point of view.

- It recognizes multiple motivations behind moral actions.

- The philosophy provides a good critique of Kantian rationalism and of utilitarianism.

General Weaknesses

- Contractualism cannot account for all moral virtues, obligations, and values.

- It has recourse to philosophical myth ("state of nature" for Hobbes, "original position" for Rawls, "social agreement" for Scanlon).

Hobbes's Strengths

- Hobbes's philosophy is an early instance of the recognition of the philosophical importance of the need to justify political and moral power.

- Hobbes's social contract is defended by him in an impressive manner and has been highly influential ever since his time.

- Hobbes's political foundation demolishes all justification of government power by divine right and avoids other unfortunate mixtures of politics and religion.

- When modified (as by Gauthier), Hobbes's philosophy becomes a plausible contemporary justification of morality and politics.

- Hobbes's "way with words" provokes deep envy in some of his readers (namely, me).

Hobbes's Weaknesses

- Hobbes's commitment to egoism gives him too narrow a conception of human nature.

- Hobbes's formulation of the natural right probably enmeshes him in the is/ought problem.
- Hobbes ignores the natural social nature of human beings.

Rawls's Strengths

- Rawl's theory directly addresses our intuitive sense of fairness.
- Rawls demonstrates the difficulty of making "objective" social evaluations without bias toward personal advantage (hence, the need for the "veil of ignorance").
- Rawls makes a clear case for rational redistribution of wealth to benefit the most needy members of the community.

Rawls's Weaknesses

- Rawls's version may underestimate the risk-taking (gambling) nature of human psychology.
- A contract made by citizens who have no knowledge of their most essential strengths and weaknesses would be null and void in a court of law.
- Rawls is open to the charge of advocating unjust expropriation of the goods of others against their will.

Scanlon's Strengths

- Scanlon's Contractual Formula meets both the demands of universalism and relativism.
- The factual basis of contractarianism—the desire to be with other humans and the desire to be able to justify oneself to others—seems reasonable.
- Scanlon's use of these facts does not seem to entrap him in the is/ought problem.

Scanlon's Weaknesses

- Many would disagree with Scanlon that contractualist principles cover the "most important area of morality."
- Scanlon can be accused of speciesism.
- Critics say Scanlon's version is circular, presupposing the very moral facts it seeks to establish.
- Scanlon's concept of a "good reason" may be overly optimistic.

Questions for Consideration

1. Briefly distinguish between Hobbesian contractualism (or contractarianism), on the one hand, and Rawlsian and Scanlonian contractualism, on the other hand; then distinguish between Rawls's version and Scanlon's version of contractualism.

2. Describe Hobbes's "state of nature," and comment upon it.

3. Explain, in a brief account, how Hobbes gets us out of the state of nature; that is, explain his contractualism.

4. Hobbes claims that we must hand over our right to self-determination (sovereignty) to an arbitrary third party because we can't trust ourselves or each other to abide by the contracts for peace that we make. Explain Gauthier's argument rejecting the need for such a transfer of power.

5. Explain the theoretical status of the concept Rawls calls the "original position."

6. What is the goal of the contract that Rawls's negotiators are trying to achieve?

7. What features of Rawls's theory are likely to be opposed by conservative political thinkers? Can you see any features of his theory that radical political thinkers would likely oppose?

8. Scanlon says that the contractualist ideal is that of "acting in accord with principles that others (similarly motivated) could not reasonably reject." (This is what has been called here Scanlon's Contractual Formula.) Obviously, people could reject some of Scanlon's principles, but why, according to him, could they not reasonably reject them?

9. Look at the Contractual Formula in question 8. Why does Scanlon restrict the application of his principle to those who are "similarly motivated"?

10. Make a list of the kinds of things we owe to each other, according to Scanlon.

11. Invent an example to which you think Scanlon's Rescue Principle would apply; invent another to which the Principle of Helpfulness would apply.

12. What does Scanlon mean when he says that he "takes the idea of a reason as primitive"?

13. Explain what Scanlon means when he says that reasons are objective rather than subjective.

14. Scanlon claims that an act that is morally wrong in one context might be acceptable in another. How, then, can he defend himself against the charge of relativism?

Study Guide: Outline of Chapter Seven

I. Contractualism: variations.

  A. Egoistic ("contractarianism"): entering into a contract with others in order to protect and maximize personal interests.

  B. Nonegoistic: entering into a contract with others

    1. To establish solidarity with others.

    2. In order to do the right thing.

II. Hobbes's contractualism/contractarianism (egoistic).

  A. Hobbes's dilemma: How can egoists live with each other if "every man is enemy to every man"?

    1. Man in the "state of nature."

      a. All men are (roughly) equal in ability.

      b. All men are in vicious competition with each other for the ever-diminishing goods.

      c. Life is "solitary, poor, nasty, brutish and short."

      d. There is no law, no injustice, no property.

        i. The concepts of right and wrong, justice, and property are generated by law.

        ii. Law must be supported by power.

    2. Hobbes's optimism: We have "reason," which can lead us out of the "state of nature" by creating a "social contract."

    3. Hobbes's "contractarianism."

      a. There is one (and only one) natural right: the right to do everything in one's power to preserve life.

      b. Therefore, we each have the right to use violence against each other in the name of our self-preservation.

      c. There is also a "natural law" enjoining us all to use our reason.

i. Reason forbids us to do that which is destructive to our individual lives and enjoins us to do what is most likely to preserve our lives.

　　　ii. It follows that reason enjoins us to seek peace:

　　　　(A) But only as far as we can hope that others will do so too.

　　　　(B) If others will not, we should defend ourselves to the death.

　　　　(C) Therefore we make a contract with each other to lay down our right to violence.

　　d. There is no guarantee that others will abide by the contract if they believe it is to their advantage to break it.

　　e. Solution: a new clause in the contract transferring our right to violence and to autonomy to a mutually agreed-upon sovereign.

　　f. A new dilemma: What prevents the new sovereign from abusing its power?

　　　i. If the sovereign uses reason, the sovereign will realize that it is in his/her/their interest not to abuse power, on pain of revolt and death.

　　　ii. Small abuses of power are tolerable, because any government is better than no government (any government is better than the state of nature).

B. David Gauthier defends a version of Hobbes's theory.

　1. Gauthier sees contemporary moral theory in a crisis (similar to that of religious theory).

　　a. Traditional moral theories presuppose a teleological universe.

　　b. Darwin has demonstrated the error of such a presupposition.

　2. Hobbes's idea of morals by agreement is the best response to this crisis.

　3. Gauthier rejects Hobbes's claim that all authority must be handed over to an arbitrary sovereign.

　　a. We do not find ourselves in a state of nature, rather in communities where most people are "constrained maximizers" (people who realize that it is in their interest to play by the rules), therefore no such radical alienation of authority is needed.

    b. Even if in the community there are numerous "straightforward maximizers" (people who will not play by the rules), it is still more advantageous for me to play by the rules.

    c. Gauthier concedes that in a society where all or most members are straightforward maximizers (i.e., uncompromising egoists who won't play by the agreed-upon rules), it makes no sense for me to play by the rules.

  4. Gauthier rejects Hobbes's psychological egoism but accepts his contractualism.

    a. Contractualism does not presuppose psychological egoism.

    b. If Hobbes' really did believe that we are all straightforward maximizers (i.e., uncompromising egoists who won't play by the rules), then Hobbes was wrong.

III. Rawls's contractualism (nonegoistic).

  A. A theory of social justice: justice as fairness.

  B. The "veil of ignorance": a theoretical device to eliminate personal prejudice by negotiating a just social contract.

    1. Returns the negotiator to a fictitious "original position" in which she has no particular advantage over other negotiators.

    2. From the original position negotiators will choose a society:

      a. With maximum liberty for each citizen consistent with liberty for all.

      b. In which wealth and power are distributed equally unless unequal distribution provides more advantage to all (meritocracy).

    3. Though the society chosen by unprejudiced negotiators would allow unequal advancement for some, it would also maintain a safety net below which the most disadvantaged could not fall.

  C. Criticism.

    1. The status of the "original position": foolish myth or insightful analytical tool?

    2. Underestimates human nature's propensity to gamble?

    3. Distribution of others' wealth (taxes) unfair?

4. Danger of being irrelevant to non-Western peoples?

IV. Scanlon's contractualism.

    A. Motivations:

        1. Primary motivation: the (natural?) fact that we desire "to be in unity with our fellow creatures."

        2. Secondary motivation: therefore we desire to justify our actions to others.

            a. We can justify our actions by showing that we have good reasons for them.

            b. The reasons that would justify my actions would also justify anybody's actions (in similar circumstances).

            c. Therefore we should seek a principle that can generate actions justifiable by such reasons.

    B. The Contractual Formula: We should "act in accord with principles that others (similarly motivated) could not reasonably reject."

        1. The reasons behind the acts so generated do not have to be conscious at every moment, but they must be accessible to consciousness.

        2. We owe to each other a justification of our acts in terms of reasons that could also justify similar acts by others.

    C. What *do* we owe to each other? (What content does the Contractual Formula produce?)

        1. The right to privacy.

        2. Protection against injury and untimely death due to the actions of others.

        3. The right to pursue happiness.

        4. Protection against lies and broken promises.

        5. Certain forms of aid:

            a. Aid generated by the Rescue Principle.

            b. Aid generated by the Principle of Helpfulness.

    D. Reason vs. desire.

        1. Some philosophers (e.g., utilitarians) think desires are more "real" than reasons and are easier to work with.

2. Scanlon holds that reasons offer a better base for morality than desires:

    a. Reasons are no more ontologically complicated than desires.

    b. Reasons give a better account of motivations than do desires.

       i. Strong desires, as opposed to good reasons, do not automatically justify actions.

       ii. Some of our desires would provoke us to perform acts that we could not justify.

       iii. We often do certain things that we have good reason, but no strong desire, to do.

E. Contractualism does not cover the whole of morality, only those parts dealing with right and wrong (what we owe to each other), viz., the most important part of morality.

F. Contractualism does not cover

    1. Certain features of sexual morality.

    2. The virtues.

    3. Our moral attitudes toward the nonhuman world.

G. Scanlon and Kant.

    1. Similarities: Both believe that reasons are objective and universalizable.

    2. Differences:

       a. Kant holds that both the form and content of ethics is ultimate.

       b. Scanlon holds that the Contractual Formula is ultimate:

          i. Principles derived from the Contractual Formula may be negotiable in some cases.

          ii. The content (specific acts) derived from the principles may legitimately vary from situation to situation and are negotiable.

       c. Scanlon rejects Kant's "formalism."

          i. Kant derives ethics from the very rules of rationality.

          ii. Scanlon grounds his ethics in the human desire for unity, which guides moral negotiations.

H. Scanlon and utilitarianism.

   1. The Contractual Formula (act on reasons that will justify your actions to others) and the principle of utility (act so as to promote general well-being) sometimes overlap.

   2. Though Scanlon acknowledges the occasional overlapping, he rejects utilitarianism as reductive and unreasonable.

      a. Not every moral value reduces to well-being.

      b. Not every attempt to promote well-being has morally satisfactory consequences.

      c. Some acts are wrong independently of the issue of general well-being.

      d. Utilitarianism's demands are unrealistic.

I. Contractualism and relativism.

   1. Two kinds of relativism:

      a. Benign relativism: Values are relative, but nevertheless have some authority over those who share the "way of life" that they govern.

      b. Skeptical relativism: There are no objective values, nothing to be right or wrong about.

   2. Benign relativism can be refuted by showing that

      a. Customs and traditions are "optional."

      b. Members of societies governed by customs and traditions sometimes have good reason to reject some of those customs and traditions as immoral.

   3. Skeptical relativism can be refuted by showing that there are some universal principles.

   4. What is correct about relativism:

      a. "Defensible moral standards can vary in content."

      b. But this fact can be accounted for by "parametric pluralism" without falling into relativism—content differs but not form.

J. Contractualism and the is/ought problem.

   1. Does contractualism run afoul of Hume's Guillotine and/or the naturalistic fallacy?

a. Scanlon bases his theory on two (natural?) facts:

   i. The human desire for unity.

   ii. The human desire for justification.

b. Scanlon does not try to *deduce* his moral facts from these natural facts.

   i. Scanlon's moral facts are *conventional* facts (agreements to give to each other what we owe).

   ii. These conventional facts presuppose but are not deduced from those natural facts.

2. Contractualism does not run afoul of the is/ought problem.

K. Criticism of Scanlon's contractualism.

  1. Is contractualism circular—does it presuppose the very moral facts it claims to establish? Scanlon says no, because

    a. Contractualism does not try to generate new moral values, but to clarify logically existing ones.

    b. All successful moral theories must presuppose a moral point of view; no *theory* by itself can cause amoralists to accept a moral point of view.

  2. Does Scanlon put more moral weight on "good reasons" than they can hold? Stuart Hampshire poses the questions

    a. In the eighteenth century, didn't many people of good will justify slavery by appealing to "good reasons" that others accepted?

    b. Don't many moral advancements come about through conflict rather than agreement?

  3. Is the moral field covered by contractualism too small to provide enough space for a genuine moral theory?

For Further Reading
Primary Texts

Hobbes, Thomas. *Leviathan: Or, the Matter, Forme and Power of a Commonwealth Ecclesiasticall and Civill.* 1651. Oxford and New York: Oxford University Press, 1998.

Rawls, John. *A Theory of Justice.* Cambridge, Mass.: Harvard University Press, 1971.

Rousseau, Jean-Jacques. *The Social Contract and Discourse*. 1762. Trans. G. D. H. Cole, London: J. M. Dent and Sons, 1982.

Scanlon, T. M. *What We Owe to Each Other*. Cambridge, Mass., and London: 1998.

Secondary Sources

Darwall, Stephen, ed. *Contractarianism/Contractualism*. Oxford and Malden, Mass.: Blackwell, 2003.

Gauthier, David. *Morals by Agreement*. Oxford: Clarenden Press, 1986.

Gauthier, David. "Why Contractarianism?" In *Contractarianism and Rational Choice*, ed. Peter Vallentyne, 15–30. Cambridge: Cambridge University Press, 1991. Reprinted in Darwall, 91–107.

Matravers, Matt., ed. *Scanlon and Contractualism*. London and Portland, Or.: Frank Cass, 2003.

Stratton-Lake, Philip, ed. *What We Owe to Each Other*. Malden, Mass. and Oxford: Blackwell, 2004.

Notes

1. E.g., Stephen Darwall, ed., *Contractarianism/Contractualism* (Oxford and Malden, Mass.: Blackwell Publishing, 2003), 4.

2. E.g., Darwall. See note 1.

3. Thomas Hobbes, *Leviathan: Or, the Matter, Forme and Power of a Commonwealth Ecclesiasticall and Civill* (Oxford and New York: Oxford University Press, 1998). Future references to this work will be included parenthetically in the text.

4. "Omit" here means "commit."

5. David Gauthier, *Morals by Agreement* (Oxford: Clarenden Press, 1986). Selections from Gauthier's book are reprinted in *Contractarianism/Contractualism*, ed. Stephen Darwall (Oxford and Malden, Mass.: Blackwell, 2003), 108–37. Citations here are from Darwall. Future citations will be designated as MbA and included parenthetically in the body of the text.

6. David Gauthier, "Why Contractualism?" originally published in *Contractarianism and Rational Choice*, ed. Peter Vallentyne (Cambridge: Cambridge University Press, 1991), 15–30. Reprinted in Darwall, 91–107. Citation here is from Darwall, p. 97. Future citations will also be from Darwall. They will be designated as WC and be included parenthetically in the body of the text.

7. John Rawls, *A Theory of Justice* (Cambridge, Mass.: Harvard University Press, 1971). Future references to this book will be included parenthetically in the body of the text.

8. Robert Nozick, *Anarchy, State, and Utopia* (New York: Basic Books, 1974).

9. T. M. Scanlon, *What We Owe to Each Other* (Cambridge, Mass., and London: Harvard University Press, 1998), 190. Future references to this book will be cited parenthetically in the body of the text.

10. Scanlon himself does not name his basic idea the "Contractual Formula," but the idea appears often in numerous forms throughout his book. I will adopt the term for the sake of easy reference. (It cannot be called the Contractual *Principle*, because the moral principles Scanlon discusses are generated by this "formula.")

11. E.g., Gary Watson, "Some Considerations in Favor of Contractualism," in Darwall, 249–69, p. 259.

12. As I said earlier, there really is no word in classical Greek that corresponds to our word "morality." Plato used the word *dikaiosyne*, but there is no precise English translation for that word either. It is usually translated as "justice, " but in the context in which Plato asks the question in Book I of the *Republic*, the word "morality" still works best.

13. Stuart Hampshire, "The Reason Why Not," *New York Review of Books* vol. 46, no. 7 (April 22, 1999): 6.

14. Stuart Hampshire, *Justice is Conflict* (Princeton: Princeton University Press, 2001).

Glossary

(Boldfaced type indicates terms that are cross-referenced within the glossary.)

adaptation The Darwinian process according to which genetic mutations and/or random combinations from the gene pools of individual organisms produce new physical characteristics in the offspring of these individuals. If these novelties prove to be more suitable for survival and reproduction in a given environment than were those of the offspring's parental generation, adaptation takes place. Adaptation can lead to **speciation,** the creation of new species.

aesthetics Sometimes refers to judgments about beauty. More commonly, the philosophy of art: the branch of philosophy that investigates questions such as What makes something a work of art? Are there absolute values in art, or are artistic judgments always relative? Can there be rational debates about judgments concerning art, or are such judgments based only on preference? What is the status of art among other human intellectual and creative endeavors?

agency In ethical discourse, an agent is the individual who acts with intention, responsibility, and effect.

agnostic In a religious context, designates a person who claims not to know whether God exists. In other fields as well, an agnostic denies either that knowledge of specific entities is available or that it is possible.

altruism As a descriptive category, designates acts that are in the interests of others at the expense of the **agent**'s own interests. As a moral doctrine, the view that in certain circumstances one ought to sacrifice one's own interests for the interests of others.

analytic philosophy The view that, in philosophy, logical analysis and analysis of meaning must be prior to the construction of philosophical theories about the world. Analytical philosophers believe that certain key concepts in ordinary language and in scientific, moral, religious, and **aesthetic** discourse are philosophically vague or misleading. Philosophical problems can be solved and pseudophilosophical problems can be dispelled through the clarification of these concepts. The theories that analytic philosophers do generate tend to be demonstrations of the logical relationships among these different realms of discourse rather than grandiose **metaphysical** schemes. Although many of the pioneers of this school were Continental Europeans, the movement has become primarily an Anglo-American one.

analytic proposition A **proposition** whose negation leads to a self-contradiction. For example, the proposition that squares have four sides is analytic because its negation, that squares do not have four sides, is a self-contradiction.

anarchy The social state of chaos produced by the collapse of civil authority.

androcentrism The prioritizing of the interests of males over the interests of nonmales.

anthropocentrism The perspective that sees reality only in terms of human interests.

anticlericalism Opposition to the power of religious institutions and their influence in public affairs.

apologetic An intellectual defense of a **proposition,** argument, or theory that is under attack.

a posteriori A belief, **proposition,** or argument whose truth or falsity can be established only through observation. Classical **empiricism** was an attempt to show that all factual knowledge about reality is derived from observation, usually from **sense data.**

a priori A belief, **proposition,** or argument whose truth or falsity can be established independently of observation. Definitions, arithmetic, and the principles of **logic** are usually held to be a priori. Classical **rationalism** was an attempt to show that all significant knowledge about the world is based on *a priori* truths, which most of the rationalists associated with innate ideas—knowledge present at birth.

areté A Greek word appearing often in the works of Plato and Aristotle, usually translated as "virtue," but sometimes as "quality" or "excellence."

atheist A person who denies the existence of God or gods.

atomism The first atomic theory, created by the **pre-Socratic philoso-phers** Democritus and Leucippus, according to which everything in reality is composed of atoms, conceived as indivisible, irreducible basic units of matter that have the characteristics of size, shape, and location, moving along law-determined paths, sometimes coagulating with other atoms, sometimes colliding with them.

beg the question A circular kind of reasoning that presupposes in the premises of an argument the very conclusion that the argument is supposed to prove (e. g., to "prove" that murder is wrong, when the very word, "murder," means wrongful killing).

behaviorism The theory that only observable, objective features of human or animal activity need be studied to provide an adequate scientific account of that activity. References to mental states such as plans, goals, and intentions (all of which are unobservable and unconfirmable) have no place in such scientific accounts. Usually associated with the psychologist—or behavioral engineer, as he preferred to be called—B. F. Skinner (1904–1990).

big bang theory The **cosmological** theory that the matter currently existent in the universe (e.g., atoms and subatomic particles) was caused in a massive explosion that took place at the beginning of time as we know it. Sometimes called the "atomic bake."

brute facts Simple facts in the world that can be expressed without reference to human mental states or to **conventional facts.**

Calculus of Felicity (or Felicific Calculus) Jeremy Bentham's name for an arithmetic test he invented for evaluating the various amounts of pleasure and pain that would be produced by future acts one might choose. The analysis of the prospective acts in terms of the seven categories in the test determine which acts one should choose.

Cartesian Anything having to do with the philosophical, mathematical, or scientific ideas of the seventeenth-century French philosopher René Descartes.

categorical imperative In Kantian ethics, designates an absolute obligation imposed upon us by our rational nature. There are several formulations of this demand, but its best-known expression is "Act only according to that maxim by which you can at the same time will that it should become a universal law."

causality Explanation of events or processes in terms of the mechanics of cause and effect. Causal explanations are usually represented in terms of natural laws. Contrast with **teleological** explanations.

compatibilism *See* **soft determinism.**

consequentialism A view motivating certain ethical theories such as utilitarianism according to which the moral worth of an act is determined primarily by the act's consequences.

conventional facts Facts (usually) about human activity explained in terms of institutions, conventions, or mores; for example, legal institutions or marriage conventions.

cosmology The study of the cosmos. The creation of philosophical or scientific theories of the origins, structure, and content of the universe.

deconstruction A theory of texts (philosophical, legal, scientific, fictional) according to which, because of the volatile nature of thought and language, almost all texts can be shown to "deconstruct" themselves—to undermine and refute their own theses. Or, deconstruction is the activity of demonstrating that a particular text undermines and refutes itself. Usually associated with the late French philosopher Jacques Derrida.

deflationism A view held by certain philosophers who believe that it is a mistake to try to generate a full-bodied theory of truth. Rather, they claim, the "problem of truth" is a pseudo-problem. Truth and falsity are not **metaphysical** entities. The expression, "X is true," can always be restated in nonproblematical ways.

deontology The study of moral obligation, that which is binding. Immanuel Kant's moral theory is deontological because of the centrality in Kant's system of the **categorical imperative,** which always reveals one's duty.

determinism The view that every event is caused (*see* **causality**). Every event follows inevitably from the events that preceded it. There is no randomness in reality; rather, all is law governed. Freedom either does not exist (**hard determinism**) or exists in such a way as to be compatible with necessity (**soft determinism**).

deus ex machina A phoney solution. Literally "god from a machine." Greek dramatists of inferior quality would create complex plots loaded with difficult problems, and then, with the use of a machine, drop a god onto the stage (played by an actor on a cable) who solved the problems supernaturally.

ego In Freudian theory, the name of the rational, mostly conscious, social aspect of the psyche, as contrasted with **id** and **superego.**

empirical Having to do with the observational nature of certain kinds of facts. *See also* **empiricism.**

empiricism The **epistemological** view that true knowledge is derived primarily from sense experience (or, in "purer" strains of empiricism, exclusively from sense experience). The classical empiricists were the seventeenth-century British philosophers John Locke, George Berkeley, and David Hume.

Enlightenment A philosophical movement of the eighteenth century characterized by the belief in the power of reason to sweep away superstition, ignorance, and injustice.

epistemology Theory of knowledge. The branch of philosophy that answers such questions as What is knowledge? What, if anything, can we know? What is the difference between knowledge and opinion?

essence The feature or set of features of a thing or an idea that constitutes what the thing or idea is—its **necessary condition.**

euthanasia Mercy killing; aiding in the painless death of individuals suffering from painful, terminal diseases.

fatalism The view that an inescapable preordained fate or destiny awaits each individual. A form of **determinism.**

feminism The sociopolitical theory and practice defending women's dignity and rights against patriarchal or otherwise male-dominated power structures that have denied legal and social equality to women, and have demeaned, marginalized, and constricted women throughout history.

the Forms In Plato's **ontology,** the Forms constitute the highest level of a four-tiered division of reality. Everything that exists below them—in the conceptual world, physical world, or the world of mere appearance—is dependent upon the Forms, which are models (**essences,** universals, archetypes) of all reality. Forms are eternal, unchangeable, and the ultimate object of all philosophy.

genes Transmittable units of organic matter carrying hereditary traits, found at certain points on microscopic rod-shaped bodies called chromosomes, whose function is to carry these genetic units.

hard determinism The view that **determinism** is true and that therefore freedom and responsibility do not exist. Contrast with **soft determinism** and **libertarianism.**

hedonism A theory of motivation according to which the driving force behind all acts either is pleasure (psychological hedonism) or ought to be pleasure (moral hedonism).

Hellenic Referring to Greek culture (art, philosophy, politics, etc.) during the so-called Golden Age of Greece, roughly during the several centuries preceding Aristotle's death (in 322 B.C.E.), followed by the **Hellenistic** period.

Hellenistic Referring to Greek culture (art, philosophy, politics, etc.) during the two centuries after the death of Aristotle (in 322 B.C.E.), in the aftermath of devastating wars among the Greek city-states, the ravages of the plague, and foreign intervention. Contrasted with the **Hellenic** period, which preceded it.

homocentricism Theories and practices that have prioritized the value of human animals over the rest of the kingdom of nature.

hypothetical imperative In Kantian ethics, designates a rational pragmatic (as opposed to moral) rule of action; its general formulation is "Whoever wills the end, so far as reason has decisive influence on his action, wills also the indispensably necessary means to it that lie in his power." It is a "hypothetical" imperative because in specific cases it is formulated as an "if . . . then" hypothesis: for example, "*If* you want to be healthy, *then* you should eat well."

id In Freudian theory, the name given to the mostly unconscious, antisocial, "animal" self, containing the primitive sexual and aggressive drives, and motivated by the "pleasure principle." Contrast with the **ego** and the **superego.**

ideology Propagandized political philosophy.

immoralist A person who is either incapable or unwilling to be bound by morality.

indeterminism The view that there are such phenomena as uncaused events and that therefore **determinism** is false.

intuitionism The view that a faculty of intuition allows us to understand things without the conscious use of reason. Or, the view that certain primary ideas (ethical, epistemological, metaphysical, or mathematical) are grasped directly and immediately with the aid of instruction, **deduction,** or analysis.

is/ought problem The claim first articulated by the eighteenth-century Scottish philosopher David Hume that no **proposition** containing prescriptive language (language telling us what we ought to do) can be logically deduced from propositions containing only descriptive language (language describing features of the world).

Lamarckism The biological theory derived from the French naturalist Jean-Baptiste Lamarck in the generation before Darwin according to which the process of evolution is explained in terms of biological transmission from parent to offspring of characteristics acquired by the parents during their lifetime. These transmittable characteristics can be the result of effort, injury, habit, use or disuse of limbs, and so on.

libertarianism The view that **determinism** is false and that freedom exists.

logic The branch of philosophy that studies the structure of valid inference; a purely formal discipline, interested in the structure of representation and argumentation rather than in its content.

Marxism A political or philosophical doctrine based on the writings of the nineteenth-century German philosopher Karl Marx: politically a form of communism, philosophically a form of **materialism** known as historical or dialectical materialism.

materialism The view that all reality can be shown to be material in nature (e.g., that "minds" are really brains, and that "mental states" are really brain states). Sometimes called "physicalism."

maxim In Kantian ethics, designates a personally chosen rational policy or rule that can guide action. A maxim that can be **universalized** is one that is consistent with moral obligation. "Never lie" and "always lie" are both possible maxims, but only the former can be universalized without contradiction.

meritocracy As used in this book, a political system in which social and economic status has been earned by talent and work.

meritoriousness The state of desert, of deserving something.

meta-ethics A kind of ethical discourse whose function is not to articulate moral advice but to analyze the meaning and the logic of moral concepts, such as good, evil, right, wrong, obligation, and duty.

metaphysics The branch of philosophy that attempts to construct a general, speculative worldview: a complete, systematic account of all reality and experience, usually involving an **epistemology,** an **ontology** (theory of being), and ethics, and an **aesthetics.** (The adjective "metaphysical" is often employed to stress the speculative, as opposed to scientific or commonsensical, features of the theory or assertion it describes.)

monism The **ontological** view that ultimately there is only one thing, or one kind of thing, in the universe.

moral egoism The ethical theory that the primary moral obligation is to oneself and that, therefore, one ought to pursue one's own interests above the interests of any other person, group, or thing. *See also* **psychological egoism.**

mutation A chemical alteration, usually sudden, in a heritable gene or chromosome of an organism. It is sometimes caused by external events such as radiation, sometimes by internal mechanical events such as the crossing of chromosomes, and it results in altered physical characteristics in the offspring of the parent whose reproductive system has suffered this genetic alteration. In biological theory, mutations play a large part in explaining the evolution of new species.

natural fact As used in this text, names facts other than **conventional facts**; includes **brute facts,** but also general laws of nature.

naturalism The **ontological** view that all is nature, that there are no supernatural or unnatural phenomena and that, therefore, the methods employed in the natural sciences are efficacious in fields other than science as well.

naturalistic fallacy An alleged logical error detected by the twentieth-century philosopher G. E. Moore. According to Moore, the fallacy is committed by anyone who attempts to define the word "good" in terms of natural features of the world, such as "The 'good' is pleasure." The fallacy is revealed by demonstrating the nonsensical conclusions implied by such definitions.

necessary condition X is a necessary condition of Y if Y cannot exist in the absence of X (or, if X and Y are **propositions,** if Y cannot be true if X is false). For example, oxygen is a necessary condition of combustion. *See also* **sufficient condition.**

necessary connection A logical relation between two sequential ideas or **propositions** "p" and "q," such that one cannot assert "p" and deny "q" without self-contradiction. Also called a relationship of "strict entailment."

nominalism The theory of meaning and language according to which the classes of objects named by abstract nouns and adjectives are determined conventionally or even arbitrarily rather than being determined by real **essences** in nature.

nonconsequentialism Ethical theories are nonconsequentialist if they claim that the moral value of an act is not primarily determined by the results of that act but resides in the act itself, or in the motivation or intention behind the act.

normative Having to do with attempts to establish norms or standards or with prescribing rules.

noumenal world In Kantian **metaphysics,** designates the ultimate reality that exists behind the world as it appears to us through the gridwork of time, space, and **causality.** We humans are constitutionally ignorant of the structure and content of the noumenal world.

ontology Theory of being. As an adjective—ontological—having to do with the status or the category of being: for example, what is the ontological status of reflections in a mirror and of rainbows? Are they real, or are they mere appearances?

open concept A concept or idea that cannot be exhaustively defined, even though it can be generally understood; a concept whose **necessary conditions** cannot be stated (e.g., game, love, art).

oxymoron A figure of speech containing components that are in direct conflict with each other, such as "hot ice," or the "sweet sorrow" of Romeo and Juliet.

Peloponnesian War A devastating, prolonged war fought from 431 to 404 B. C. E. among the city-states of ancient Greece, mainly between Athens and its allies and Sparta and its allies, terminating in victory for the Spartans.

phenomenal world In Kantian philosophy, the world as it appears to us through the gridwork of time, space, and causality—an objective world, but not equivalent to the **noumenal world,** which is ultimate reality.

phenotype In biology, the physical organism that is the result of its genetic inheritance (called a genotype) interacting with the physical environment that the organism finds itself occupying.

philosophy of science That branch of philosophy that studies the key concepts of scientific discourse, as well as its methods, models, and practices, querying their meanings, implications, and the logical relations among them.

pluralism The **ontological** view that reality is composed of a multiplicity of things or different kinds of things and that this multiplicity cannot be reduced to one category (**monism**) or two categories (dualism).

political philosophy That branch of philosophy concerning itself with the legitimacy of government and the organization of humans governed by law. Political philosophy overlaps social philosophy, which is usually seen as concerning itself with theories of justice.

polytheism The belief in many gods, contrasted with monotheism (one god) and with **atheism** (no gods).

postmodernism As used here, a term designating a contemporary posture of skepticism concerning the values of traditional philosophies and institutions, fascination with popular culture and the domination of technology over human endeavors, and dwelling on **semiotic** strategies that prioritize signs and images over substance and truth, reproduction over originality, and representation over reality.

pragmatism An American philosophy flourishing at the beginning of the twentieth century, claiming that the meaning of an idea or **proposition** can be established by determining what practical difference would be produced by believing the idea or proposition to be true and that the truth of the idea or proposition can be established by determining that belief in the idea of the proposition "works"—that it places the person who believes the idea or proposition in a more satisfactory relationship with the rest of her beliefs and experiences.

pre-Socratic philosophers The philosophers of early Greece who flourished before Socrates (469–399 B. C. E.) and who meditated on the ultimate nature of being, unlike Socrates who was more concerned with the world of human activity.

principle of falsifiability A criterion of scientific meaning set forth by Sir Karl Popper according to which a **proposition** or theory is scientific only if its wording would allow recognition of the kind of evidence that would refute or falsify the theory. The implication of the principle is that every true theory must rule out some possibilities; any putative theory that is compatible with every possible state of affairs is no theory at all.

principle of uncertainty A theory in quantum mechanics created by the twentieth-century German physicist Werner Heisenberg, according to which the location, velocity, and direction of subatomic particles (electrons, neutrons, etc.) cannot all be known simultaneously. The implication of the principle is that the traditional theories of **causality** in physics must give way to statistical models.

principle of utility (or of happiness) The founding principle of utilitarianism, defended by Jeremy Bentham and John Stuart Mill, according to which we should only perform acts that help achieve the goal of "the greatest amount of happiness for the greatest number of people."

proposition As employed in this text, whatever is asserted by a sentence. The sentences "It's raining," "Es regnet," and "Llueve" all assert the same proposition.

psychological egoism The theory of motivation claiming that the object of every action is the self-interest of the agent. According to this theory, altruism is impossible.

quietism The psychology or philosophy of inaction. Doing little or nothing is better than doing something. Don't just do something; stand there!

rationalism In the broadest sense, philosophies committed primarily to reason. More precisely, the **epistemological** view that true knowledge is derived primarily from reason (or exclusively from reason in the purer strains of rationalism). Reason is conceived as the working of the mind on material provided by the mind itself. In most versions, this material has the form of innate ideas. Therefore, for rationalists, the purest type of knowledge is *a priori.*

realism As used in this text, the theory of language and meaning holding that the entities named by nouns, including abstract nouns, are real entities in the world that have **essences**; opposed by **nominalism.**

reductio ad absurdum Reduction of a theory or **proposition** to an absurdity by showing that its consequences are impossible or ridiculous.

reductionism The attempt to show that all objects and events distinguishable at one level of analysis can be reduced to simpler objects and events at a more basic level of analysis (e.g., the attempt to demonstrate that all physical objects can be analyzed in terms of molecular structures or that molecular structures can be analyzed in terms of atomic structures).

relativism In **ethics** and **aesthetics,** relativism is the view that there are no absolute values; all values are relative to time, place, and culture. In **epistemology,** relativism is the view that there are no absolute truths; all truths are relative to time, place, and culture.

semantics As used in this text, theory of meaning.

sense data A sense datum is that which is perceived immediately by any one of the senses prior to interpretation by the mind. Sense data include the perception of colors, sounds, tastes, odors and textures, pleasures and pains. Classical **empiricism** claimed that sense data are the source of all true knowledge.

sexual selection In Darwinian theory of evolution, designates a process by which genes are passed on, not by "natural selection," but by individual choice based on the attraction of opposite-sexed members of a species for each other, as when a female elk "chooses" as a partner the male with the largest antlers.

skepticism (or scepticism) The denial of knowledge. General skepticism denies the possibility of any knowledge; however, one can be skeptical of certain fields of inquiry (e.g., **metaphysics**) or specific faculties (e.g., sense perception) without denying the possibility of knowledge in general.

sociopath A person suffering from a pathology that prevents interiorization of moral and social instruction, sometimes aggressively antisocial.

soft determinism (sometimes called **compatibilism**) The view that **determinism** is true but is compatible with freedom and responsibility.

solipsism The view that the only true knowledge that one can possess is the knowledge of one's own conscious states. According to solipsism, there is no good reason to believe that anything exists other than oneself.

sophists A group of philosophers—or, more accurately, rhetoricians—contemporary with Socrates who traveled through ancient Greece teaching argumentative skills as the vehicle to political power. Philosophically, the sophists defended relativism, **skepticism,** and subjectivism.

speciation In evolutionary theory, indicates the process whereby individual offspring are distinct enough from their parents that their birth represents the creation of a new species.

speciesism The view that bestows one natural species (usually the human species) with moral and/or **ontological** qualities superior to those of other species.

straw man argument An argument attacking views falsely attributed to an opponent; an attack on views that no one actually holds.

strict entailment *See* **necessary connection.**

sufficient condition P is the sufficient condition of Q if the presence of P guarantees the presence of Q (or, if P and Q are **propositions,** then if the truth of P guarantees the truth of Q). For example, the presence of mammary glands in an animal is a sufficient condition for designating that animal as a mammal. (It is also a **necessary condition** for doing so.)

superego In Freudian theory, the component of the psyche that counteracts antisocial desires and impulses of the **id** by attaching conscious and unconscious feelings of guilt to them.

synthetic *a priori* According to Immanuel Kant, a **proposition** is *a priori* if it cannot be confirmed or refuted by sense observation, and it is synthetic if it makes factual assertions about the visible world. Hume claims that such a synthetic *a priori* truth is impossible, but Kant believes that they do exist.

synthetic proposition A **proposition** is synthetic if it makes assertions about facts in reality, and if its negation does not lead to a self-contradiction. For example, the proposition that Jupiter has a square moon is synthetic, even though it is false, because it asserts something about the real world and because its negation, that Jupiter does not have a square moon, is not self-contradictory; generally contrasted to **analytic proposition.**

tautology A repetitive or redundant **proposition.** For example, definitions are tautological because their predicates form the equivalency of the term being defined: "A sister is a female sibling." Each side of the copula "is" constitutes the equivalent of the other side. Similarly, "A sister is a female" and "a sister is a sibling" are also tautologies, though they are not definitions. *See also* **analytic proposition.**

teleology The existence of purpose, intention, and design, or the study of the evidence for the existence of purpose, intention, and design in the universe. A teleological explanation is an explanation in terms of goals, purposes, and intentions, and is contrasted with a **causal** explanation, which looks for mechanical relationships rather than purpose.

telos The Greek word for goal.

the Terror The period of the French Revolution between 1783 and 1784 when the ruling faction of the revolutionary government executed thousands of its perceived enemies and even former allies by firing squad and guillotine. Eventually, the leader of this faction, Maximilien de Robespierre, was also sent to the guillotine.

Thanatos In Greek mythology, the god of death. In psychoanalysis, the death instinct, a suicidal drive that Freud finds in all living matter.

truism A self-evident truth; a platitude.

universalizability A moral principle or a rule, or **maxim,** is universalizable if it can be recommended to all individuals without producing a self-contradiction. Universalizability is a moral criterion in Kantian ethics (the **categorical imperative**) and in Christian ethics ("Do unto others as you would have them do unto you").

utopianism Any political theory motivated by the belief that perfection is possible in the building of human societies.

Index

Locators in **boldface** denote the first appearance of terms in the text that also appear in the glossary.